C0-AVN-976

THE CHURCH'S PUBLIC ROLE

THE CHURCH'S PUBLIC ROLE

Retrospect and Prospect

Edited by
Dieter T. Hessel

WILLIAM B. EERDMANS PUBLISHING COMPANY
GRAND RAPIDS, MICHIGAN

$9-

BR
115
.W6
C575
1990

Copyright © 1993 by Wm. B. Eerdmans Publishing Co.
255 Jefferson Ave. S.E., Grand Rapids, Mich. 49503
All rights reserved

Printed in the United States of America

Library of Congress Cataloging-in-Publication Data

The Church's public role: retrospect and prospect / edited by Dieter T. Hessel.

p. cm.

Papers from an ecumenical symposium held at the Princeton Seminary Continuing Education Center, Sept. 1990.

Includes bibliographical references.

ISBN 0-8028-0647-3 (pbk.)

1. Church and the world — Congresses. 2. Church and social problems — Congresses. 3. Sociology, Christian — Congresses.

I. Hessel, Dieter T.

BR115.W6C575 1990

261'.1'097 — dc20 92-27234

CIP

Contents

Preface

This book completes a unique and timely — though certainly not exhaustive — inquiry into *what* mainstream churches of North America have been doing, and ought to do, to effect social transformation. It illumines aspects of the twentieth-century experience of these churches as they have sought to make a faithful, effective public witness. It also suggests *how* this role of the church may be carried out in a new era.

The concluding chapter highlights the dialogue between social ethics and religious history that shaped this book, and it draws some implications for strengthening the public role of the church. Special thanks are due to James Hudnut-Beumler, then director of the undergraduate program at the Woodrow Wilson School of Public and International Affairs, Princeton University, for coauthoring the last chapter and for helping to recruit the religious historians who participated.

Origins of This Project

This collaborative work emerged from papers prepared for an ecumenical symposium on "The Church's Public Role: Retrospect and Prospect" that occurred in late September 1990 at the Princeton Seminary Continuing Education Center. The authors, steeped in the discipline of Christian ethics or of church history, were asked to bring their considerable breadth and depth of experience to bear in exploring alternative perspectives on this topic. Their research was commissioned by the Lilly Endowment as an aspect of that foundation's ongoing study of the current status and future prospects of churches in the United States. I am grateful to Robert Lynn and Craig Dykstra, who succeeded him as vice president of the Religion Division of the Lilly Endowment, and to Program Officer James Wind, for support of this endeavor.

In my first conversation with Bob Lynn about the idea of this symposium, I noted that relatively little research had been funded on this subject, compared to major grants for congregational and denominational studies. Yet the *big story* of mainline churches in twentieth-century North America is their continuing effort to engage public affairs faithfully and effectively. What aspect of twentieth-century American Christianity could be more important than the church's social witness, examined in its strengths and weaknesses? Shouldn't the church's public role — recent and future — get more direct attention at the beginning of a new era?

The stated purpose of the ecumenical symposium was "to explore aspects of public engagement by churches in response to a changing social situation and major theological movements." Both historians and ethicists were invited "to offer alternative perspectives on issues raised by and lessons learned from the efforts of mainstream American Christianity to make a public difference in the 20th century."

Those who participated in the conversation experienced the special benefits of cross-disciplinary reflection on this subject. In addition to the authors of these chapters, the symposium involved an equal number of other seminary and college teachers of religion or of ethics as well as church leaders. In each symposium session our method was to feature one presenter's overview of the paper's argument, followed by a designated respondent's brief comments, then general discussion. Four of the responses are included in this book to indicate the value of reasoned dialogue about the church's public role. One of the respondents during the seminar, David Ramage, Jr., graciously welcomed me at McCormick Theological Seminary, Chicago, as a visiting scholar and teacher of Christian social ethics during 1991 when I was also finishing editorial work on this volume.

In late summer 1991 the authors revised and updated their papers for publication in the light of the symposium dialogue and editorial suggestions relating to publication plans. All of us are indebted to Bill Eerdmans for taking a personal interest in offering this book at a time when few religious publishers have been paying much attention to *basic* questions of the church's mission in society, as distinct from printing books on particular social issues.

The Presbyterian Committee on Social Witness Policy, of which I was director from 1987 to 1990, assumed some on-site costs of the symposium at the Princeton Seminary Continuing Education Center, and added a modest subsidy to a Lilly Endowment grant for editing and publishing this book. I am pleased to acknowledge support of this endeavor by Gordon Douglass, Committee chair, and Dana Wilbanks, a committee member who convened the symposium and contributed chapter 2.

Features of This Book

The most distinctive contribution made by this book is to combine a look back with a look ahead, utilizing the tools of historians and ethicists. For the most part, this was done in a noncompartmentalized way. Contributors from both disciplines offered a retrospective assessment of the church's public role. For example, chapters 3, 5, 6, 10, and 15 — all by ethics teachers and researchers — provide important historical background to orient all of us regarding where we have come from as we begin to think harder about where we are going and the way to journey there. Meanwhile, some of the historians (e.g., the authors of chapters 7, 12, and 13) are not shy about recommending particular steps to take as a public church!

In the book as a whole, it is evident that the retrospective look is more substantive and detailed, while the prospective proposals remain general, tentative, or even conflicted. From these chapters we cannot derive one definite approach to carrying out the church's public role, but we do gain essential perspective and can discern elements — sometimes in tension — of an agenda for the church's public witness in a rapidly changing society.

We invite readers joining this history-ethics dialogue to weigh our retrospective insights and prospective recommendations in the process of thinking through the church's public role today. Beyond that, let researchers take note! Here is a goldmine of observations and endnotes for church leaders and scholars to pursue. A particularly noteworthy contribution this volume makes to researchers is its extensive current review of sources pertaining to *ecumenical* public witness (listed in notes for chapter 8). That homework resulted from a special investment of a limited budget. We hope it will lead other scholars to pursue the subject in depth and help to upgrade journalistic approaches that have so often been stereotyped or simplistic.

Another feature of this book is that it concentrates on evaluating and projecting the role of church bodies and councils. We focus on what has been and ought to be done in the corporate social witness of the church, including particular churches, networks, agencies, and asssociations. That is a large enough topic for more than one book. Consequently, in these pages we are not trying to provide a practical manual on "how to" do social ministry in and through the congregation. That is the subject of other books, including one I recently revised (see chapter 1, n. 34). Numerous denominational and ecumenical resources also address that need in particular ways. We do suggest strongly, however, that leadership development for social ministry in these times must become more than practical by giving careful attention to the historical roots and ethical issues, as well as the foundational and directional questions, being explored here.

D.T.H.

Contributors

Gonzalo Castillo-Cardenas is professor of Theology and Culture at Pittsburgh Theological Seminary. A native of Colombia, he has specialized in Latin American liberation theology.

Donald L. Drakeman teaches in the Politics Department of Princeton University, and is president of Medarex, Inc., a biotechnology company. As an attorney and historian of American religion, he has assisted religious groups and has served as an amicus curiae in church-state litigation.

Janet F. Fishburn is professor of Teaching Ministry and American Church History in the Theological and Graduate Schools of Drew University, Madison, N.J. She is the author of *The Fatherhood of God and the Victorian Family: A Study of the Social Gospel in America* (Philadelphia: Fortress, 1982), and *Confronting the Idolatry of Family: A New Vision for the Household of God* (Nashville: Abingdon, 1991).

J. Bryan Hehir is professor of Christian Ethics, Georgetown University, and counselor for Social Policy, U.S. Catholic Conference, Washington, D.C. A prolific author of scholarly articles, Hehir is an authoritative interpreter of Roman Catholic moral thought and was instrumental in drafting the Bishops' pastoral letter, *The Challenge of Peace: God's Promise and Our Response* (Washington, D.C.: U.S. Catholic Conference, 1983).

Dieter T. Hessel is an ethicist and educator who served on the national staff of the Presbyterian Church (U.S.A.) between 1965 and 1990 as coordinator of social education and then as director of social witness policy. He is the author of *Social Ministry*, rev. ed. (Louisville: Westminster/John Knox, 1992), and editor of *After Nature's Revolt: Eco-Justice and Theology* (Minneapolis: Fortress, 1992), as well as *Social Themes of the Christian Year: A Commentary on the Lectionary* (Geneva, 1983). In 1992 he was a resident member of the Princeton Center of Theological Inquiry. Currently he is director of an ecumenical Program on Ecology, Justice and Faith supported by the MacArthur Foundation.

James Hudnut-Beumler is an historian of American religion who is now a program associate in the Religion Division of the Lilly Endowment. While working on this volume he was director of the undergraduate program at Princeton University's Woodrow Wilson School of Public and International Affairs. He is completing a book on religion and social criticism in the 1950s.

Christian T. Iosso recently received his Ph.D. in Christian social ethics from Union Theological Seminary, New York. From 1979 to 1984 he was on the staff of the United Church of Christ and the Presbyterian Church. He has specialized in ecclesial and economic ethics, including issues of corporate responsibility, and recently directed a public witness project for the National Council of Churches.

Lois Gehr Livezey is dean of Doctoral Studies and professor of Christian Ethics at McCormick Theological Seminary, Chicago. She brings a background of process theology and interest in feminist ethics to bear on issues of human rights in contemporary society.

Edward LeRoy Long, Jr., is emeritus professor of Christian Ethics and Theology of Culture at Drew University Theological School, Madison, N.J. He is known especially as a premier historian of ethics, and is the author of numerous books, including *A Survey of Christian Ethics*, rev. ed. (New York: Oxford Univ. Press, 1967).

Eugene Y. Lowe, Jr., is dean of students, Princeton University, and a specialist in American religious history, concentrating in nineteenth- and twentieth-century studies.

Peter J. Paris is professor of Christian Social Ethics at Princeton

Theological Seminary and liaison with the Princeton University Afro-American Studies Program. He is the author of *The Social Teachings of the Black Churches* (Philadelphia: Fortress, 1986) and in 1991–92 was president of the Society of Christian Ethics.

David Ramage, Jr., is president of McCormick Theological Seminary and its professor of Church and Ministry. He has previous experience in the pastorate, as a leader of the Presbyterian Board of National Missions, and as director of the New World Foundation, N.Y.

Max L. Stackhouse is professor of Christian Social Ethics, Andover Newton Theological School, affiliated with the United Church of Christ. He is the author of many books, including *Ethics and Urban Ethos* (Boston: Beacon, 1973); *Creeds, Society, and Human Rights* (Grand Rapids: Eerdmans, 1984); and *Public Theology and Political Economy* (Grand Rapids: Eerdmans, 1987).

Ron Stief is executive director of the Center for Ethics and Economic Policy in Berkeley, Calif., focusing on issues of tax policy, deregulation of industry, and U.S. foreign policy, trade, and agriculture. In the 1980s the center trained more than ten thousand individuals and fifty organizations in advocacy for economic justice.

Ronald H. Stone is professor of Social Ethics at Pittsburgh Theological Seminary and author of *Christian Realism and Peacemaking* (Nashville: Abingdon, 1988). Reflecting a career-long interest, his analytical biography, *Professor Reinhold Niebuhr*, was published by Westminster/John Knox in 1992.

Dana W. Wilbanks is professor of Christian Ethics at Iliff School of Theology, Denver, Colo., and coauthor of *Decision Making and the Bible* (Valley Forge, Pa.: Judson Press, 1975). A frequent contributor to social policy studies of the Presbyterian Church (U.S.A.), he is currently focusing on Christian ethics and immigration policy.

Making a Public Difference after the Eclipse

Dieter T. Hessel

What does it take for mainline churches, facing troubling, wrenching times, to make more of a public difference — to leaven a pluralistic, fermenting society with a transforming spirit, and to participate in movement toward an eco-just world? This question comes to the foreground as these same churches experience a human energy crisis due to membership loss and institutional decline, and blurred vision of their social mission to the nation. No individual scholar or church leader can fully answer this complex, freighted question. Pursuing it requires collaborative research into the changing relation of churches to North American society, and reflective assessment of competing proposals regarding the appropriate public role(s) of the church. Here is my initial contribution to the conversation.

I begin with a brief examination of the continuing place vs. displacement of mainstream Protestantism in the United States. After deconstructing the view that mainstream churches are now sidelined or impotent, my paper underscores the constructive public role of ecumenically minded churches as part of a reemerging independent sector. If such a possibility is to be actualized, however, the churches must give special attention to three urgent tasks: to regain and enliven contextual theological focus in a rapidly changing society, to formulate and teach a coherent social ethic, and to develop a vigorous witness to the nation that better utilizes ecclesial resources and mobilizes members to carry out this mission.

Reexamining the Sociology on Mainline Churches

How ought we to understand the changing relation of the church to North American society? The first step is to examine critically what sociologists of religion have been saying, particularly in the literature regarding a "third disestablishment" of the mainstream Protestant churches.[1] A careful reading of the relevant books and articles raises serious questions about the disestablishment thesis, which typically culminates in a discouraging theme, easily co-optable by neoconservatives, that the "mainline is now on the sideline." But has a "massive power shift" toward conservative religion actually occurred in the United States? And have mainline Protestant churches become impotent?

Critical analysis reveals that several sociologists of religion writing about a new mainstream Protestant disestablishment have overgeneralized about these churches from member opinion surveys. The opinion survey questions they analyzed have to do with the social issues that cluster around status politics in America — status politics being the struggle for social honor and public respect through symbolic cultural crusades.[2] Sociologists focusing on religious defenders of an old worldview ignored what the churches of the ecumenical movement said, and what their advocacy networks were doing, about foreign policy questions and economic justice issues. In short, neither the peacemaking nor the justice agenda emphasized by mainstream churches in the 1980s was taken into account in prominent books that portrayed a new disestablishment of progressive Protestants and that announced a major power shift toward New Right religion.

In my view, there was little warrant for declaring religious conservatism as embodied in the New Christian Right to be on the verge of triumph across the land. The very real influence of neoconservative presidents, representatives, and Supreme Court justices does not mean that neoconservative *religion* captured America's soul. A plural, secular society has its own priorities. Moreover, as James Davison Hunter notes, conservative churches taken as a group did not mushroom in

1. My homework on that subject appears in "Mainline Protestantism Sidelined?" *Christianity and Crisis* 50/13 (Sept. 24, 1990): 293-98.

2. See Kenneth D. Wald, Dennis E. Owen, and Samuel S. Hill, Jr., "Evangelical Politics and Status Issues," *Journal for the Scientific Study of Religion* 28/1 (March 1989): 1-16.

membership during the 1970s and 1980s,[3] and their political activism crested after holding the media spotlight for awhile. Now they look, again, like a rear guard.

Even in the area of most intense New Right political activity — to outlaw abortion — temporary victory presages a losing war. Today's pro-life crusade to thoroughly recriminalize abortion and to restrict the reproductive rights of women is likely to parallel the main religious effect of the temperance crusade decades ago. The Prohibitionists were so uncivilly sure of divining *the* moral position, so instrumental in (mis)using theology, so willing to constrict individual decision making that they undermined the church's mission in society generally. One significant, unintended consequence was to intensify trends toward the secularization of American culture, convincing an increasing number of educated folks to dismiss moralistic religion along with its impractical, hypocritical social agenda.[4]

Meanwhile, American society has become even more publicly secular as it has become more religiously and ethnically diverse. Protestants in the United States are now only about one-third of the population, compared to two-thirds at the beginning of the century.[5] In the changing relationship between mainstream Protestant churches and American culture, continuing secularization coupled with expressive individualism are much more potent factors than has been the New Religious Right. In fact, the conservative denominations are not far behind the progressive churches in having, among their faithful adherents, restive members who want looser ties to established theological authority and will distance themselves from "a fanatical devotion and adherence to faith and an incivility and intolerance toward any deviation, practical or theological."[6]

The thesis of a new disestablishment, as presented by Wade Clark Roof and William McKinney in *American Mainline Religion*

3. James Davison Hunter, *Evangelicalism: The Coming Generation* (Chicago: Univ. of Chicago Press, 1987).

4. See Robert Moats Miller, *American Protestantism and Social Issues, 1919–1939* (Chapel Hill, N.C.: Univ. of North Carolina Press, 1958). Chapters on "A Footnote to the Election of 1928" and "The Conservatism of the Churches in the Thirties" document the crass partisan politics practiced by Christian Prohibition crusaders.

5. Peggy L. Shriver, "The Waiting World Parish," an unpublished paper of the National Council of Churches, 1991, has an overview.

6. Hunter, *Evangelicalism*.

(Rutgers, 1987), and Robert Wuthnow in *The Struggle for America's Soul* (Eerdmans, 1989) already feels outdated. Their overviews of church member opinions read like snapshots of the early 1980s, when, for a while, right-wing televangelists and political lobbies, building networks of conservative church members, did effectively exploit issues of status politics. But focusing so much analysis on short-term developments produced a double eclipse that obscured what else the churches were thinking and doing during the 1980s, and blurred the longer term pattern of church-culture interaction.

Eclipse is a more relevant image of what happened to the churches because it is realistic about the recent public obscurity of progressive denominations and politics, while it has nonfatalistic implications for the future. That image also calls attention to the scarcity of vital religion as a formative source for public ethical consciousness to meet the future. Hans Jonas ponders the implications:

> It is moot whether, without restoring the category of the sacred, the category most thoroughly destroyed by the scientific enlightenment, we can have an ethics able to cope with the extreme powers which we possess today and constantly increase and are almost compelled to wield. . . . Only awe of the sacred with its unqualified veto is independent of the computations of mundane fear and the solace of uncertainty about distant consequences. However, religion in eclipse cannot relieve ethics of its task; and while of faith it can be said that as a moving force it either is there or is not, of ethics it is true to say that it must be there . . . because humans act, and ethics is for the ordering of action and for regulating the power to act.[7]

Roof and McKinney and related disestablishment theorists were too narrow in focus and too short-range in time frame. Along with other alert participants and observers, they could see a pattern of reticence in the public behavior of mainline churches during the 1980s. And they could certainly point to important statistics of "birth dearth," rising median age of the U.S. population, and membership decline in the ecumenical denominations (e.g., mainstream Presbyterian churches increased average membership age to 50 as they suffered roughly 25 percent membership attrition during the last 25 years). But moving from those data to generalized disestablishment

7. Hans Jonas, *The Imperative of Responsibility: In Search of an Ethics for the Technological Age* (Chicago: Univ. of Chicago Press, 1984), p. 23.

talk with reference to the mainline has done little to illumine the challenge or appropriate ways to respond.

Rather than to key ecclesial thinking to a disestablishment myth, it makes more sense to focus on the following realities: (1) A wider spectrum of churches and religious networks have entered the political playing field — often with high-tech networks of communication and sometimes with major financing by patrons of the far right. Aggressive single-issue groups with that kind of support have more power to block healthy social change for awhile than to install any major plan for restoration of the old ethos. (2) The mainstream denominations feel less certain of their ability to influence American culture and politics in situations where secularists and fundamentalists bifurcate public opinion. Yet a significant number of progressive church members and congregations cannot be described as marginal in their power to shape community institutions or to influence politics. (3) Just how much of a public difference any body of Christians, or several churches acting together, will make in particular moments of social witness is uncertain, but mainstream churches do have resources — message, members, and money — to undertake creative, courageous social mission, when they give priority to such involvement.

Recovering a Constructive Public Role

So where are the churches now in relating to late twentieth-century society? We see that the churches have become more uneasily pluralistic even as they remain capable of moving beyond the ideological straitjacket of strident individualism and the ethical confines of restrictive moralism. When it comes to influencing the public, however, all churches have been losing ground — whether they be conservative Protestants, Mormons, and Roman Catholics who overplayed their hand on particular social issues, or liberal and moderate Protestants who sometimes failed to assert their voice. "In a nation that is anxious about its future, all churches are likely to experience nasty, even irrational, conflict. All must struggle to live graciously with moral ambiguity in social policy and personal decision making, . . . while trying to live in covenant with the powerless."[8]

8. Hessel, "Mainline Protestantism Sidelined?" p. 298.

Given this social situation, ecumenical and conservative churches alike share a responsibility to: (a) accept and value diversity of membership in an increasingly pluralistic society (e.g., soon more than one-third of American society will be people of color, and the work force will be even more of a rainbow); (b) restrain crusading habits of repressive moralism or tendencies to exclude people who are different; and (c) act in solidarity with the powerless to challenge unjust institutional practices and empower movements for change.

To care for civil well-being by fostering an inclusive and just community that values reasoned moral discourse is a constructive, broadly "liberal" religious task par excellence. Churches need to show their commitment to this agenda lest they be perceived on the one hand as closet theocrats who would treat sins as crimes, or on the other hand as mere Cheshire cats with bodiless progressive smiles. The constructive alternative is to become agents of mature dialogue, decision, and implementation on tough issues of social policy and practice.

Meanwhile, however, (mis)perception has tended to become reality in ecclesiastical politics, with disestablishment talk functioning as a drag on public engagement. The reasoning goes, "Because we are less visible, let's not try to do very much, or even think hard about our public role." Some church leaders and scholars of religion offer that rationale for mainline churches to mute or even to abandon social policy witness. Theirs is not often a blatant call for social quiescence, as one would hear from neoconservatives, but the rhetoric heard in church gatherings and the ecclesial agenda recommended by some scholars points away from vital social mission.

I have in mind, for example, the views of church historian and Louisville Seminary president John Mulder, who coordinated a denominational case study of Presbyterians. Mulder thinks the denomination developed a serious problem in the 1960s when the church "just reduced its commitment to evangelism. . . . The big shift was away from what is sometimes called 'word evangelism' — testifying to your faith — to 'deed evangelism' — the social-justice agenda of the church." The denomination attempted to respond faithfully to "horrendous struggles and crises" over civil rights, the Vietnam War, Watergate, the feminist movement, peacemaking, and the environment. "The Presbyterian Church undertook to lose its life for the sake of the world, in many, many ways," Mulder says. "It was all very idealistic and filled with commitment. . . . But it turned its back on a lot of areas of its life that contribute to the building and the nurturing of the church." Therefore, church leaders at all levels should chart a middle course that involves much less social engagement and much more attention to membership recruitment and family life.[9] One could summarize that agenda, echoing a biblical image, as inviting the church to seek its own life — and lose vigorous witness.

I see several difficulties with asking church leaders and members to accept a peripheral or middling social role and to retreat into worshiping, winsome fellowships apart from public struggles for justice and peace. First, the rationale for doing so is based on a dubious account of the church in society over the last thirty years — a story line that exaggerates the extent of earlier commitment to costly mission and ignores the comprehensive parish education, including youth and family programming, that was the chief strength of mainline churches throughout the 1950s and 1960s. Neither deed nor word evangelism as such, but holistic worship-education-mission was and is the most promising thrust of healthy churches.

Second, the chuch during the 1970s and 1980s fell into bad habits about which Mulder's account is silent. It overlooks the ecclesiastical self-preoccupation with reorganizing that has dominated denominational life since the early 1970s and has put off a generation of potential leaders. Mulder also ignores the deterioration of teaching-enabling ministry as clergy acquiesced to a therapeutic, chaplain-counselor model of ministry.

Third, the lack of theological coherence to this agenda is striking, preoccupied as it is with institutional indicators and balance. "Balance," far from being an important Christian ethical category, is more akin to moral neutrality, or to being lukewarm (Rev. 3:16). What would be a balanced presentation of, or moderate response to the struggle for human rights, or issues of torture, terrorism, abuse of power, racial and gender injustice, poverty, hunger, ecological destruction? How can churches of the Reformed tradition — the heirs of John Calvin and John Knox — disconnect from socially transforming engagement?

Fourth, and ironically, this invitation to retreat from public life misses an important societal trend — a revival of the independent sector in North American life. Surprisingly, churches have never had a greater opportunity and responsibility to make a public difference.

9. See the Lilly Endowment Occasional Report, *Progressions*, Jan. 1990.

This is a special time for the churches to focus on new developments and urgent problems in the society and world around them. Precisely at this time, leaders of congregations, regional church bodies, denominational agencies, and ecumenical groups need to pay more attention to larger social dynamics that are shaping cities, counties, and states, as well as national and international well-being.

An important trend to see in our pluralistic society is the larger social role that devolves on the private and independent sectors. Voluntary organizations have a crucial public task, as long noted by James Luther Adams and recently reemphasized (though less imaginatively) by Peter Drucker.[10] In a pluralist society with the government facing severe financial constraints even as social needs accumulate and public cynicism intensifies, relatively autonomous elements of the private sector such as business, university, professions, health providers, and the media are reasserting their interest — though not necessarily for the common good. The social responsibilities of powerful private institutions and of individuals working in them need to be clarified in relation to basic ethical claims and urgent societal needs.

This gives an increasingly important role to religious and other nonprofit groups in the "third" sector of voluntary, nongovernmental organizations, or "human change institutions." While Drucker has a rather domesticated view of the religious community's role in a changing society, and fails to recognize the responsibility of churches and synagogues to be both prophetic and pastoral,[11] he highlights the crucial social significance of the independent sector across the progressive-conservative spectrum. The potential for cultural reform increases as third-sector organizations reemerge to pose alternative visions of a better future, to provide citizen training, to foster community rebuilding, and to work for constructive public policy change. The special leadership role of the church within the independent sector is to embody ethical vision and reliable presence.

10. The significance of voluntary organizations for the public task of religious social ethics is the main interest of James Luther Adams, *Voluntary Associations: Sociocultural Analyses and Theological Interpretation,* ed. J. Ronald Engel (Chicago: Exploration Press, 1986). Peter Drucker, *The New Realities* (San Francisco: Harper & Row, 1989), pp. 195ff., underscores a revival of the independent sector in American life. Reflections on the subject also occur in annual forums of a Washington-based organization, "The Independent Sector."

11. Drucker, *New Realities,* p. 203, is enamored with the "large pastoral church." In *Christian Century* (Oct. 4, 1991), he was quoted as telling a group of church leaders to stick to pastoral ministry and to "Just say no" to social involvement.

Mainstream denominations have been slow to discern their reconstructive role in society, and lately have not thought much about developing their third-sector linkages in order to make a public difference (beyond providing a few safe social services). All the wisdom garnered in earlier decades of social mission regarding public-private-independent sector partnerships and effective methods of community organization and development has relevance. It suggests how the church, in alliance with other independent sector organizations, can respond to the crisis of human deprivation and community deterioration in North America.

The church is called to work for *shalom* — to be a laboratory of vital new community. Knowing that the world is "an intricate organism created by God for the benefit of all creatures, and a home within which humans experience life's highest purpose," the church becomes alert to ominous social developments that contradict the promised future, and acts hopefully on "a vision handed down by its confessional heritage, which describes a new world that has begun to infiltrate the old, like healing into a sick body."[12]

In this light, one cannot overstate how sociologically *and* theologically pertinent it is for mainline churches to break out of the ecclesial cul-de-sac into which the disestablishment mind-set and related denominational timidity have placed them. To pursue the mission of social transformation and reconstruction is just the opposite of retreating to the margins. It requires that the churches recover theological-ethical vigor by nurturing members in kingdom values while working with low-power groups as well as holders of institutional power to rebuild community life and to revitalize government.

Regaining Contextual Theological Focus

Along with a thoughtful critique of mainline-to-sidelines thinking and recovery of an independent public role, another related church discipline is to develop contextual theological focus in a changing society. Rapid changes are occurring in the world and in the United States that deserve the church's concentrated social concern and response.

12. Paul D. Hanson, *The People Called: The Growth of Community in the Bible* (San Francisco: Harper & Row, 1986), pp. 499, 512; and chap. 15, "The Biblical Notion of Community: Contemporary Implications."

I have just mentioned two of these changes: pluralist society and third-sector responsibility. These have worldwide significance as more countries struggle to establish stable democracy while trying to meet basic human needs under conditions of ethnic conflict, a widening rich-poor gap, and continuing arms race.

Another major change (now my particular vocational focus) is a people's movement worldwide to attend to ecological integrity within the ongoing struggle for social justice. The environmental crisis challenges prevailing paradigms of theology, life-style, and economic progress. It requires a postmodern, eco-just way of being and doing.[13]

The church is called to embody the good news that in Christ, the world is reconciled, the far off are brought near, dividing walls are broken down, and all become members of one household of God (Eph. 2). As Larry Rasmussen puts it,

> the ancient image of the world as *oikos* — a single public household — now has empirical reality . . . [and] can guide our sense of public responsibility. . . . The material and managerial well-being of the public household *(oikonomia);* the promotion of the unity of its family as a single family *(oikumene);* the knowledge of the envelope of life the household is part of, and dependent on (ecology); and the trusteeship of the household *(oikonomos)* — these are dimensions of a public vision of and for the church in our time.[14]

A crucial public role of North American churches is to think through and to embody a social vision for this time and place, "to become purposively and profoundly contextual."[15] Contextual thinking seeks *both* to become critically conscious of the contemporary situation and our social location in it, *and* to engage this historical moment from the standpoint of a witnessing community of faith.[16]

Contextual thinking involves listening to a range of voices from the powerless to the powerful, but for Christians there is more to it than being situationally alert. As Paul Lehmann described it, "The

13. See D. Hessel, ed., *After Nature's Revolt: Eco-Justice and Theology* (Minneapolis: Fortress, 1992).

14. Larry Rasmussen, "The Near Future of Socially Responsible Ministry," in *Theological Education for Social Ministry,* ed. D. Hessel (New York: Pilgrim, 1988), pp. 27-28. Also see Letty Russell, *Household of Freedom* (Louisville: Westminster/John Knox, 1987).

15. Douglas John Hall, *Thinking the Faith* (Minneapolis: Augsburg Fortress, 1989), pp. 234-35.

16. Ibid., p. 96, offers a similar definition of contextuality.

complexity of the human situation with which a koinonia ethic tries seriously to deal is always compounded of an intricate network of circumstance and human interrelationships bracketed by the dynamics of God's political activity on the one hand and God's forgiveness on the other. It is always in such a context that Christians undertake to determine what to do in the world."[17]

Contextual ethical reflection requires theological reflection linked with social analysis that would grasp the common meaning of our lives. According to Beverly Wildung Harrison, "An analysis is theological if, and only if, it unveils or envisions our lives as a concrete part of the interconnected web of all our social relations, including our relations to God. . . . An inclusive social theory is required to ground our theological analytical work because the new global system controls the life and death prospects of all of us . . . in the the poorest and the richest nations, in villages and in urban centers everywhere."[18] Such social analysis, of course, must attempt to remove ideological blinders that, in overdeveloped Western societies, almost automatically subordinate social needs and ecosystems to the harsh requirements of market economic theory and practice. Meanwhile the national economic accounting systems completely miss the continent's and world's accumulating environmental deficit.

> In sector after sector, we are consuming our natural capital at an alarming rate — the opposite of an environmentally sustainable economy. . . . As economist Herman Daly so aptly puts it, "there is something fundamentally wrong in treating the earth as if it were a business in liquidation." . . . We are depleting our productive assets, satisfying our needs today at the expense of [nature's web and] our children.[19]

Space does not permit a discussion of why modern economy is so voracious in consuming the environment, except to note that the

17. Paul Lehmann, *Ethics in a Christian Context* (Harper & Row, 1964).

18. Beverly Wildung Harrison, *Making the Connections: Essays in Feminist Social Ethics,* ed. Carol S. Robb (Boston: Beacon, 1985), p. 245. The quotation is within an excellent chapter on "Theological Reflection in the Struggle for Liberation."

19. Lester Brown, "The New World Order," *State of the World, 1991* (New York: W. W. Norton, 1991), pp. 8-9. Also see Herman E. Daly and John B. Cobb, Jr., *For the Common Good: Redirecting the Economy Toward Community, the Environment, and a Sustainable Future* (Boston: Beacon, 1989); and Hazel Henderson, *The Politics of the Solar Age: Alternatives to Economics* (Indianapolis: Knowledge Systems, 1988).

tendency to organize the world according to outmoded ideas of economism is at root a faith crisis. It exposes an underlying religious issue regarding appropriate human behavior within the web of interdependent creation. The Judeo-Christian tradition emphasizes human responsibility, derived from God's loving covenant with all created beings, to be caring and sharing stewards, acting in faithful and fitting ways for the good of the whole.[20] But the sinful inclination of alienated human beings is to seek unlimited abundance. "The classical name for this [lust] is *concupiscentia*, concupiscence — the unlimited desire to draw the whole of reality into one's self,"[21] and to devour it.

The church's social witness and ministry need to show livelier contextual theological focus on the urgent priorities of the new planetary age. Reflecting on the eternal here and now where God interacts with a dynamic creation, theology clarifies the part human beings have to play in a drama whose outcome is open. Of particular interest today is the sense that we live at the turning of an age in which assumptions that were taken for granted are seen to be part of an obsolete worldview, and there is widespread concern about the future. The contextual responsibility of the church in this crisis is "to keep human beings truthful and at the same time hopeful. . . . A truly contextual theology will be a critical theology; for it can serve the biblical God in its social context only by naming the inadequacy and the dangers of the illusion its society tries still to cling to," and by witnessing to the commonwealth of God inaugurated by Jesus.[22]

This theology has implications for social statements by mainline church bodies, which otherwise tend to become cheap and flat — cheap in declaring themselves on an array of particular issues that the church intends not to do much about; and flat in adopting unimaginative or incremental policy recommendations that reflect little self-criticism and do not challenge prevailing ideology or social practice. Significant social witness requires a depth dimension that speaks to the crisis of our time. It means looking straight at the deadly, idolatrous characteristics of a society and world system that have

20. See Charles S. McCoy, "Creation and Covenant: A Comprehensive Vision for Environmental Ethics," and J. Baird Callicott, "Genesis and John Muir," in *Covenant for a New Creation*, ed. Carol S. Robb and Carl J. Casebolt (Maryknoll, N.Y.: Orbis, 1991).

21. Paul Tillich, *Systematic Theology*, vol. 2 (Chicago: Univ. of Chicago Press, 1957), p. 52.

22. Hall, *Thinking the Faith*, pp. 190, 195.

deliberately ignored or tragically dropped many of their best opportunities to achieve justice, peace, and integrity of creation. Quality social witness must also articulate an alternative vision of a humane society where high value is placed on freedom with equity and a "sustainable sufficiency for all."[23]

Developing a Coherent Social Ethic

Closely related to the task of regaining contextual focus is the responsibility to formulate and teach a coherent ethic pertinent to current issues of social policy and practice. Of course, this task is not easy in a setting where we are bombarded with information explosions about every major social problem, and where there is intensified methodological ferment about what is morally normative.

Perhaps the most radical challenge to inherited traditions of ethics, both theological and secular, comes from feminist moral theorists, who contend that the root cause of socioeconomic domination of both women and nature is the masculinist or andocentric worldview. In sharp contast, an ecofeminist ethic "invites us to affirm our interconnection with all of life, while at the same time acknowledging the distinction between ourselves and other living beings. . . . It is an appeal to attend to nature in order to detect, not what we might want from her, but rather, what she might want from us. It is, in short, an invitation to *re-spect* nature, literally to 'look again.'"[24]

This example of ferment in moral theory illustrates the challenge of teaching and embodying a social ethic that is religiously grounded, experientially authentic, and offers clear norms that are communicable to the public. Historic quadrilateral sources of authority — Scripture, tradition, reason, and experience — remain pertinent to truthful ethical reflection;[25] today we should view them nonhierarchically as aspects of an interactive process. The responsibility of

23. See *Keeping and Healing the Creation*, prepared by the Eco-Justice Task Force (Louisville, PCUSA, 1989), chap. 5.

24. Marti Kheel, "Ecofeminism and Deep Ecology," in *Covenant for a New Creation*, pp. 146, 160. Kheel, who is a leader in animal liberation, distinguishes sharply between an ecofeminist ethic and deep ecology, though both challenge anthropocentrism.

25. See Max Stackhouse, *Public Theology and Political Economy* (Grand Rapids: Eerdmans, 1987), chap. 1.

today's church is to comprehend the socially dynamic implications of contemporary human experience and new scientific truth interacting with the faith claims or profile of faithfulness articulated in Scripture and tradition and illumined by other ancient religious ways.

Within the process of discerning what is morally authoritative, there is a discrete social ethical task. A church body or group involving Christians confronted by an event or policy issue that demands response needs to: analyze the human and social situation — gaining familiarity with the issues, impacts, persons, and powers involved; examine the theological vision expressed in Scripture, tradition, and contemporary theology that illumines this situation; form middle-range principles that approximate the religious vision and apply to the particular problem; and choose specific policy options and programs of action to support.

The core of the church's social teaching is represented in middle-range principles that interrelate theological vision and social reality while undergirding specific responses. It is essential for the church making a social witness to articulate ethical principles that apply or enhance loving justice in contextual action and reflection intended to express moral character and engage real public problems. Otherwise the church burns over the territory with one issue statement, briefing, or action after another, without giving church members and the larger public a clear sense of basic Christian social goals and the faith community's reasons for taking particular stands. Scattershot witness does not satisfy the quest for moral meaning in a world of complexity and suffering; it is more likely to encourage local churches and regional governing body committees to tour issues episodically or casually (dilettantism).

It is necessary, then, to correct the habit of doing issue "touring" or "pronouncing" (more words with few deeds) on disparate issues. The qualitatively better way, let us emphasize, is *not* to stop taking definite positions on urgent social policy choices; rather the task is to concentrate thought and action — to develop particular policy positions and education and action programs in Christian ethical depth. In fact, that kind of social involvement nurtures faithfulness.

The task of exploring and teaching a social ethic becomes all the more urgent in a postmodern situation where there could soon be "no common language in which to discuss the common weal," as theologian George Lindbeck puts it. He ponders the educational implications, though not the explicit task of teaching a social ethic. Lindbeck highlights the need for scriptural knowledge and awareness of biblical images to help form the aesthetic imagination and enrich public discourse. He proposes a deliberate strategy of inculcating "the patterns and details of [Bible] sagas and stories, its images and symbols, its syntax and grammar, which need to be internalized if one is to imagine and think scripturally."[26]

Lindbeck, however, does not call for churches to follow through publicly; he contends that "a Christianity faithful to its origins does not seek cultural and the consequent social power. Ambitions of this kind are forbidden to the servants of a crucified Messiah." Instead, the cultural mission should remain "an accident or by-product of the Christian community's faithfulness in attending to its own language and life [including] service to others."[27] This proposal has similarities to that of Stanley Hauerwas, who calls the church "to be a social ethic" rather than to shape social policy.[28] Lindbeck states a similar agenda in softer terms, proposing that churches become "communal enclaves," which are concerned with socialization and mutual support but not with social rights or public entitlements. The focus is on loving nurture, not social justice.

This approach has an historical blindspot and an obvious problem. The blindspot is that we have been there before, particularly with continental Protestantism during the 1930s. This approach implicitly returns to two-sphere thinking about the church as a community that fosters interpersonal love while leaving struggles for justice and the shaping of social policy to the orders or institutions of government and business. The communal enclave intends something else, of course — namely, to become an alternative community. But a separated, personalistic existence does not engage societal forces or the institutional realities of big organizations in policy conflict.

That brings us to the obvious problem: enclave churches would further disconnect from public discourse and involvement. In the same symposium where Lindbeck proposed this circumscribed social agenda for the churches, Rowan Williams observed that "intensive

26. George Lindbeck, "The Church's Mission to a Postmodern Culture," in *Postmodern Theology,* ed. Frederic B. Burnham (San Francisco: Harper & Row, 1989), pp. 48, 52.

27. Ibid., p. 54.

28. See Stanley Hauerwas, *A Community of Character: Toward a Constructive Christian Social Ethic* (Notre Dame: Univ. of Notre Dame Press, 1981), pp. 68-86; and a continuation of this logic in idem, *The Peaceable Kingdom* (Nashville: Abingdon, 1983), as well as Hauerwas and William Willimon, *Resident Aliens* (Nashville: Abingdon, 1989).

in-house catechesis" will not suffice. "Unless these 'enclaves' are also concerned quite explicitly with the problem of restoring an authentically public discourse in their cultural setting, they will simply collude with the dominant consumer pluralism and condemn themselves to be trivialized into stylistic preferences once more. The communal enclave, if it is not to be a ghetto, must make certain claims on the possibility of a global community, and act accordingly."[29]

Churches need to bring ethical judgment to bear in the public arena because their ministry, like that of Jesus, is a worldly activity with justice implications. In John 10, building on Ezekiel 34, Jesus says, "I came that they may have abundant life. . . . I have other sheep that do not belong to this fold. . . . So there will be one flock, one shepherd." A shepherd, biblically understood, cares for the weak, sick, crippled, strayed, lost, and takes preventive action to keep them from becoming mere prey. The prophetic purpose of pastoring is to "to feed them in justice" and to establish "a covenant of peace" (Ezek. 34:16b, 25a).

To participate in this public mission, church bodies, members, and staff must learn to "play away from home," as Williams aptly puts it. Their language must engage the public, including the public policy community, without at the same time reducing their speech to the level of vague civil Esperanto that obliterates distinctive Christian theological-ethical norms.

Let me offer a concrete example. At the suggestion of a Senate committee staffer in 1989, I arranged to send to each member of the U.S. Congress a copy of *Keeping and Healing the Creation,* a study book for which I was administratively responsible. It profiles the eco-justice crisis, and then explores its theological meaning and ethical norms for response that move toward a healthier social paradigm. A few senators and representatives began utilizing its categories, particularly the theologically disciplined ethical guidelines presented in the last chapter of the book. These same guidelines, including our discussion of "sufficiency" and "participation," percolated into secular writing about appropriate responses to the environmental crisis, which prior to 1991 focused almost exclusively on the singular norm of "sustainability."[30] Eco-justice ethics rooted in biblical covenant thought brings these norms together.

So it certainly does matter whether and how well the church

29. Rowan Williams, "Postmodern Theology and the Judgment of the World," in *Postmodern Theology,* p. 101.

30. E.g., Alan Durning, "Asking How Much is Enough," *State of the World, 1991,* pp. 153ff.

learns to play away from home, alert to dynamic analogies between the original faith story and current social choices. One way to proceed in public witness, Williams suggests, is to "so rediscover our own foundational story in the acts and hopes of others that we ourselves are reconverted."[31] This is one way to discern within contemporary social struggles the transforming power of Christ.

Only an authentic witness and ministry, immersed in a community of social action and reflection alert to shared public responsibility, establishes the right of Christians to be heard or even the possibility of Christians uttering a renewing word. To cultivate such authenticity, congregations and larger church bodies as well as theological institutions should be

> equipping us for the recognition of and response to the parabolic in the world — all that resists the control of capital and administration and hints at or struggles for a true sharing of human understanding in art, science and politics. [Theology] should also equip us to speak and act parabolically as Christians, to construct in our imagining and our acting "texts" about conversion — not [mere] translations of doctrine into digestible forms, but effective images of a new world like the parables of Christ. . . . [This] presses us further into the disciplines of listening — to our own untheologized memories and context, to the particularity of where we are, and to the efforts at meaning of the rest of the human race.[32]

Part of the church's educational task — reflected in the upsurge of interest in narrative theology and ethics — is to help form new images of the world by linking the biblical stories about God's action and human conversion with contemporary stories of personal-social pilgrimage. This is a familiar method — holding the Bible in one hand and in the other today's newspapers coupled with what we know from experience, giving special attention to texts of faithfulness. If the objective is to make a public difference, the church must do something more than retell the story. That something more, in response to an individualistic society and personalistic church, is to teach and embody a coherent social ethic that grapples with issues of justice across a range of particular policy issues and social practices.[33]

31. Williams, in *Postmodern Theology,* p. 105.

32. Ibid., pp. 110-11.

33. For examples of this function, see "Conscience and Justice: Interpreting the Social Teachings of the Presbyterian Church," *Church and Society,* Nov.-Dec., 1990.

One can reasonably object that church bodies are not well suited to the role of clarifying, let alone teaching, a coherent social ethic. Moral reasoning by committee has severe limits, as we know too well. Still, the social teaching task remains a crucial requirement. In order to make more of a public difference in a pluralist society, church committees developing social statements need to articulate middle-range ethical principles that link theological commitments to social analysis, and thus help all who discuss such reports, including public officials, to grasp where and why to move.

Similarly, church-based social education and action groups need to cultivate theological-ethical quality throughout their work. Quality, not quantity, is crucial now. Socially engaged sectors of the churches recently have relied so much on forming and servicing issue-focused advocacy networks that the basic task of leadership development for social ministry has been neglected. To teach church leaders and members a coherent ethic and holistic ways to utilize all modes of ministry[34] is basic to rebuilding the infrastructure for social witness in this new era.

Making a Public Witness to the Nation

The most urgent responsibility of the churches is to concentrate directly on developing a vigorous public witness to the nation. Such a witness to policymakers at all levels of government should be designed to foster community rebuilding and justice-oriented federal policies in this post–cold war era. The need here is for issue-transcending social analysis coupled with historical and theological vision. The cold war became a hackneyed but resource-consuming melodrama that concealed the real world. Now, after the cold war, the question is: How will the people of the United States, including church people, develop a coherent vision — a new story — of themselves in the world and embody that new story locally? Ours is a time for self-definition regarding who this people are and would like to become. It could be a time of new reformation rather than of tired restorationism. The church has a prophetic and pastoral role to play

34. D. Hessel, *Social Ministry,* rev. ed. (Louisville: Westminster/John Knox, 1992), sketches themes of a Christian social ethic and develops a holistic approach to the congregation's public ministry.

in shaping social vision. But this will not happen if the churches continue their routine pattern of making scattered social policy statements and leaving implementation merely to those who may be interested with whatever time or money they might be able to find.

Church bodies should continue to debate and adopt social statements — well done and implemented with seriousness. That, however, is the exception. For the most part, social witness by the churches remains routinely marginal to both ecclesial and public life. Church members and public officials alike pay relatively little attention to them as guides for social policy. The more controversial study papers and resolutions frequently become procedural issues — rather than matters of substantive discussion — with factions in the church arguing about the fairness of the process by which they were developed. This is hardly what was intended by leaders of the mainline denominations in twentieth-century America as they evolved toward a more serious social witness effort. Let me explain.

During the six decades from 1930 to 1990, a number of social ethicists and church leaders became more sophisticated about the task of making a public policy witness, and deliberately attempted to institutionalize a changing model. First the churches broadened their social concerns by seeking to apply the ethical idealism of the social gospel to a range of economic justice and international issues. On this basis a commitment to action for the public good gained strength in the churches. This "social trend," as John Bennett described it after World War II, meant: (1) greater emphasis on the decisiveness of social institutions and policy — a common recognition that "no degree of depth in theology and no degree of warmth in piety can compensate for failure in social sensitivity"; (2) acceptance of radical change in which no social structure is ordained by God a priori; and (3) an attempt to see the world from the viewpoint of oppressed and deprived groups or classes.[35] In a century that began with the social gospel and is concluding with the flowering of various liberation theologies, a continuity of commitment to social ministry is quite evident.

In between, under the influence of Reinhold Niebuhr's Christian realism, the churches of the 1950s and 1960s developed a model of social education and action that sought reform of social relations and structural justice. In turn the model evolved toward making an effec-

35. John Bennett, *Christian Ethics and Social Policy* (New York: Scribner's, 1946), pp. 1-12.

tive corporate witness through social analysis, advocacy, and coalitional linkage. Some denominations such as the United Presbyterian Church in the USA attempted to foster a "social policy development and implementation" model as a more institutionally serious witness than the characteristic "pronouncement" habit of church bodies.

But the model of corporate social witness has foundered on the rocks of: (1) a constant struggle to gain legitimacy for developing a social policy posture, repeatedly forcing the church to face inward; (2) a tendency to fragment or domesticate the witness by confining it programmatically to issue-focused networks that could be ignored by most of the church; and (3) lack of concentration on a strategic public witness to entities of the federal government and the nation's opinion influencers through full use of ecumenical partnerships and denominational resources. On this last point I must also note the remarkable lack of progress in linking the institutional resources of denominations and the expertise of members for the sake of making a social difference.

If we really are entering a new, postmodern era while experiencing national uncertainty if not decline, then it behooves the mainline churches to think much harder about, and to plan directly for, a witness to the nation that focuses their own social mission activity to make more of a constructive public difference. Such an approach requires quality contextual thinking, coherent development of social ethical vision and norms, and concentration on priorities for reform of domestic and foreign policy. It also challenges the church's tendency to pull back from public engagement in a self-defeating attempt to concentrate on taking care of its own members' needs or ecclesiastical business, while the society changes and everywhere

> the Spirit moves to give and renew life, to unmask idolatries in church and culture, and speaking through voices of peoples long silenced, impels the church to work with others for justice, freedom and peace.[36]

36. The concluding affirmation adapts phrases from lines 52, 69-71 of a new "Brief Statement of Faith" placed in the *Book of Confessions* by the 1991 General Assembly of the Presbyterian Church (U.S.A.).

The Church as Sign and Agent of Transformation

Dana Wilbanks

What are the implications of recent developments in Christian social ethics for understanding the church's public role? In exploring that question my focus is on normative proposals for the church's relation to the public arena rather than an analysis of prominent sociological interpretations of mainline churches, as important as this literature is (see chapter 1). I am interested in this topic not only because of its obvious pertinence for social ethicists but also because of my experience in social policy formation committees in the Presbyterian Church (U.S.A.). I am especially intrigued with what the various changes in our sociohistorical context and in the perspectives of Christian ethicists might mean for the way we envision the public role of mainline Protestant churches for the days ahead.

Students of contemporary Christian social ethics cannot help but be struck by the recent proliferation of diverse perspectives. The current scene is considerably more complex than the days when the primary options were perceived as realism, idealism, and Roman Catholic social thought. At least three directions have particular pertinence for a consideration of the church's public role.

The first direction is provided by liberation theology and ethics. According to this perspective, North American churches have identified their view of public responsibility too closely with "the American project." Churches have been far too uncritical of the impact of the United States' power on the poor and oppressed of the world. Rather than attempt to adopt the social location of the policymakers in positions of power, the churches' public engagement should be shaped by the standpoint of powerless peoples. What is needed is a radicalization of Christian social witness. Although some contemporary Christian ethicists maintain that North American power is, on balance, used for good in the world, liberation ethicists argue that the United States is not an agent of humane reform but is instead a major political and economic force behind entrenched systems of injustice.

The second direction is represented by ecclesial theologians and ethicists. According to this perspective, North American churches have given insufficient attention to their public significance as a distinctive community in the world. For some critics this means that the church's corporate role needs to be developed more thoroughly in contrast with individualistic notions of Christian social responsibility. For others, the very notion that Christian ethics should be concerned with changing society's institutions and policies through political activity is fundamentally wrong. Instead, according to this view, Christians should seek to nurture the kind of community of faith that can be a distinctive presence and witness in the world.

The third direction is provided in the thought of public theologians and ethicists. According to this perspective, North American churches have permitted themselves to become increasingly marginalized in their society. They have accepted and fostered the dualistic notion that the language of Christian faith is only appropriate in Christian circles but not in the spheres of public life. Consequently, churches have not recognized and claimed their public significance, including the potentially public import of Christian symbols and beliefs. Instead, North American Christians in their corporate existence should exemplify their deepest communal convictions and seek to shape the normative perspective of the broader social ethos.

When these directions are viewed in the context of the recent remarkable changes in international relations, a basis is provided for revisioning the church's public responsibility. With breathtaking suddenness, the walls between East and West came tumbling down in 1989. Almost no outside interpreter had anticipated these revolutionary changes, or that they would occur nonviolently for the most part. Astonishingly, the cold war is over as the dominating characteristic of international relations. This is a moment of grace given to the human community; it provides the opportunity for creative initiatives for justice and peace. Unfortunately, thus far, as tragically demonstrated in the Persian Gulf, the United States has continued to act as a hegemonic power relying primarily on overwhelming military force. Nonetheless, churches now have unparalleled opportunities to contribute to shaping a world in which the mutual hostility and threat of war between the United States and the former Soviet Union is not the determining reality.

Liberation Thought: Analysis of Dominance and Struggle for Transformation

First, I believe churches need to appropriate the social analysis, criticism, and historical projects of liberation theology in determining their public responsibility. In liberation thought, social, economic, and political structures are examined critically with the expectation that they serve the privileged at the expense of the poor and powerless.[1] Social analysis informed by a hermeneutics of suspicion seeks to illumine the dynamics of injustices, expose their ideological rationalizations, and point toward the kinds of systemic changes required to benefit the poor. Liberation thought insists that human sinfulness must be understood in terms of unjust patterns of human interrelationship that distort the mutuality for which persons are created. Social analysis is theologically vital as it focuses on unjust power relations that manifest rebellion against the liberating and reconciling reality of the God of history.

The contribution of liberation thought to an understanding of the church's public responsibility is immense. Churches doing social ethics need to begin their consideration of social responsibility with the concrete experience of suffering rather than the vantage point of policymakers.[2] This drives Christians to understand why the poor are poor and to act for the kinds of changes that are required to embody hope in social contexts of despair. Attentiveness to the cries of the poor leads to suspicion about the morality or the necessity of the existing social order. It leads to viewing the social situation from the perspective of the powerless and marginalized. The ethical presumption of the church lies with the poor rather than with the powerful or with a stance of presumed neutrality.[3]

1. See Thomas Ogletree, "The Activity of Interpreting in Moral Judgment," *Journal of Religious Ethics* 8 (Spring 1980).

2. See Beverly Harrison, *Making the Connections,* ed. Carol S. Robb (Boston: Beacon, 1985), pp. 54-80; Karen Lebacqz, *Justice in an Unjust World* (Minneapolis: Augsburg, 1987), pp. 148-54.

3. The meaning of "poor" and "oppressed" in liberation thought is complex while it is also concrete. See Enrique Dussel's discussion: "The poor are the *nothing,* the non-being, of 'this world' " (*Ethics and Community* [Maryknoll, N.Y.: Orbis, 1988], p. 55);

The social analysis of liberation thought helps to identify the primary sociohistorical challenge for the contemporary church. While it is important to subject each particular source and manifestation of injustice to thorough analysis (e.g., race, gender, class), it is not helpful to seek to determine which is the most pernicious. Instead, the various liberation theologies together point to the distorted and alienated relationship of *dominance* itself as the heart of injustice. They stress that dominance is manifested in particular, concrete, and often interrelated ways.[4] The analysis of dominance is responsive to the suspicion that unjust social relations are rooted in disproportionate power. For example, Cornel West argues that the modern historical project itself is characterized by the interrelation of various manifestations of dominance: white, male, Northern imperialistic hegemony, militarism, heterosexism, and environmental exploitation.[5] According to liberation thought, unjust power relations become structured in systems; hence systems themselves must be subjected to fundamental criticism and transformational action. It is insufficient to propose reforms in particular social sectors when systemic transformation is theologically and ethically required.

In the light of this analysis, one can interpret the various historical movements for liberation in the twentieth century as struggles to overcome specific systems of dominance. The moral promise in such movements is for mutuality and interdependence to replace dominance as the primary mode of social relationship. In a single lifetime we have experienced the crumbling of colonialism, the inter-

---

"*These here-and-now poor* are *concrete* persons, objectively determinable in real worlds, that of Aztecs, Incas, Chinese, Bantus, capitalists, socialists. . . . Everyone knows, in each *concrete* situation, who are poor and oppressed, who have fewer opportunities, goods, values, rights, and so on" (ibid., p. 76).

4. For further elaboration of the importance of "domination" for social ethics, see ibid.; Sharon D. Welch, *A Feminist Ethic of Risk* (Minneapolis: Fortress, 1990);

Gibson Winter, *Liberating Creation: Foundations of Religious Social Ethics* (New York: Crossroad, 1981). Dussel interprets sin in terms of domination and argues that domination "is the relationship that institutionally establishes a definite relationship between persons" (*Ethics*, p. 79). Welch believes oppression is rooted in white society's attempts to control other nations and peoples (*Feminist Ethic*, p. 19). She critiques the "erotics of domination," which is the glorification of absolute power, an orientation that she attributes to religious beliefs in a sovereign and omnipotent God (pp. 111-16). Winter regards domination as characteristic of the symbolization and "distorted spirituality" of the modern age. He contends that "an infinite drive to increase dominion conceals earthly creatureliness, threatening its own destruction through the very acquisition of power" (*Liberating Creation*, p. 115).

5. See Cornel West, *Prophesy Deliverance* (Philadelphia: Westminster, 1982).

national repudiation of racist ideologies and systems, and the surge of a global movement to overcome patriarchal dominance and sexism. Moreover, there is now a demonstrable heightening of international awareness of how human dominance over the earth has brought us nearer to ecological crisis and perilously close to ecological disaster.

In liberation thought these movements to transform historical systems of dominance are interpreted as signs of God's humanizing activity in history. God is the God of life, overcoming the forces of death, which come in concrete forms of economic, political, military, and social oppression and repression in the everyday lives of many of the world's peoples. Jesus is the embodiment of God in personal existence, disclosing God's special identification with the struggle of the poor and manifesting that truly human existence is realized in solidarity with the poor. Justice is therefore a theologically based imperative for transforming relationships from patterns of dominance and alienation to genuine mutuality and reconciliation. For example, Beverly Harrison understands justice "as the rightly ordered relationships of mutuality within the total web of our social relations."[6] Liberation ethics clearly represents a transformative perspective of advocacy on behalf of the poor and oppressed with a vision of just community as the trajectory of God's redemptive activity in the world.

Yet with all the positive historical changes to transform long-entrenched systems of dominance, many remain. Racism and sexism continue in powerful and often subtle forms. Apartheid dominance remains in South Africa at cruel cost to the black population. Ethnic and religious conflicts in various societies point to other manifestations that dominance may take in the years to come. Even though very positive changes have occurred in Europe, worldwide gaps between rich and poor, both inside Northern countries and between the relatively affluent Northern countries and brutally poor Third World countries, are appalling. With all the trumpeting about the failures of socialism and the successes of market economies, too little attention is being given to the failures of capitalism, or democratic societies with market economies, to secure economic justice.

Liberation thought challenges churches to embrace a transformative role in the public arena. Churches are to participate in overcoming systems of dominance that block historical possibilities for justice. Churches need to identify and contribute to the specific his-

6. Harrison, *Making the Connections*, p. 253.

torical projects of liberation that bear the greatest promise for the poor, recognizing that the initiative and leadership in such projects is to be found in communities whose primary social location is with the poor. This view of the church's public role clearly requires a sharply critical stance with regard to "the American project" in the world. The implications of liberation ethics for North American churches are radical and controversial. It is no easy task to open churches to this theological vision of public responsibility. Fundamental changes are required of us all. Convictions about God's call to seek justice with the poor must be an outflowing of authentic piety requiring *metanoia* and inner transformation as well as public engagement in social transformation.

Although many church members will resist this vision, many others will respond, indeed, have already responded: for example, persons involved in Witness for Peace in Nicaragua, the nuclear weapons freeze campaign, women's support groups, environmental protection efforts, and social ministries with the homeless. The most powerful recent expression of the North American church's transformative role in the public arena is the story of the black struggle for freedom. The breadth of the impact of that story was visible in songs and signs from the courageous Chinese student protesters in Tienanmen Square to the nonviolent protests in Leipzig.

The North American church has in various times and places participated in the public struggle for transformation both through critique of the injustices of dominance and committed advocacy for the justice of mutuality. The challenge and opportunity for exercising this public role persist in our own historical context.

Furthermore, North American churches can be challenged and inspired by the creative growth of basic ecclesial communities in other contexts. These are at once worshiping and supportive communities, nurturing the development of persons into historical subjects empowered by faith. Persons learn and practice the skills of participating in decision making and exercising community leadership. The base communities are a force for life among the oppressed. The authorities often perceive their very existence as a threat. Indeed, basic ecclesial communities provide an alternative to the structures of dominance, and they empower persons to begin the long struggle for systemic change. They can teach North American churches about the integral relation of piety, community, and social transformation.[7]

7. See Ana Maria Tepedino, "Feminist Theology as the Fruit of Passion and

Ecclesial Ethics: The Church as Communal Sign of Transformation

Questions remain, however, about the relation of a liberation perspective to the church's public role and what is usually experienced in the life of many mainline congregations. This contrast leads to reflection on the second direction in contemporary Christian social ethics, namely, the emphasis on the church itself in calls to Christian social responsibility. Particularly influential is the proposal for narrative ethics provided by Stanley Hauerwas.[8] He has had a major impact on many ethicists in shifting attention from methods of decision making and from public policy questions to issues of the moral character of Christians and churches. For him the social analysis of disproportionate power is not very interesting ethically. What is interesting is the collapse of foundations for ethics in the modern world, the confusing and incoherent array of moral messages in contemporary society, and the persisting presence of violence. He argues that theological ethics should be concerned with the development of the Christian story as the coherent and truthful narrative that can shape the character of Christians within the particular and distinctive community of the church.

The church is pivotal for Hauerwas because the Christian story is about the ways God creates a people who are able to live nonviolently in a violent world. The church should pattern its life after the life of Jesus. When it is faithful to the life of Jesus the church is a radically distinctive sociohistorical community in the world. The church should not be concerned with trying to change the world. It should seek to witness to the truth about God's ways with the world and recognize that it is precisely in such faithful witness that God brings the eschatological future of the peaceable kingdom into history. The Christian life is a deeply communal one. Hauerwas clearly regards the church's calling as an adventurous journey of faith in which

---

Compassion," in *With Passion and Compassion*, ed. Virginia M. M. Fabella and Mercy Amba Oduyoye (Maryknoll, N.Y.: Orbis, 1988), pp. 165-72. She emphasizes the importance of women's leadership in basic ecclesial communities, "in the movement to create an alternative to this wasteful, consumerist, individualistic, and hedonistic society" (p. 166). Basic ecclesial communities are vital relational contexts for women to live out their commitment to life in all its varied aspects.

8. See especially Stanley Hauerwas, *The Peaceable Kingdom* (Notre Dame: Univ. of Notre Dame Press, 1983).

Christians embody in their life together such virtues as truth telling, forgiveness, hospitality to the stranger, patience, and hope.

What are the implications in Hauerwas's thought for the church's public role? Hauerwas objects to the criticism that he is a sectarian. I am inclined to agree with him. In his view the church should not, indeed cannot, withdraw from the world. The point is to engage the world and to challenge the world with a different ethical perspective, one that is not merely a set of ideas but is incarnate in a specific human community. The church is to be that community which represents a different way of living in the world. This is precisely its contribution to the public arena. Hauerwas's position is consistent with "the intentional motif" in the history of Christian ethics.[9] It is a version of the parallel or alternate institutions model of social change developed by sociologists, except that it is not advocated as a pragmatic means to change the social order.

Hauerwas is most consistent with the sectarian tradition in his seeming skepticism about or even opposition to efforts to change the world. Here he has clearly broken with the social change orientation of the social gospel and Christian realist tradition. Not only does he base his position on theological grounds; he also seems to call into question the assumption of political liberalism that it is possible to change the world qualitatively through political action. Here he is in league with other disillusioned postmodern thinkers who doubt that projects aimed at societal transformation amount to very much. Instead, hope in a public sense can best be inspired by the existence of alternative communities that demonstrate that it is possible to live in a different way than the presumed necessities and conventions dictate.

I believe that Hauerwas's ethics have great value. His arguments that Christian convictions are important in shaping the moral life, that the church should embody these convictions in its own life, and that the church should be a distinctive witness in the world need to be affirmed. He challenges social ethicists to take the church seriously, which often they have failed to do.[10] Yet one need not conclude that this is the *only* social ethical task.

9. See Edward LeRoy Long, Jr., *A Survey of Christian Ethics* (New York: Oxford Univ. Press, 1967), pp. 252-90.

10. Yet the renewed interest in ecclesiology by Christian social ethicists can be readily seen in the 1980s. See, e.g., Dieter T. Hessel, *Social Ministry*, rev. ed. (Louisville: Westminster/John Knox, 1992); Peter Paris, *The Social Teaching of the Black Churches* (Philadelphia: Fortress, 1985).

Thomas Ogletree is more convincing when he points to the ecclesial radicalism of the New Testament as the communal embodiment of the eschatological vision of God's promise in Christ. The theological and ethical import of this vision extends to the whole world and is to be brought to bear through struggles for historical transformation. Churches are to live according to the new age of Christ in the midst of the old age, drawing taut the tensions this necessarily produces, embodying in their own life and seeking for the world the radical inclusiveness of God's future.[11] In this contrasting view, the calling for the church is indeed to fashion in its own life together a community reality that incarnates in history its beliefs about God's purposes for the world. Yet it is also to be an agent of historical transformation as it brings its faith to bear in concrete struggles to change the world, to seek for the world the realization of the vision it is called to manifest in its own life.

The life and thought of Martin Luther King, Jr., emphasizes that the most fundamental tension in Christian ethics is not between the world and the church but between the future and the present.[12] For King, the black struggle for freedom, rooted in the spirituality of the black church, was to model in its organization and strategies the future for which it works and, at the same time, to seek the realization of that future through social and political action. My point is that the challenge to shape in the church itself a community of justice and mutuality is integral to, not in opposition to, the Christian responsibility to contribute to overcoming patterns of dominance in the contemporary world. It is noteworthy that Hauerwas is silent about the challenge of King, who in certain respects shares his view of Jesus and nonviolence but clearly believes this can be embodied in sociopolitical efforts to transform the world as well as provide norms for the church's own life.

The attention to ecclesiology in recent Christian ethics is very important for reconsidering the church's public role. The creative contribution of Hauerwas is to focus on ecclesiology as the concrete and communal embodiment of God's peace in history. Christians are called to be innovative in their own communities by fashioning non-

11. See Thomas Ogletree, *The Use of the Bible in Christian Ethics* (Philadelphia: Fortress, 1983), pp. 175-205.

12. See Martin Luther King, Jr., *A Testament of Hope: The Essential Writings of Martin Luther King, Jr.*, ed. James Melvin Washington (San Francisco: Harper & Row, 1986).

dominant patterns of relationships and organizational structures, not only to press these norms on other institutions. It is a profoundly significant *public* contribution for churches to model inclusiveness, hospitality to strangers, justice, and mutuality. Christians who focus only on purportedly pragmatic strategies of social change may well miss the potential power of providing alternatives to the dominant models of social organization and human relationship. For example, the Presbyterian Church has increasingly sought to insure that each social policy recommendation includes actions related to the church itself as well as to appropriate public institutions and officials. Beyond this it may be important for denominations to give special priority to stimulating and supporting innovative efforts of congregations to implement in their own life the visions they seek to commend to the world.

The argument that the modeling role of the church is publicly significant makes the point that the church's responsibility is diverse and frequently subtle. The specifically political effort of Christians is one way to engage the public realm. But there are other ways as well, and these may be corporate as well as individual. For example, the sanctuary movement in the 1980s demonstrated the powerful relation between compassionate service and political struggle in the church's public witness. Sanctuary was primarily a response to the vulnerability of Central American refugees, designed to protect specific refugees yet also to communicate their plight to the broader national community. It was a corporate decision, involving the whole congregation. It was a symbolic act, demonstrating the public potency of vital symbols. Many who were involved in sanctuary ministry did not eschew political action but recognized the importance of making hospitality visible in churches as well as working for change through political processes. This is an example of the kind of imaginative corporate exercise of public witness that is often available to the church and that deserves further attention.

Public Theology: Transforming the Public Ethos

The third direction in contemporary Christian social ethics is represented by public theology and ethics. It is sharply critical of a dualistic outlook among Christians in which theology is regarded as pertinent to the church but not to the public realm. In this perspective, not only has theological discourse been withdrawn from the public sphere but it has become increasingly "strange" even to persons in the church. Professors in theological schools often lament the inability of students "to theologize" about contemporary life. If theology is a nonpublic language, however, it is not likely to be any more understandable to people in churches than it is to "secular" persons. Theology has become an esoteric language for the few. The chief contribution of Max Stackhouse's ethics is his insistence on the public significance of Christian theology.

Stackhouse opposes dualistic notions about the relation of theological ethics and human societies by illumining the ways that normative intellectual traditions are concretely embodied in cultural mores and structures. The analytic task of social ethics is to describe and interpret the implicit as well as explicit creeds that shape human communities. He defines a creed as "a doctrine held to be true, embraced with commitment, celebrated in concert with others, and used as a fundamental guide to action."[13] The constructive task is to articulate and advocate the normative perspective of theological ethics in the public arena, that is, to shape contemporary societies by the creed of Christian theological ethics.

Stackhouse's theological ethics is explicitly rooted in the biblical covenant tradition, particularly as it is articulated historically in the trinitarian creed of the Christian church[14] and rendered normative in a synthesis of liberal and Puritan influences in modern North American society. The theological content is rich, involving interpretations of God as parent, son, and spirit. Clearly central is the righteous sovereignty of God in creation and history — judging as well as sustaining and transforming human existence. This theology gives rise to a normative perspective on human rights that stresses the equal value of every human person, the freedom of persons from determination by psyche and culture, the relativization of authorities and the right to resist absolutism, ongoing and transforming criticism of social reality, the value of rationality, and the necessity of social space for such values to flourish.[15] He has also shown how this theological orientation gives special signifi-

13. See Max L. Stackhouse, *Creeds, Society, and Human Rights* (Grand Rapids: Eerdmans, 1984), p. 2.

14. Idem, *Ethics and the Urban Ethos* (Boston: Beacon, 1972); idem, *Creeds*.

15. Idem, *Creeds*, pp. 267-82.

cance to the norm of stewardship for shaping contemporary political economies.[16]

Theological ethics, therefore, is not only pertinent for the life of the church and for influencing the conscience and behavior of Christians but is explicitly normative for the public realm as well. Attempts to identify ethical norms that are areligious or religiously neutral are deeply flawed because they ignore how norms necessarily arise from convictions about the holy. Christian theological beliefs and ethical norms need to be articulated publicly as a compelling normative perspective for evaluating and shaping the full breadth of society's structures. Stackhouse further departs from many contemporary colleagues when he firmly rejects the notion that the normativity of theological ethics is relative and communally particular. He maintains, for example, that Judeo-Christian theological ethics provides the basis for a universal ethic of human rights in the contemporary world.

The implications of Stackhouse's thought for the public responsibility of the church are quite clear. The church is to represent and advocate a public theology as the normative basis for society and its institutions. Churches should no longer be diffident about speaking theologically in public. Stackhouse is not interested in establishing or reestablishing a kind of Christian institutional dominance in diverse societies. He is explicitly critical of imperialist expressions of Christianity.[17] In his proposal Christian theology can provide a normative foundation for a democratic and pluralistic society without functioning in a dogmatic or sectarian way. He is convinced that public discourse about theological ethics is critically important because religious commitments and perspectives are the strongest determinant of the character of societies. Theological ethics is precisely the basis on which public debate needs to turn.

I agree with Stackhouse that an important element in the church's public role is to learn how to speak theologically in public, to propose the embodiment of these norms in its own life and in the wider public ethos — and to do so in ways that do not presume privileged access to truth, or express religious authoritarianism or intolerance toward creedological traditions of other particular communities. Churches need to attend to the language of public discourse

16. Idem, *Public Theology and Political Economy* (Grand Rapids: Eerdmans, 1987).
17. Idem, *Creeds*, pp. 59-60, 75.

and to contribute their theological understandings in normative public debate. In the influential study of Bellah, et al., the authors point to the impoverishment of language about public commitments.[18] People may be involved in public life in vital ways but do not have the vocabulary to account for it. There is no need for an enrichment of the language used in the public arena, so that the symbols, myths, and visions of particular communities, non-Christian as well as Christian, are welcomed in public discourse rather than excluded. I would emphasize more than Stackhouse the values of dialogue between Christian theology and other religious traditions in shaping public theology. Even so it is not sufficient for churches only to advocate public policy objectives or to support pragmatic strategies to accomplish these objectives. They must also seek to contribute to the enrichment and vitalization of public discourse that is fundamental to the moral promise of human communities.

At a city college I recently participated in a team-taught course with a rabbi and a professor of public policy on "Religion and Public Policy." Most of the students already had careers and were deeply involved in politics. For example, one was a staff member in the office of a U.S. senator from Colorado. Another was the staff director of the American Civil Liberties Union in Colorado. Generally, they were much more interested in what I could inform them about specific Christian beliefs (e.g., God, Christ, sin, eschatology) *and* how Christians related these beliefs to public policy questions than they were in my attempts to "translate" Christian understandings into more generalized moral and political language. They stated explicitly that they wanted religionists to represent their religious perspectives, not merely advocate a particular policy position. Although there was some Moral Majority bashing in the class, they were not rebelling against Christian pretensions to ethical dominance (as perhaps an earlier generation was). Instead they were curious and reflective about how Christian and Jewish beliefs might contribute to moral deliberation about public issues.

Stackhouse emphasizes another point as well. He regards the surest institutional protection for ongoing social reform to be the legally protected space for voluntary associations to organize and assert their convictions publicly. Where this space is protected, the churches have an especially important opportunity to exercise a transformative influ-

18. See Robert Bellah, et al., *Habits of the Heart* (Berkeley: Univ. of California Press, 1985).

ence on society. Churches are to nourish their capacities to shape the public ethos. Stackhouse is openly critical of the failures of North American churches (indeed, ecumenical Christianity) to engage in a public struggle over the explicit and implicit creeds that are to be determinative in public life.[19] Churches should be active agents in seeking those changes in society that would embody their deepest creedological perspectives on God and the human community.

In entering into public discourse about policy questions it is also important for churches to attend to the spirit of society and to seek to nourish and vitalize spiritual resources for social transformation. Widespread cynicism and apathy in American society manifest diseases of the spirit that need healing. Spiritual qualities of hope, generosity, and public-spiritedness are required for a vital public life. Mainline churches could learn much from African American churches about ways to address public issues with imaginative appropriations of biblical imagery while nourishing, sustaining, and empowering people for the difficult, frequently frustrating, and sometimes dangerous work of social transformation. Martin Luther King, Jr., provides profound insights into the content of a transformative public theology while also emphasizing how essential it is to minister to the spirit of human communities.

Implications for Churches

I am arguing here that the church's public role and responsibility is a transformative one. The church's theology calls and equips it to be both an agent and a sign of God's redemptive love. The church's role is not a matter of either/or but of both/and. Moreover, this role is not to be understood as an ahistorical ideal but as a vision of the promised future that bears on present options and possibilities. In the current historical context I have suggested that a particularly pressing challenge for the church is to engage in the analysis and critique of dominance, and through modeling and public advocacy to struggle for the transformation of dominance into justice, mutuality, and inclusive community, including community with the earth and nonhuman life.

This understanding of the church's role is in basic continuity with the social gospel and Christian realist tradition in advocating

19. Stackhouse, *Creeds*, p. 281.

participation in social change as a requirement of the gospel. It seeks to build on that tradition by attending to the challenge of liberation theology to overcome the dynamics of dominance, the challenge of ecclesiological ethicists to emphasize the public significance of the church as a distinctive sociohistorical community, and the challenge of public theologians to make explicit the normative implications of Christian discourse for the public arena.

Moreover, historic Protestant convictions about the relation of church and state can continue to inform and empower mainstream Protestant churches' engagement with the public order. God is at the center of public life as well as of church life, ordering civil institutions for human well-being. When the state serves the purposes ordained by God, Christians are to cooperate with the state in their realization. But when the state acts in ways contrary to these purposes or, even more seriously, systematically and persistently violates God's righteousness, Christians are called to a posture of criticism and even, on occasion, resistance. For Protestants, Christians are called to serve God in the public order both in cooperation and criticism, support and dissent, dependent on theological and ethical discernment in each context, guided by the Holy Spirit.

In conclusion, let me summarize some of the primary points in the above analysis and comment on several possible implications for churches.

First, churches need to contribute their particular theological and ethical convictions to broader public discourse. This will require experimentation as the churches learn to express their theology of transformation in varied public arenas. Churches do not have to accept the thesis that they are increasingly marginalized in their public influence. Indeed, one can make a strong case that churches made an important contribution in the 1980s to public debate about U.S. nuclear weapons policies. In that decade, for the first time since the inauguration of the nuclear era, the moral and political legitimacy of the nuclear arms race was seriously challenged and weakened. Local churches were very likely among the primary settings where moral deliberation on the arms race occurred. Often they were struggling with ways to express their theological convictions about peace in public as well as in church arenas. Churches can function as communities of moral deliberation on public issues and can help shape the public ethos through more energetic and intentional engagement.

Second, in their public witness, churches need to focus on an analysis of dominance and advocacy for social transformation. Of course, many public issues are appropriately matters for the churches' attention. But the pressing historical challenge of our context is to overcome the injustices of class, race, and gender dominance while also establishing a creation-affirming relation between humans and the rest of nature. It is crucial that churches have a focus; otherwise they too easily dissipate their energies in an endless list of particular issues and causes. North American churches can most faithfully discern their public role through a direct engagement with the poor and the readiness to be transformed by this encounter.

Third, churches need to be engaged in service ministries as an integral dimension of congregational life. In an important sense, of course, all aspects of congregational life can be understood as social ministry.[20] Here I have a more precise meaning in mind. Insofar as members of churches are involved in ministries with the poor (e.g., with the homeless, hungry, refugees, battered, AIDS patients, medically indigent, severely disabled), they are opening themselves to the experience and perspective of the poor. It is through service ministries that North American churches can be most concretely engaged with the poor and nurture the experiential basis for a transformative public witness. At the same time, reflection on the experience of service ministries is essential. Direct involvement in service ministries does not automatically lead to enhanced sensitivity to systemic injustices.[21]

Fourth, churches need to educate and equip their members for creative public involvement. Churches can no longer take for granted that members know how to participate in public life, much less seek to transform it. The General Assembly of the Presbyterian Church (U.S.A.) called its members to "the extraordinary use of ordinary means" to change the U.S. government's nuclear weapons policies.[22] Even though the dangers of the cold war have been receding, the same

20. See Hessel, *Social Ministry.*

21. In September 1989, I heard Carl Dudley speak to this point. He is director of a Church and Community Project of the Center for Church and Community Ministries at McCormick Theological Seminary. His field research has led him to conclude that there is a barrier between commitment to service and commitment to justice. The one does not automatically flow into the other. Indeed, it has been difficult to join the two. This critical issue deserves further attention.

22. See General Assembly (200th), Presbyterian Church (U.S.A.), "Christian Obedience in a Nuclear Age," *Minutes* (Louisville: Office of the General Assembly, 1988), p. 490.

political imperative applies to proliferating arms sales and to the scandalous contrasts of rich and poor in the world. A transformational politics is required. Churches need to accept corporate responsibility for training members to be agents of transformation.

There is a long-standing debate in Christian social ethics between those in favor of changing society through established processes of party politics, elections, and lobbying and those who seek change through the mobilization of peoples. Although I do not believe it is necessary to choose between these strategies, I believe greater weight should be placed on generating involvement in grass-roots organizations and movements that are seeking transformative change. Churches need to help people explore modes of public participation that go beyond "politics as usual." In addition to fostering the exploration of innovative public strategies, churches need to provide the pastoral nurture and support that enable people to persist in their engagement over the long term — indeed, for a lifetime.

Fifth, churches need to model in their own communal life their convictions about God's transformative activity in the world. An example of the public significance of this role came to light in the revolutionary changes in East Germany in 1989. For over a decade many churches in East Germany had been studying and practicing peacemaking with little expectation that their efforts would be translated into public policy.[23] Yet because of the work *within* churches, when the opportunity arose the churches were able to contribute their commitment to nonviolent change within the growing public resistance to the East German government.[24]

In a social policy statement adopted by the 1988 General Assembly of the Presbyterian Church (U.S.A.), the members were challenged to participate in "projects of reconciliation" similar to Witness for Peace in Nicaragua during the 1980s.[25] These projects would place church members in contexts of harsh conflict in order to make the resort to violence less likely and to provide bridges for resolving the

23. See Pedro Ramet, *Cross and Commissar: The Politics of Religion in Eastern Europe and the USSR* (Bloomington and Indianapolis: Indiana Univ. Press, 1987), pp. 80-96.

24. See John P. Burgess, "Church in East Germany Helps Create die Wende," *Christian Century* 106 (1989): 1140-42; Barbara G. Green, "An 'Incomparable Chance' for GDR Churches," *Christianity and Crisis* 50 (March 5, 1990): 55-57.

25. See General Assembly (200th), Presbyterian Church (U.S.A.), "Christian Obedience," p. 494.

conflict without violent confrontation. The modeling role of the church is far more potent than some pragmatically oriented persons have realized; yet it must be developed with imagination, clarity, and boldness.

Sixth, churches need to seek social transformation through ecumenical and coalitional organizations and networks. In their public role, churches should both cultivate and represent the broadest expressions of distinctive Christian witness and support and work with non-Christian groups who share a similar social vision.

In the current situation, a particular challenge for ecumenical Christianity is to form an organization (both transnational and interdenominational) oriented toward public action that is shaped by Christian convictions about God's liberating activity on behalf of the dominated. The church is a transnational community, but there are few institutional expressions of the church's global inclusiveness. Moreover, opportunities for clergy and laity to participate in the development of denominational social policy or to represent denominations in current ecumenical organizations (like the National Council of Churches and the World Council of Churches) are exceedingly limited. A different kind of ecumenical organization could draw support from denominations but provide a channel for Christian public witness that is outside particular denominational polities. The need is to make Christian public theology and action international, and to make it more broadly participatory. Such an initiative would not replace other avenues for political involvement and Christian social action but might be envisioned as an ecclesial form through which Christians could intentionally and explicitly bring their religious convictions to bear on public life in an interdependent world.[26]

26. Two decades ago, Max Stackhouse proposed the institutionalization of an ethics of just peace as an alternative ecclesiology to the institutionalization of the "ethics of necropolis" (*The Ethics of Necropolis* [Boston: Beacon, 1971]). This idea has never received the attention it deserves.

A Response

David Ramage, Jr.

It is a pleasure to be part of a conversation that is seeking ways to express radical hope and focused love and that strives to find both pragmatic discipline and embodied truth seeking action. There is here no serious question of the proposition that faith in action is in some way accountable to the dispossessed and that truth as revealed in the life, death, and resurrection of our Lord is profoundly dialectical. I say this with appreciation because my personal background is one of activist, pragmatic administrator and mission strategist. I am not a scholar, although I care about intellectual rigor, clarity, focus, and integrity. I must caution that in the messiness of acting in the world it is hard to find clarity about either truth or sin; one learns to hope and struggle in the midst of large measures of moral ambiguity. One can, however, seek solidarity with authentic experience, which is where agendas and priorities should ultimately be forged.

As I respond to Dana Wilbanks and Dieter Hessel, I must assert first my appreciation for these forceful presentations. Both have brought particular clarity to their positions, and they share many views.

Wilbanks's review of our dynamic sociohistorical context reminds us of the theological journey, and his description of changing understanding of public and private faith responsibilities is helpful. He is on solid ground in his strong defense of liberation thought as not only useful but theologically vital. I affirm the clarity of his assertion that social criticism and transformational action is essential to the church's role and that ultimately reform strategies are insufficient signs of God's humanizing activity in history. He offers a powerful and insightful description of the voices that perceive the seeds of disaster in the modes of dominance that characterize our social behavior.

He refers to voices such as Martin Luther King, Jr., Cornel West, and others. I wish he had been able to develop from these reflective thinkers and others who have been engaged in faithful action and the search for justice a more complete framework of thought and a practical rationale for action.

I am afraid that while I found his careful description of Hauerwas's work interesting and challenging, it was neither convincing nor was it helpful in relation to the subject of this conversation. Wilbanks's own insistence on important symbols, clear myths, and articulated vision as legitimate modes of communication in the public realm does provide a framework for utilizing Hauerwas's insights in the service of public justice and peace. His reminder that Martin Luther King, Jr., insisted that the church be both a community of justice and mutuality and accept responsibility to be active in overcoming patterns of dominance in the modern world serves the argument well.

Wilbanks's helpful unpacking of Stackhouse's conviction that contemporary societies must be shaped by Christian theological ethics, consistent with affirmations hammered out and articulated in the creeds of the churches, makes very clear how troubling is the suggestion of a normative relationship between church and society in our contemporary complex social reality. Stackhouse offers much to challenge and even excite interest, such as the role of voluntary associations in protected space and the norm of stewardship for shaping political economics. But ultimately the implied dominance of creedal thought over the insights derived from mutual struggle is unacceptable to me. I stand with Wilbanks in his commitment to a transformative role for the church and for Christians in society. I suspect that his case could have been made even stronger if he had fully recognized the critical importance of experience in particular contexts of struggle as a necessary learning and analytic framework.

Dieter Hessel's clear vision of what the mainline churches need to do to be publicly active and accountable is impressive. He has a position and he argues it forcefully. He takes on what he sees as the opposition directly and names the alternatives as he sees them. He rejects status politics, but he himself may be infected with the disease. What is faithful and how to live faithfully in the public sphere are not about how to oppose those who disagree or who regret or deny such faithfulness. We should concentrate more on bringing forth from gospel, tradition, and serious analysis a dialogue among contending thoughts, attitudes, and efforts to find faithfulness.

Hessel points out that arguments about the marginalization of the church are not only a diversion but a strong disincentive to the faithfulness that is possible in the ways and with the influence available to the church. Such arguments help to keep the church from being where it belongs: with the truly marginalized, wherever else it also lives and serves.

Hessel argues that the liberal-conservative struggle in the churches is a diversion from accepting the reality of an emerging plural society, where many if not all feel culturally and politically marginalized and are asking questions like: Where do we belong? With whom? And how? What is needed is not a return to any exclusive or dominant authority but to find for ourselves a legitimate and authentic voice in a plural conversation.

Hessel makes a plea for an enlarged commitment by the church to social mission that is engaged and real. Hessel's plea for us "to renew a normative Christian ethical framework in dynamic interaction with today's social realities" is on the right track. But the use of "normative" by both Wilbanks and Hessel is troubling for me. The very heart of social responsibility in a complex, multicultural world of many particular contexts of meaning and reality makes the use of "normative" language problematic. A norm is defined as correctness, as trying to establish rules for all, of reflecting assumptions or favoring an assumption. Its intent is to set a standard, serve as a model, prescribe a pattern. It is a standard based on a given, a past, or a real value. These are the definitions of Webster. The very nature of today's social reality and of this conversation calls into question the idea of "normative." By whose standard or authority or assumption should we be normative? Careful analysis and reasoning can inform the struggles but not create the norms. It may be wise to remind ourselves that Marxist analysis was and is a useful tool in analytic understanding, but Marxism as embodied in state socialism (communism) is a tragically failed experiment.

I am grateful that Hessel has introduced me to Rowan Williams with his emphasis on a dynamic and authentic interaction of act, event, context, persons, and community, and with his welcoming appreciation for imagination and the possibility of successive reconversions to gospel understanding and commitment that keeps us in the public place with our witness.

In each place, with each particular set of contenders, we have to seek the appropriateness of thought and action. Context is as important as creed. Pragmatism must come to the fore in a new way if we are to move beyond the ideologies that so quickly becomes idolatries. Imaginative new approaches to public discourse and communication must be found and tried. Vision and myth and symbol must be revalued.

Wilbanks urges us to engage in public participation and pastoral nurture at the same time. I endorse that fully, for how else can we do the analysis, seek the clarity, remember the truths, and tell the stories that faithfulness requires?

If I had time I would press further, mostly with affirmation for these thoughtful presentations. May they help us to encourage legitimate and authentic voices that are inclusive, not exclusive; that point to the integrative and integral; and that seek coherence, not competition or domination.

My bias in the search for the church's public role is not only to bet on the remnant of the faithful or on the hope for an idealized, revitalized institution but to seek a focused, targeted, clear, and purposeful direction for those who would be faithful in the struggle, working with those who have need, in our present situation.

The Public Role of the Black Churches

Peter J. Paris

The principle of autonomy underlies the life and mission of the black churches. From the time of their birth up to the present day, the black churches have stood in their respective communities as symbols of independence from white domination, quietly transmitting by their ubiquitous presence the spirit of dignity and self-respect. As will become evident in the course of this chapter, both the principle of autonomy and its impact on the black community are deeply rooted in religious, political, and moral values.

By the beginning of the eighteenth century, most white Christians in America were generally agreed that Africans were not fully a part of the human species and consequently should not be converted to Christianity. Accordingly, the earliest missionaries to America from Spain, France, and England concentrated their energies on the evangelization of the Indians, with little or no concern for the spiritual life of the African slaves. During the Great Awakenings, many Christian revivalists (especially Methodists and Baptists) had come to believe that African slaves should be converted to Christianity and began focusing attention on that goal.

Most slaveholders at the time opposed such activities because they assumed that Christianity implied free citizenship. Hence they believed that the experience of religious equality in church membership would cause slaves to aspire to civil equality as well. When they became convinced, however, both by law and by custom that Christian conversion did not necessarily imply any such change in a member's civil status, some relaxed their opposition for at least two reasons: (1) their own personal conversion sometimes caused them to see the evangelization of their slaves as an expression of their Christian compassion; (2) their gradual conviction that the system of slavery could function more efficiently with converted slaves because the latter would likely cultivate the virtues of truth telling, honesty, and patience, the lack of which among slaves constituted a major disciplinary problem.

Thus by the middle of the eighteenth century the membership of many white churches included slaves because whites were unwilling to permit racially separate associations, fearing slave involvement in abolitionist activity. Further, most whites continued to believe in the inferiority of blacks and resented any semblance of equality that might be implied by the latter's membership in their churches. Hence the custom emerged of relegating slaves to segregated status within white churches: separate seating arrangements, receipt of holy communion after the whites had been served, neither voice nor vote in matters of church governance. In spite of these restrictive conditions, however, some of the slaves gained considerable status as preachers, praised by both whites and blacks for their oratorical excellence.

The Black Church Independence Movement came into existence through the agency of freed slaves in Northern cities. Unwilling at first to form racially separate organizations lest they be viewed as racists, their founders eventually agreed to the proposition that their choice to separate themselves from the white churches was not racist but rather a religious and moral refusal to comply with racist practices that robbed them of human dignity in the house of God. Convinced that compliance with racism compromised their understanding of the Christian faith by denying the parenthood of God and the kinship of all peoples, they felt obligated both theologically and morally to separate themselves from such blasphemy and to establish alternative churches that would institutionalize the principles of God's parenthood and humanity's kinship.[1]

From the beginning, black churches have rejected racism, viewing it as the paramount sin of the white churches. Hence they have never had policies of exclusion or segregation based on race or ethnicity. Rather, every independent black church that chose to separate itself from its white counterpart from the time of the American Rev-

1. For a full discussion of this principle and its institutionalization in the black churches see my *Social Teaching of the Black Churches* (Philadelphia: Fortress, 1986), chap. 1.

olution up to the present time did so as a religious and moral response to the sin of institutionalized racism. Deliberately removing themselves from the social practice of racism constituted the public role of the black churches at the moment of their birth. This originating principle enabled them to provide an independent space for their people to worship God and to serve the needs of their people in accordance with their own desires and choices. Faithful devotion to the principle of racial autonomy enabled them to construct alternative religious institutions with the unique aim of serving the well-being of blacks in every dimension of their common life. This factor alone differentiated them completely from the white churches, which had never been primarily concerned with the well-being of black Americans, whether slave or free. Accordingly, the black churches have always exercised multifaceted roles in the black community since no area of life was excluded from its purview.

Being the only independent institution in the community that was owned and controlled by blacks and dedicated to the maintenance and enhancement of the community's well-being, the black churches played a role in their communities analogous to that of governments. No other institution served the good of the black community. Theologically and morally legitimated by all blacks, the churches not only founded schools, colleges, seminaries, hospitals, publishing houses, newspapers, insurance companies, banks, countless social clubs, and the like, but they institutionalized the most basic moral values of the community and provided the role models for community leadership. In fact, for generations the black churches have been the training ground for ecclesiastical, political, civil rights, and educational leadership, and countless numbers of professional singers, musicians, and artists got their initial support, encouragement, and promotion from the churches. In short, throughout the nineteenth and much of the twentieth century, the black churches inevitably had a role to play in virtually every good thing that occurred in the lives of black people. From a sociological perspective, E. Franklin Franzier spoke of the church as the primary agency for social organization and social cohesion following emancipation.[2]

One basic reason why the black churches have flourished is clearly their unadulterated commitment to the good of the black

2. See E. Franklin Frazier, *The Negro Church in America* (New York: Schocken, 1964), pp. 82ff.

community. They alone provided blacks with opportunities for leadership, achievement, self-esteem, and racial pride. They alone became the primary locus of identification for their people. Someone once wrote that in parts of the rural South blacks used to equate their denominational membership with their nationality. Thus one cannot overemphasize their commitment to the principle of racial autonomy. It alone enabled blacks to gain a significant measure of freedom from the control of and dependency on whites.

Many have leveled strong criticisms on the black churches by claiming that in the post–Civil War period they forsook their prophetic orientation of the antebellum era in favor of focusing their energy on institutional maintenance functions.[3] Most of these critics clearly had a limited understanding of the sociological meaning of the varied functions of the black churches, including that of institutional maintenance. Their many functions became evident to the nascent Black Panther Party in the 1960s, which at first condemned the black churches for their so-called accommodationist orientation but later retracted those statements when they discovered that the black churches were the only places in the black community willing to allow them to use their facilities for implementing their children's free-breakfast program. Thus the Black Panthers discovered that black churches had the capacity to support certain programs of other groups bent on serving the well-being of the community whether or not they agreed with all their purposes. Their prophetic principle of origin and its continued efficacy in their life and mission has disposed them to lend moral support and encouragement to similar prophets in the black community, whether or not they arise from within the churches.

One of the many effects of racism on American culture is that the internal life of black America has been hidden from whites. This has had both positive and negative results. Positively, the concealment has kept whites at bay and prevented their interference. Negatively, however, the ignorance of whites relative to black America has confirmed them in their presumptions that nothing of value took place in such independent spaces as the black churches. In fact, many assumed that blacks were devoid of the capacity for either creative

3. This criticism was made repeatedly by the progenitors of the black theology movement. See James H. Cone, *Black Theology and Black Power* (New York: Seabury, 1969), pp. 103ff.; see also Gayraud S. Wilmore, *Black Religion and Black Radicalism* (New York: Doubleday, 1972).

thought or constructive action and that whatever purposes they had were poor facsimiles of those of whites. In contrast, blacks were infinitely more knowledgeable of whites than vice versa by virtue of the substance of their education and the dynamics of their employment situations.

Ideal Types of Black Churches

I have demonstrated elsewhere four ideal typifications of African American religious leadership and their embodiment in four major mid-twentieth-century leaders. I have called these types pastoral, prophetic, political, and nationalist.[4] I contend that each leadership type is correlated with an African American ecclesiastical tradition that issues either directly or indirectly from the Black Church Independence Movement of the late eighteenth century.

Pastoral and Prophetic

From the beginning of their history the pastoral and prophetic types of ecclesial associations have dominated the life of the black churches. As ideal types no historical representation of them is ever perfect. Each historical instance of the particular type is always ambiguous, containing elements of more than one type. In fact, depending on the circumstances of any particular situation, any and all of the types may have inhered in any one person or church. Yet, in the main, a leader or a church will likely exhibit the logic of one of the types as its characteristic style.

1. Historically, the *pastoral* type is the oldest, having emerged and long endured in the heart of slavery before the independent churches were born. Its function has been that of proclaiming the grace of God to all and affirming the fundamental goodness of the nation. While recognizing and condemning racism, it has tended to view its perpetrators as the few, not the many. This type has always abhorred societal conflict, which it sees as the precursor of bitterness, hatred, and violence. Optimistic in outlook, it has consistently challenged blacks to be more self-respecting, industrious, honest, thrifty,

4. See the new introduction in the 2nd ed. of my *Black Leaders in Conflict* (Louisville: Westminster, 1992).

self-reliant, morally virtuous, and hopeful that a better day will surely dawn because of God's providence. Accordingly, these types of churches focused primarily on saving souls and nurturing their people in the survival skills of patience, hope, and goodwill toward their oppressors.

It is important to note that the theological and moral substance of the Independent Black Church Movement is deeply rooted in what E. Franklin Frazier called the "Invisible Church." In the context of slavery the conditions were not present for legitimate associations among slaves, so slaves responded by organizing secret meetings. Although these clandestine gathering frequently aided and abetted the efforts of many to escape from slavery, their primary purpose was that of celebrating the goodness of God and encouraging one another through these supportive communities in which the principal activities were praying, preaching, singing, and testifying.

These meetings clearly concentrated on serving the intra-associational needs of the members by strengthening their moral and spiritual capacities. Thus these meetings aimed at the cultivation of moral virtues and spiritual devotion the acquisition of which was thought to result from the inspiration received from regular attendance and participation in those gatherings. That objective has continued to characterize the ethos of those black churches whose members are daily threatened by the devastating constraints of poverty, racism, and psychological and social alienation. Those whose lives are being constantly diminished need the moral support derived from being closely related to others in like circumstances. The character of this ministry is largely communal in nature, and the people are helped and sustained by one another as they all seek to develop the capacity to face personal suffering in a constructive way. These churches may rightly be called spiritual support groups. Acts of praying, singing, and testifying manifest signs of the transcendent Spirit that helps them overcome adversity. This community attributes its life to the grace of God, and hence it never ceases "praising God."

The political expression of this pastoral type has often been called accommodationist — that is, it submits to the design of racism. I hold that the submission was never complete and often more appearance than reality. The resiliency of the human spirit enabled blacks to devise creative ways of resisting the oppressor's definition of the race as genetically inferior to whites. Consequently, more often than not, blacks concealed their beliefs and feelings about themselves and acted deceptively by utilizing forms of speech and action that pleased their overseers but were not truly expressive of their own internal being. In that way, blacks resisted the demand to participate in their own destruction as humans. Hence I contend that the appearance of submission in the eighteenth and nineteenth centuries was largely formal, calculated to deceive — objective form was separated from subjective meaning. This separation enabled the race to submit themselves partially to the racist practices of the day. Booker T. Washington has been the most prominent exemplar of that style since his unforgettable 1895 Atlanta Compromise Speech. Black educational institutions, professional organizations, and welfare agencies have tended to exhibit a similar accommodative style, as have most of these pastoral churches bent on helping their people discern ways of making the best out of a bad situation in order to survive in the midst of incredible odds.

2. The *prophetic* type proclaims the justice of God and condemns all forms of injustice, especially that of racism. Accordingly, it boldly criticizes both the nation and the churches for straying from the authentic biblical understanding of humanity and the values of the founding fathers as immortalized in the U.S. Constitution. Interestingly, both the pastoral and prophetic traditions appeal to common sources of legitimation. Unlike the former, however, the latter believes that redemptive ends necessitate direct conflict with the forces of evil. The dominant ethos of the priestly churches is that of pastoral ministry characterized by celebrative worship expressed in dynamic preaching and rhythmic song and music. The dominant ethos of the prophetic churches is that of social ministry, often called "protest activity" in the service of enhancing social justice via a similar liturgical pattern of powerful preaching and exuberant music and song.

Historically, this prophetic form of leadership and ecclesiastical form emerged publicly with the birth of the Negro Convention Movement in the 1830s. The civil rights struggles of the post-emancipation period are deeply rooted in the abolitionist tradition born in the Negro Convention Movement. Amid much debate and controversy over strategies and tactics, both abolition and civil rights have been close to the heart of the black churches. In fact, the relationship between the churches and civil rights activities has been so close that many scholars have wrongly concluded that the black church is little more than a political organization promoting racial justice. Frederick Douglass, W. E. B. DuBois, Martin Luther King, Jr., and Jesse Jackson represent some of the race's greatest leaders in this area. Various abolitionist societies, the National Association for the Advancement of Coloured People, the Southern Christian Leadership Conference, and many others were virtually spawned and nurtured by the black churches.

It is important to reiterate that the pastoral and prophetic types (along with the others) are not mutually exclusive, certain sociological theories notwithstanding.[5] Emphasis on the logic of each type implies that the other is secondary in importance. Yet I contend that these types are not antithetical but complementary: the strength of the one represents the weakness of the other. Further, neither repudiates the dominant emphasis of the other. Since each tends to be correlated with an economic class factor, their differing life-styles usually result in very little face-to-face contact.

From time to time various sociological factors have caused these two types to become significantly united in institutions that I call "Missed Churches." Many of the major historic black congregations in large urban centers exhibit this character.

Not surprisingly, the spirit of the pastoral-type churches provides the moral and spiritual foundation for the prophetic churches, which, in turn, have tended to have more resources of education and finance with which to launch protests against the societal forces of racism that afflict all blacks in varying degrees of intensity but especially those who are exceedingly poor. The mutual interdependence and cooperation of both of these church types was graphically demonstrated in the mass rallies of the civil rights movement under the leadership of Martin Luther King, Jr. On those occasions the atmosphere was continuously charged with the testimonies and prayers of the faithful, the moving beauty of the spirituals, the guttural exuberance of the gospel songs, and the persuasive oratory of dynamic preaching. These provided the means by which blacks were woven together into a harmonious whole embued with a common mission that they zealously affirmed. Thus folk artists and professional musicians, civil rights leaders and welfare recipients,

5. E. Franklin Frazier, Benjamin Mays, and others have explained black churches as products of socioeconomic forces. Accordingly, in their views the lower economic class is more likely to be concentrated in the pastoral churches while the prophetic churches are more likely to be composed of middle-class members. Further, these sociologists have tended to view religion as the preserve of the former type and to see the middle class as gradually evolving away from religion toward a humanism represented in a self-conscious orientation to political matters.

movie stars and rural farmers, poor people and middle-class folk sang, prayed, joined hands, and marched together in their quest for a racially just social order. In that movement many whites joined with blacks and thereby expressed their belief in and commitment to the struggle for a common humanity.

The black churches have consistently desired and sought the embodiment of racial justice in the public institutions of the larger society. By instituting the principle of autonomy in their own racially separate spaces, the black churches have represented a prophetic critique of the American society that had consistently denied first-class citizenship to any persons of African descent. The realization of that goal has constituted the continuing mission of the black churches and all others who identify with the task of constructing a just social order totally devoid of racism.

Political and Radical

The above discussion of the pastoral and prophetic types of black churches and their corresponding political expressions in accommodationist and legitimate protest respectively has been extensive because those styles have characterized the history of the independent black churches up to the present era.[6] It remains now to discuss the logic of the political and radical types and to assess their import.

3. Although all the ecclesial types are political since each is concerned with the character and shape of the social order (which, incidentally, is the subject matter of politics), the type I call *political* refers to the narrower and more common usage of the term, namely, electoral politics or government. This political type is closely related to the prophetic, and political scientists have long been aware of the close relationship between civil rights protest activity and politics per se.[7] This close relation should not be surprising since the aim of the

6. A good summary of the literature on the black church that reveals two basic poles of thought about the churches (i.e., the black church as a protest institution and as an instrument of political pacification) is found in John Brown Childs, *The Political Black Minister: A Study in Afro-American Politics and Religion* (Boston: G. K. Hall, 1980), chap. 2.

7. James Q. Wilson described this close relationship between black civic leaders and black politicians as one that was endangered in the light of his view of the rise of a new class of black leaders. See *Negro Politics: The Search for Leadership* (New York: Free Press, 1960).

former has always been that of effecting the full participation of blacks in the body politic.

During the brief period of Reconstruction following the Civil War, the black churches were fully engaged in the art of electoral politics via voter education and registration, as well as encouraging clergy and lay leaders alike to run for political office. During the periods of exclusion from political participation both prior and subsequent to Reconstruction, the various pastoral and prophetic functions of the black churches served as prepolitical conditions for the eventual rise of their political function. The conditions for the latter were set by the mass exodus of blacks to Northern urban centers that began around the turn of the century.[8] The dynamics of congregational governance and leadership style within the churches combine to constitute prepolitical conditions that readied the race for democratic politics in urban areas.

I have the following dynamics in mind: Black churches have always been social centers in the black community and meeting places for virtually every forum concerning the welfare of the black community. The typical black pastor has enormous influence in the black community, functioning as a kind of governor in all religious and moral matters. The vast majority of black Americans belong to churches with a congregational style of governance, which is excellent training for democratic politics. The black pastor must be a good politician within the confines of the church (i.e., know his or her people personally, serve their needs well, and encourage their participation in the church's life and mission) in order to maintain the maximum support of his or her constituency. And the black churches have always been models of racial autonomy and racial self-respect.

From one period to another, the protest churches made use of every legitimate means they could discover in their quest for adequate laws that would effect racial justice in all areas of public life. Their struggles for civil rights clearly also prepared the way for black participation in electoral politics. Thus both the pastoral and prophetic styles of black church leadership have been and continue to be positively related to the American political process and have been strongly

8. A good discussion of this demographic change and its impact on the access of blacks to urban politics is found in Martin Kilson, "Political Change in the Negro Ghetto, 1900–1940's," in Nathan I. Huggins, Martin Kilson, and Daniel M. Fox, *Key Issues in the Afro-American Experience* (New York: Harcourt Brace Jovanovich, 1971), pp. 167ff.

supportive of black candidates for political office. Unfortunately, many scholars misunderstood this fact for a full generation or more following Gunnar Myndal's depiction of the black churches as politically dysfunctional due to what he and others called their "otherworldly" orientation.[9] I contend that the black churches have never been solely "otherworldly," appearances notwithstanding.[10]

Lest there be some doubt about the matter, I contend that the black churches have more than a little capacity to be pragmatic in thought and action; they have a clear sense of the relation of means to ends. Their experience in various struggles for increased economic justice for blacks has been preparatory to disposing them toward the art of public confrontation, debate, negotiation, use of the black media, etc. In short, such experiences in mobilizing support for a public issue and, from a position of strength, negotiating a resolution of that issue, are evidences of democratic politics in practice.[11] Several representatives in the U.S. Congress and many more state representatives manifest the ease with which black churches and pastors lend their support to electoral politics.

American electoral politics is basically local in its focus. That is, local constituencies send representatives to the seat of government to represent and act for their particular interests. Since black representatives are elected mostly by predominantly black electorates, the black churches often feel uncomfortable advocating proposals that will benefit blacks only because the essence of their faith is to proclaim "good news" to the world at large, not merely to a specific locale.

9. See Gunnar Myrdal, *An American Dilemma: The Negro Problem and Modern Democracy,* vol. 2 (New York: Pantheon, 1972), chap. 40. Interestingly, Myrdal's understanding of the black churches was based on the interpretations of several black scholars who assisted him, chiefly Benjamin E. Mays and J. G. St. Clair Drake. These interpretations were destined to dominate the literature of the black churches for the next generation.

10. This argument is fully developed in my *Social Teaching of the Black Churches,* chap. 1.

11. The Reverend Leon Sullivan's ministry at Zion Baptist Church in Philadelphia issued in his renowned "Selective Patronage Campaign" and the eventual birth of the Opportunities Industrialization Center (OIC), which became the model for Jesse Jackson's Operation Breadbasket, the precursor to his People United to Save Humanity (PUSH). A good introduction to Sullivan's ministry is contained in J. DeOtis Roberts, *A Theological Commentary on the Sullivan Principles* (Philadelphia: The International Council for Equality of Opportunity Principles, Inc., 1980), chap. 1. One of the best studies of Jesse Jackson's style is in Roger D. Hatch, *Beyond Opportunity: Jesse Jackson's Vision for America* (Philadelphia: Fortress, 1988).

Further, the nature of their protest tradition has been characterized by the quest for racial justice that, they argued, when realized, would benefit the nation as a whole, not blacks alone. Thus, unlike the prophetic struggle against racism, which was deeply grounded in a universal understanding that all humans are equal under God and hence should be treated similarly in the body politic, the parochial aspect of electoral politics is often problematic for them. As a result, black representatives often find themselves more at ease advocating policies that will have a broad effect on the body politic.

In other words, blacks see black representatives in government primarily as watchdogs for racial justice, a moral value they ought never to compromise. Secondarily, blacks view their representatives as agents of patronage for their specific constituencies. This accords well with the universal principles of the black church tradition both in its pastoral and prophetic styles. That is, black representatives rarely advocate any issue that is strictly local in every respect. Rather, they inevitably seek to show how its local expression is indicative of a larger problem, the resolution of which would enhance the moral life of the society as a whole.

4. Finally, the logic of the *nationalist* type differs decisively from that of the other three and is thus related differently to the traditions of the black Christian mainstream. Since I cannot here present an in-depth description of the nature of that mainstream, suffice it to say that it is characterized by the belief that eventually racial justice will be realized in the United States. This belief implies a temporary character for the idea of the Independent Black Church Movement, which had always justified itself solely as being a necessary Christian moral response to the immoral racist practices of the white churches. Evidence of its good faith has been its unequivocal opposition to every form of racism and its willingness to welcome whites to its congregations both as visitors and as members. In its extreme form, the logic of this nationalist tradition clearly represents the polar opposite of the black Christian mainstream. Of course, its proponents adhered to its logic variously.

The basic principle of difference between the nationalist and the mainline traditions has been the former's belief that America is incurably racist and any attempt to reform its character will necessarily fail. Further, this tradition firmly believes that blacks must regain a strong sense of racial identity and self-respect, which they lost as a result of slavery and its aftermath. In addition, however, this tradition believes that the necessary enlightenment of the race can occur only through racial separation, racial pride, racial self-determination, and the inculcation of a new ideology rooted in a renewed appreciation for African values. Elements of this tradition can be found in virtually every period of black American history but most clearly in the Africa emigrationist vision of such men as Martin Delaney, Bishop Henry McNeal Turner, Alexander Crummell, Edward Wilmot Blyden, and Marcus Moziah Garvey, to mention only a few. All of these held that the liberation of Africa was a necessary condition for the liberation of black Americans, and each advocated the importance of black American agency in actualizing African sovereignty through Christianity, commerce, and civilization. The African missionary enterprises of the independent black denominations also represented modified examples of this tradition.

Rebellion expressed itself in a variety of slave revolts (most notably those led by Nat Turner, Gabriel Prosser, and Denmark deVesey) and in the teaching of such men as David Walker, Henry Highland Garnett, and all those who advocated liberation from slavery by any means necessary, including the use of violence.[12] Yet it appears that no Christian institutions came into being for the purpose of effecting freedom via violence. Nevertheless, it is important to note that the pre–Civil War underground organization called the Knights and Daughters of Tabor was founded by an A.M.E. minister, the Reverend Moses Dickson, and aimed at the military overthrow of the slavocracy. In general, however, black Americans have not viewed rebellion as a viable response, possibly because of their minority status and (unlike Native Americans) because they were brought involuntarily to America and thus have had less sense of spatial belonging.

Many of the marks of this nationalist freedom tradition are evident in the black theology movement, which is presently less than three decades old. This movement began with James H. Cone's book *Black Theology and Black Power*, a Christian apologia for black power and a prophetic demand that theology serve the end of black liberation. The movement initially aimed its prophetic challenge at the black "quietist" churches, the racist practices of the white churches, and the theological methodologies of white seminaries. More study is

12. It is important to note that the progenitor of the black theology movement, James H. Cone, implied the legitimate use of violence in the quest for liberation in his first book, *Black Theology and Black Power* (New York: Seabury, 1969), pp. 22ff.

needed in order to assess its precise impact on those arenas. Its impact on theological studies in America and abroad has clearly been considerable, as evidenced in the number of courses presently offered in African American religious studies as compared with the very few offered twenty years ago.

In my judgment, one of the principal achievements of the black theology movement was its systematic explication of the theology of the black churches and its success in gaining legitimation for it in the curriculum of theological education. Its most decisive impact on the practical life of the churches occurred not in this country but in South Africa, where Christian opposition to apartheid desperately needed theological categories other than those provided them by their oppressors, categories that would enable them to rebut the theological justification of apartheid as provided by the Dutch Reformed Church. Accordingly, black theology enabled South African theologians to construct a contextual theology with which to proclaim a prophetic message of liberation within the context of Christian devotion, biblical exegesis, and courageous action.

It should be noted, however, that this nationalist type of black ecclesial existence differs from the pastoral, prophetic, and political types in the primacy it gives to the importance of racial identity, self-respect, African heritage, principles of independence, and self-determination. In short, this type maximizes the values implied by the distinctiveness of the African race while vigorously denying the accusation of reverse racism. Its principal aim has always been that of liberating the race from every vestige of racial inferiority bequeathed to it by white racism. Thus this type can also be viewed as a condition for the politics of self-determination either racially separate from or racially allied with whites.

The Encompassing Style of Black Religion

In many distinctive ways black religion has always manifested some characteristics of all the types discussed above but not always in the same proportion or at the same time. Similarly, black leadership styles in both the religious and political arenas have generally reflected these various styles, even though the accommodative and legitimate protest styles seem to have dominated in every period due to the predominance of the pastoral and prophetic functions of the black churches.

Since the situation of black Americans has always been circumscribed by a parameter of white racial hostility bent on preserving the systematic oppression of blacks, the churches have always struggled to maintain and to enhance the humanity of the race not at the expense of whites but whenever possible in association with them; whenever that association was not possible, they constituted "a nation within a nation," providing space for all necessary human activities in the social, economic, political, and religious spheres of life. That is, the internal life of the church provided the opportunity for human enhancement through association, and in this way blacks experienced the freedom denied them in the white world.

More specifically, the black churches have struggled to create a world of harmony wherein justice and human respect might be the controlling virtues in both personal and communal life. Hence the principles of racial self-development, self-initiative, self-determination, and self-fulfillment have been highlighted in varying ways by different churches and their leaders. In their religious life blacks have sought to justify the principles of freedom, liberty, and equality not only as constitutive for human being as such (as in the Declaration of Independence) but as harmonious with God's will. Most importantly, blacks have trusted primarily in the biblical God, whom alone they experienced as nonracist. Accordingly, all normative political activity has been evaluated in accordance with its commensurability with God's nonracist will. Blacks fully trusted none other since they, like all oppressed peoples, learned through bitter experience not to put their trust in the oppressor and to be very cautious about their own oppressed people, who might be involved in numerous forms of survival techniques that might entail varying forms of collaboration with their oppressors. In short, the religion of the black churches has always viewed freedom as both an eschatological and an historical principle, a religious and a political goal. In the main, the black churches have viewed their quest for the liberation of blacks as contributory to the liberation of all. Although the black churches have been occasionally implicated in some revolts and rebellions during times of extreme disillusionment and general despair, they have been generally committed to nonviolent resistance long before the term was popularized by Martin Luther King, Jr. In fact, the ready affirmation of the principle by the black churches evidences their familiarity with it.

In general, the black churches have enriched the public realm by keeping alive issues of social justice relative to public responsibility and citizenship rights by publicly exposing all forms of racial hypocrisy and injustice. In this respect, they have been the conscience of the nation.

The black churches emerged on the stage of history as a response to the public issue of racism that had been firmly established both politically and religiously from the beginning of the Republic. Their life and mission religiously and politically have aimed at effecting alternative ways of being in the world both religiously and politically. The Independent Black Church Movement of the late eighteenth and early nineteenth centuries represents the institutionalization of that aim religiously, and the many and varied collective activities aimed at effecting racial justice through structural societal changes expressed themselves in numerous organizations both within and without the churches. The abolition of legalized racism (i.e., racial segregation and discrimination) in the 1960s marked the successful culmination of the civil rights movement that began immediately following the Civil War. Civil rights legislation bestowed upon black Americans the long-awaited citizenship rights. Unfortunately, a residue of cultural and psychological racism continues to affect institutional decision-making processes. Meanwhile, the style of black American electoral politics has followed the formal pattern of the majority electorate, though its substance (i.e., its political agenda) has differed from that of the white electorate by giving higher priority to the role of government in protecting civil rights and effecting economic justice through full employment policies and the abolition of poverty both at home and abroad.

A Proposal

Assuming the laudable history of the black churches as institutional agents in the enduring struggle for liberation and justice, and assuming their continuing primacy as voluntary associations concerned about enhancing the quality of social justice in black communities,[13] let us turn to the contemporary moral and religious challenge that the

13. This assumption is strongly confirmed by the conclusions drawn by C. Eric Lincoln and Lawrence Mamiya in their massive empirical study of the black churches, *The Black Church in the African American Experience* (Durham, N.C.: Duke Univ. Press, 1990).

black churches need to accept if our blighted communities are to be restored to viable health. The black churches clearly have an enviable history as prophetic organizations demanding social justice via the art of moral persuasion and varied forms of nonviolent resistance. The lawful demise of racial discrimination and segregation in the public domain marks a turning point in the public mission of the churches. These must now become more self-consciously political in the narrow sense of that word: a people's deliberate choice to gain access to the arenas of authority and power for enhancing the quality of the body politic. As mentioned above, this political function is not alien to the black church tradition. Rather, it inheres in its nature.

Although the black churches have traditionally addressed all sorts of public issues and, especially during the 1970s and 1980s, have spearheaded numerous voter registration drives and voter registration campaigns (including the endorsement of candidates, campaigning, poll watching, fund raising), I contend that they must now intensify all these efforts, including the increased fielding of candidates for public office. This must now be done for theological, moral, and political reasons.

(1) Theological Rationale: The gospel of liberation and justice, long proclaimed by the black churches, implies institutionalization lest it be cast aside as an abstract, formal platitude devoid of historical expression. As the black churches constituted the original institutional loci for a nonracist Christianity in sharp contrast to their white counterparts, and as they expressed their devotion to such a viewpoint in their moral support and engagement in a myriad of organizations and associations dedicated to the pursuit of social justice, now they must continue that tradition of enriching the public realm with their self-conscious involvement in all aspects of electoral politics. Their experience in para-political activities will undoubtedly be of immeasurable help in defining public issues and mobilizing support in their behalf. Even more importantly, these churches are peculiarly capable of making good moral judgments about human character and accordingly can exercise leadership by giving their blessings to men and women of integrity who view public service as an expression of their Christian devotion.

Such a venture implies many difficulties, none of which is insurmountable. In fact, the political experience and wisdom of such church leaders as former Congresswoman Shirley Chisholm, Congressmen Walter Fauntroy, William Gray, John Lewis, Floyd Flake, Parren Mitchell,

Andrew Young, and presidential candidate Jesse Jackson (to mention only a few) constitute a reservoir for critical thought and guidance. (Note that all of these stand in the tradition of such notable Reconstruction trailblazers as the Reverend Hiram Revels, the first black U.S. senator, and the Reverend Richard Cain, who served both as state senator and U.S. Congressman. Further, the Reverend Adam Clayton Powell, Jr., who served in the U.S. Congress from 1944 to 1970, was the first of several black ministers to serve in Congress during the second half of the twentieth century.) The same black church that produced numerous prophets, educational and civic leaders, men and women of unusual practical wisdom, courage, and devotion, and countless numbers of enthusiastic supporters from all walks of life must now enhance its rhythm of social protest with the activity of political consolidation and expansion. In brief, the fathers and mothers of the liberation struggle must now pass the mantle to their successors, the "nation builders." These must occupy the seats of power in order to contribute to the task of constructing a good and just society wherein the sociopolitical structures will facilitate the well-being of all citizens and hinder none from actualizing their potential.

(2) Moral Rationale: The purpose of the good state should be that of enabling the good of all its citizens, the promotion of justice for all. Thus the purpose of good politics is ethical in nature. The black churches and their allied associations have had excellent preparation for such a moral task, evidenced in the process by which the civil rights movement under the leadership of the Reverend Martin Luther King, Jr., effected a moral revolution in the nation's legal framework. For more than a decade black church leaders rendered public service by giving persuasive moral fiber to the pressing issues of racial justice in the body politic. Their accomplishments marked the end of an era in American history and the beginning of a new epoch filled with potentiality. They must now become the torchbearers of a more substantive political agenda and exercise leadership for its actualization. The part of their prophetic tradition that should serve them well in this new mission would be the public-regarding spirit that disposes them to seek justice for all citizens rather than the few alone. In fact, Martin Luther King, Jr., predicted the need for this present moment and saw political organization as the logical step following the legal guarantee of basic civil rights. Subsequent to the nonviolent expressions of resistance to evil as boycotts, peaceful demonstrations, education, individual and collective sacrifice, he called for political organization.

> To produce change, people must be organized to work together in units of power. These units might be political, as in the case of voters' leagues and political parties; they may be economic units such as groups of tenants who join forces to form a tenant union or to organize a rent strike; or they may be laboring units of persons who are seeking employment and wage increases.
>
> More and more the civil rights movement will be engaged in the task of organizing people into permanent groups to protect their own interests and to produce change in their behalf. This is a tedious task which may take years, but the results are more permanent and meaningful.[14]

In his last presidential address to the Southern Christian Leadership Conference, King spoke of the need for political power.

> Another basic challenge is to discover how to organize our strength in terms of economic and political power. No one can deny that the Negro is in dire need of this kind of legitimate power. Indeed, one of the great problems that the Negro confronts is his lack of power. From old plantations of the South to newer ghettos of the North, the Negro has been confined to a life of voicelessness and powerlessness. Stripped of the right to make decisions concerning his life and destiny, he has been subject to the authoritarian and sometimes whimsical decisions of this white power structure. . . . The problem of transforming the ghetto, therefore, is a problem of power.[15]

King then continued his discussion of power by offering a corrective to those clergy and others who view power as devoid of love and justice. Clearly influenced by Paul Tillich, he argued, "Now we've got to get this thing right. What is needed is a realization that power without love is reckless and abusive, and love without power is sentimental and anemic. Power at its best is love implementing the demands of justice, and justice at its best is power correcting everything that stands against love."[16]

(3) Political Rationale: Several years ago the eminent political scientist Professor Charles V. Hamilton drew an important correlation

14. Martin Luther King, Jr., "Non-Violence: The Only Way to Freedom," in *A Testament of Hope: The Essential Writings of Martin Luther King, Jr.*, ed. James M. Washington (New York: Harper & Row, 1986), pp. 60-61.

15. Martin Luther King, Jr., "Where Do We Go From Here," in ibid., p. 246.

16. Ibid., p. 247.

between American political leadership and that of the black churches by arguing that both were rooted in local organizational structures primarily concerned with the well-being of their constituents. Both the political and religious leaders must maintain the trust of their people and be sensitive to their needs and willing to be public advocates on their behalf. In other words, he argued that black clergy possess all the elements for good, effective political leadership: high social respect, excellent rhetorical skills, knowledge of local issues and their relatedness to larger social problems, and good moral character. Further, black clergy have the ear of their community, and this helps immeasurably in mobilizing volunteers for electioneering purposes.

An important constraint on clergy moving quickly into the arena of electoral politics is the negative moral image that has come to be associated with professional politicians. To date this has not tarnished the character of those black clergy already in public office, and that in itself should demonstrate that holding political office does not necessarily lead to moral decline.

Accepting such a charge could lead to improved public debate on matters relative to the common good. Not since the civil rights movement has the public realm been dominated by a substantive debate about societal structures and their impact on the quality of human life. Black church leaders alone have the capacity to initiate and to mobilize widespread public debate on the devastating social problems presently threatening the lives of one-third of the nation's citizens. This debate must be waged by public policymakers, which implies the necessity of putting in office sufficient numbers of people with the mandate to make a difference. Thus the black churches must now become the loci for intensive political activity by deploying their institutional resources to the task of electing church leaders to public office, since the primary need in our day is the consolidation of the civil rights gains in more substantive public policy. Black churches alone have the leadership potential for effective actualization in the domain of public office.

Public Theology and the Future of Democratic Society

Max L. Stackhouse

As this century draws to a close and we begin to think of our responsibilities in the next, we cannot fail to note that what many Protestant leaders have thrown their lives into has come to pass. Freedom of religion is more widely established, and governments dominated by royal lineage, colonial power, and both fascist and communist ideologists have been defeated. In many ways, the prospects for a democratic future are positive, if fragile. Eastern Europe, Latin America, Africa (including South Africa!), and large parts of Asia inch toward democratic national polities. And in the West, families, the law, the media, and economic institutions — both corporations and unions — have become more and more democratic internally.

The New Shapes of Democracy

To be sure, a great difference in income and wealth remains, and has slightly increased in the 1980s in the United States and between the North Atlantic countries and those in the southern hemisphere. This is so although some regions, such as India, Indonesia, Mexico, and Brazil, have seen millions raised out of subsistence and above the poverty line for the first time in recorded history. At the same time, the vexing problems of homelessness and poverty have not been solved, and pressures on the middle classes increase, compounded by population bulges among the elderly in the West and the young in the Third World. How to deal creatively and morally with the global economy of the future is as yet undetermined. In many respects, the key issues of Christian ethics will have to shift from sex and politics to economics, technology, and culture.

Still, autocracy, elitism, and domination are less and less potent forces in the structuring of the common life, and nearly everyone seeks a partially regulated, mixed economy based heavily on corporate capitalism. Indeed, contrary to the intuitive expectations of many, the growing comparative evidence on traditional economies, mercantilist developing countries, centralized command economies, and corporate capitalism indicates that the last has produced the widest extension of democratic values into the economic sphere.[1] The new structure of corporate organization has become less centralized and hierarchical,[2] but also more democratic. The patriarchal relationships between master and slave, male and female, old and young, white and black, and boss and worker are discredited. Their moral legitimacy is broken, even where they persist.

Democracy is not the same everywhere, of course. Its forms in Canada, Japan, Italy, and the United States differ. But on the whole, the ascending patterns of democracy that we see around us involve a sense of order under law, checks and balances among centers of authority, procedures to assure the accountability of leaders to the led, a pluralism of group organizations, and the protection of the rights of worship, speech, and assembly. The last point is of special importance, if we consider that nearly all societies in human history have been dominated by two institutions above all others — the familial and political. These are the institutions that have not only controlled power and wealth but have also determined religion, culture, and most forms of human association. Thus the guarantees of the rights of religion, expression, and association that developed with modern democracy mean also the right to develop organizations for political, economic, journalistic, cultural, or professional purposes independently of governmental or patriarchal control.

In other words, it is a specific tradition of democracy — one accenting "freedom under law," not only majority rule, and distinguished by the formation of an enormous variety of organized relationships — that is presently being adopted around the world. It is a

1. For examples of contrasting standpoints that agree on this matter, see Peter Berger, *The Capitalist Revolution* (New York: Basic Books, 1986); and Severyn T. Bruyn, *A Future for the American Economy* (Stanford: Stanford Univ. Press, 1991).

2. See Robert B. Reich, *The Work of Nations: Preparing Ourselves for 21st Century Capitalism* (New York: Knopf, 1991).

pattern so familiar to Americans that we do not always recognize how rare it is in the history of the world. Indeed, it is a quite fragile experiment, based on the formation of moral communities and the cultivation of public discourse based in first principles. As we shall see, these principles developed under the impact of "conciliar Catholic" and "liberal-Puritan" influences.[3] The polities based on these could easily erode in the West and evaporate around the world if the moral, social, and intellectual infrastructure for democracy is not fostered.

A Vision of Modern Democracy

This modern form of democracy is not the kind that developed in ancient Greece — what scholars called timocracy and critics called mobocracy — with the political morality of the mass, the herd, the swarm. Nor is it that form of populist solidarity which grew out of the repudiation of religion in the French Revolution. The attempt to free humanity from the idea that we are subject to any order except that which we construct led first to the "Terror," then to Napoleon, and, more recently, to the "people's democracies" that have proved to be neither popular nor democratic — as we shall shortly discuss.

Instead, what is being adopted is a tradition of pluralist democracy that depends upon the capacity of people to transcend personal, class, gender, or national interests in some modest measure, and to recognize two realities: (1) that all people live under a common, universal moral law, giving each person a moral purpose and dignity; and (2) that we all have a spiritual capacity to form associations of commitment — societies of cooperation beyond family and political arrangements. That is, ordinary people have a fundamental ability and responsibility to bond into self-disciplining communities that can actualize moral and spiritual realities in some serious degree on earth — indeed, even in quite material institutions such as cooperatives, corporations, unions, and business associations.

The first part of this vision, that all humans live under a common and universal moral law, is near the root of all great thought. Whatever

3. I have shown how the church played a decisive role in the formation of the kind of democracy that protects human rights and provides a "public theology" in my *Creeds, Society, and Human Rights* (Grand Rapids: Eerdmans, 1984).

disagreements there may be about other matters, Christians share this insight with the various religions and with all profound philosophies. Indeed, the contending religions and philosophies of the world and the competing claims of various Christian groups can be evaluated in part accordingly as they grasp, and honor, that reality. Any perspective that denies that all humans are subject to the same moral principles — that we ought not defile what is holy, lie, cheat, rape, torture, murder, break promises, etc. — is false and untrustworthy. It cannot endure. It must not be allowed to become dominant.

The second part of this vision, that people who catch this vision have the absolute right under God and the duty before God to organize in self-governing communities of commitment and cooperation for worship, study, and witness in the society at large, without the approval of familial or political authority, is a great Social Novum brought to us by only some branches of some of the world's religions.[4] Wherever this has occurred, as happened in the synagogue of Judaism and the *ecclesia* of Christianity, we have seen the reorganization also of the ordinary structures of living — not only familial and political, but economic, cultural, educational, and technological — in a pluralistic, democratic direction.

In the West, certain streams of Christian theology have given intentional impetus to a democratic ecclesiology as it interacted, over time, with humanist philosophies of the classical, Renaissance, and modern scientific periods. Further, these have focused on the formation and constant reformation of personal and social life by accenting the radicality of sin, which equalizes all persons before God, and by calling people into communities of commitment and mutual discipline that involve concrete reallocations of time, money, and energy as well as thought and loyalty. Here is the root — seldom noted by political theorists and pundits — of the pluralistic democracy today being adopted and adapted around the world.

These streams are genuinely interested in public discourse, not only in inner piety or confessional traditions. Such streams were influential in parts of the early encounter of Christianity with Greek and Roman philosophy, in several of the orders, among those Catholics who posed the councils against the absolutism of papal authority prior

4. I have taken up this question on a comparative basis in "Democracy and the World's Religions," in *The Best of This World*, ed. M. Scully (Lanham, Md.: Univ. Press of America, 1986).

to the Reformation, those Protestants who advocated toleration in Northern Europe during the Reformation period, and those who fought for the separation of church and government in the Unites States during its formative political period. They were the forerunners of what are today called the "ecumenical," "mainline," or "conciliar" Protestant traditions.

The Religious Roots of Modern Democracy

We need not recount again here the fuller history of these developments. The evidence is overwhelming, even though much of what is taken to be scholarship today simply presumes that religion was not, is not, and could not be a formative force in the construction of a constitutional order. To be sure, some branches of Christianity opposed democracy and paid homage to the doctrine, fomented by royalty, of the "divine right of kings." Further, some have been suspicious of human rights and promoted the view that faith and reason are opposites — a convenient dogma that makes it unnecessary for them to give any basis for what they propagate as truth.

But other branches of the Christian tradition have always protested the disjunctions of faith and reason, of a God who governs only in heaven or among unworldly enclaves and a world that is to be best understood by antireligious philosophical or scientific principles without reference to moral or spiritual realities. These traditions have claimed the right under God to engage these matters in open discourse. Theology, when it is serious, is a public matter, accessible to any and pertinent to all areas of the common life.

It is in these traditions that we find the root visions that gave rise to modern, constitutional, pluralistic democracy, and turning to these sources allows us to find a better account of how it arose than we can find among those, believer or nonbeliever, who hold that democracy came with a secular repudiation of religion. In fact, it came with the repudiation of some religious orientations because other religious convictions turned out to be more persuasive with regard to what could be held to be true and more effective with regard to what could be held to be just.[5]

5. Many thinkers have accepted the antitheological account of the history of democracy by identifying it with secular theory only. See, e.g., Ronald Dworkin, *Taking*

The Public Significance of Churches

We could summarize the matter this way: ecclesiology holds the key to understanding the genesis and inner structure of modern democratic societies. Where it has focused on the mutual accountability to one another of a leader and the led under a divine mandate to service, an elected episcopacy has developed. Where leadership is more focused on a representative body of elders, it is more deeply rooted in the magisterial wing of the Reformed tradition. And where it is more participatory in form, it is more deeply rooted in the Congregational or "free-church" part of the heritage. These are today joined in most contemporary denominations — as well as in the executive, judicial, and parliamentary branches of government. In the twentieth century, they are written into the constitutions of every emerging land. They have become so much a part of the background beliefs by which modernity operates that we often forget how much ink was spilled and blood was shed to bring pluralistic democracy into being.

Ecclesiology, in turn, is fundamentally dependent on a vision of how we think God wants us to live together on earth — of how we ought to bond together, of how we ought to preserve both the awareness of particular individuality and a sense of common humanity under God, of what is worth doing with our personal and social lives. On these bases, we fumblingly come together in associations of mutual edification and discipline for the sake of a personal yet cosmic graciousness that is the source of truth and justice, and that is beyond the control of violence, domination, or death. In other words, ecclesiology at its deepest is a normative model of and for human society, based in theology and manifest in history under all the conditions of wickedness, evil, and destruction.[6]

Rights Seriously (Cambridge: Harvard Univ. Press, 1977); Alasdair MacIntyre, *Whose Justice? Whose Rationality?* (Notre Dame: Notre Dame Univ. Press, 1988); and Stanley Hauerwas, *Against the Nations* (San Francisco: Winston, 1985). This view, however, is sustained only by a neglect of the evidence.

6. This is, in one sense, simply an extension of the greatest insight of Ernst Troeltsch, *The Social Teaching of the Christian Churches and Sects*, tr. Olive Wyon, 2 vols. (New York: Harper, repr. 1960; German ed. 1911). Whatever difficulties his historicism entailed in other respects, he demonstrated that ecclesiology is the clue to the meaning of social history generally, and that it is formed by the interaction of basic religious insights with both philosophical modes of thought and the social dynamics of the common life.

Such notions have become an increasing part of Roman Catholic practice as well as of Protestant ecclesiology, as we can see in the processes informing the National Conference of Catholic Bishops' statements about nuclear war and the economy during the 1980s. They are striking in the evangelical and pentecostal movements of the Third World.[7] And even in areas of theological reflection where previous generations did not expect it, the democratic impulse is growing more quickly than can be contained.[8]

Theologically and ecclesiologically rooted democracy has now been transposed into family, educational, economic, and political forms — and indeed into the commitments people live for, die for, and, in rare but occasionally necessary circumstances, kill for. That is why modern people who have been deeply influenced by these traditions have an almost sacred view of constitutional government and of human rights, even if in the conduct of life we often remain sinners on just these points.

It is not triumphalism but the bold proclamation of what has been falsely denied and neglected by the pundits of history to say that the contemporary development of democracy around the world is the fruit of ecumenically oriented Protestant ecclesiology, formed out of the womb of a public theology, now become actual in the world. Under conditions of modernity, it has become the primary sociopolitical model of how peoples, groups, governments, and nations ought to structure their common life. The burden of proof is on any person or group that does not act democratically.

This tradition has been reinforced by the failure of socialism, which we need to examine briefly. But it faces other challenges that may prove more difficult. Its glory may wither in the face of the acid rain of doubt that clouds the horizon.

7. See David Martin, *Tongues of Fire: The Explosion of Protestantism in Latin America* (London: Basil Blackwell, 1990); and David Stoll, *Is Latin America Becoming Protestant?* (Berkeley: Univ. of California Press, 1990). These books suggest that the explosion of "neo-protestant" movements in South and Central America involves the creation of new communities of discipline and cooperation, far surpassing the numbers in the "base communities" and the vitality in the present Roman Catholic Church.

8. For careful efforts to stave off these two trends, see the marvelous work by Catholic theologian and ethicist Dennis McCann, *New Experiment in Democracy: The Challenge for American Catholicism* (New York: Sheed and Ward, 1987); and the suggestive work by the Baptist scholar William J. Everett, *God's Federal Republic* (Mahwah, N.J.: Paulist, 1988).

The Humanist Challenge: Socialism

In 1789–90, the West was shaken by the French Revolution. The shock wave reached around the world. The ancient regime, the presumed natural hierarchy of life that had been taught by philosophers and clergy, was broken. "The way things really are" appeared not to be hard, solid, fixed, settled, and universal but soft, plastic, changeable, temporary, and local. The source of distress was held to be the alliance of petrified religion, authoritarian politics, and economic privilege. And the fundamental model of how transformation happens became fixed by the vision of militants in the street confronting the high, the powerful, and the rich, storming the Bastille, and shouting: "Liberty, Equality, and Fraternity."

The shadows of great events are long. As is well known, Karl Marx mediated these ideas from the eighteenth century to the twentieth. His ideas, refined by German philosophy and English economics, captured the loyalties of millions — specifically in opposition to authoritarian regimes legitimated by dogmatic theology and a hierarchical church. Within a century, Marxism extended its sovereignty from Berlin to Beijing and its influence from the universities of North Europe to guerrillas in South America and Southern Africa.

Here was a great rejection of church and theology. The church was no longer a primary community of identity at the center of society, but a voluntary option for some. Theology was relegated to the store of human myths, not on the basis of some new religious faith, but on the basis of a denial that there could be any particular revelation that could establish a universally authentic religious faith at all. All ideas and religions and ethical philosophies and theological systems were seen to be the constructions of human imagination, and based in the group interests of those who create them. Of course, this was itself an odd faith, rooted in nothing more than human self-divinization.

Now, before our very eyes two centuries later, the harsh forms of this heritage are being overthrown precisely in those lands where Marx and the French Revolution have been most honored. China and Eastern Europe exploded, with the people crying for liberation from communist propaganda; desocialization of the society; establishment of liberal, bourgeois rights; space for a pluralism in political parties and individual life-styles; and, above all, new freedoms to organize for religious, economic, cultural, and professional purposes.

This transformation was brought about, in part, by the simple fact that the holistic, centralized system did not work. It not only failed to produce enough to meet human needs and generated a structure of the privileged few controlling the controlled many while claiming to overcome a class structure; but it also corrupted respect for the genuinely human, eroded cultural creativity in the arts and sciences, and undercut the capacity to develop a viable, modern, rational society. It led neither to truth nor to justice, nor even to socialization.

What is remarkable and utterly unexpected by most "serious" modern observers, however, is the fact that it was to the religious groups that the progressive forces turned when socialism proved to be reactionary. Solidarity found refuge in the Catholic churches of Poland. The transformation in East Germany began in the now-disestablished and democratized Evangelical churches. The Hungarian revolt was centered in the Reformed churches. In Czechoslovakia the opposition was headed by a writer whose main message on receiving the German Peace Prize was that this revolution against Marxism was won on the basis of John 1:1 — "In the beginning was the Word . . . ," not on the basis of material interests or class conflict.[9]

Just as remarkable is the fact that precisely where a strong theology and an independent ecclesiology did not exist — China, Burma, Albania, Romania, Bulgaria, Yugoslavia, and a number of regions of the USSR — democracy has not emerged as a vital prospect, and the protest against Marxism is marked above all by forms of ethnic (familistic) and nationalist (political) tribalism that threaten the now-weakened East with racial and cultural violence.

A Discredited View of the Future

In any case, we face the discrediting of the two-century-old secular theory of the future of human civilization. Implications are legion: The basic vision of a humanist path to the future is discredited in the Far East by the bloody repression of dissenters under communist regimes; in Eastern Europe by the massive exodus of people away from the system whenever and wherever they can leave or change it. Socialism, the most potent modern form of humanism, may be able to overthrow degenerate forces of old elites; but it is not able to provide

9. Vaclav Havel, "Peace Prize Address," *New York Review of Books,* April 1990.

a vision for the rebuilding of a humane society. Even in Latin America, people vote it out if they get a chance, while in South Africa and the Philippines, socialism provides the rhetoric of protest but has no serious chance of becoming the pattern of the future.

We do not yet know how deep the new distrust in the socialist vision will cut. It is likely to influence the mild as well as the harsh forms of socialism, and that includes nearly every significant version of critical theory of social change developed in the twentieth century, including the social theories of church leaders who live in democratic societies. Thus we can expect that the more progressive forces in the universities and in journalism and in prominent positions of religious leadership will be shaken by these developments. They adopted, with only modest reservations, many of the basic presuppositions behind Marx and the French Revolution — ideas, for example, that religion was essentially a projection of what were really personal needs, class interests, or social conditions; that morality was a function of the conventions developed by a society; that the relations between people are established by the dominations of class and gender but can be changed by the mobilization of human will and force. These are dying ideas. Great will be the crash of them.

How difficult it will be for all those for whom the chief conversation partner of Christianity for most of a century has been socialism — and, more broadly, the humanist, quasi-scientific, and romantic traditions of the French Revolution behind it. Although they helped correct forms of piety that had become mere masks of privilege and legitimations of the status quo, much of what they learned and what they taught is now redundant. For many it will require a major reformation of thought and loyalties if they are to avoid becoming tired dogmatists, and to recover instead a deeper and broader social-ethical dimension of theology. Even more difficult for us all will be the effort to find new ways to apply a broader and deeper view to the global system of corporate capitalism (neither individualist nor statist) that has accompanied the spread of pluralistic democracy and that will surely predominate in the post-socialist future.

The Fundamentalist Challenge: Islam

Lest anyone think that the path to the future of pluralistic democracy will be smooth, since its nearest enemy has failed as a viable option, the cunning hand of providence has brought us a confrontation that presents a deeper challenge. This challenge comes from the Black Muslims of America and the migrant workers of Europe, throughout the Arab world, North Africa, and South Asia to the islands of Indonesia. Its name is Islam. It has existed more than seven times as long as socialism, and its reach has extended as widely. If Marxism rejected theology in general, Islam represents the greatest and still perhaps the most profound specific rejection of Christianity (and Judaism) that the world has known.

Of course, much that today brings Christians and Muslims into direct and regular contact is not obviously theological. No small amount of it is transparently the result of a lust of the world powers for oil — the black gold on which the energy supplies of nearly all the industrial nations are based and which lies in abundance under Islamic soil in the Mideast. Much is at stake in the matter of oil. Some of it reflects the gluttonous life-style of the richer peoples of the world. Other parts of it are an equally greedy life-style of sheikhs whose sense of democracy and human rights is, at best, underdeveloped. These factors do not constitute a justifiable reason for current conflicts.

No, other issues are at stake. One of them is seriously prudential: A failure of supply or a hostile monopoly over it could hold millions hostage, plunge the world into recession, destroy the productive capacity of the more developed nations, and bring increased hunger to the less developed ones. But we should have learned something from the collapse of Marxist socialism and the shadow now cast on all economistic views of reality, socialist or capitalist: purely economic explanations of what drives political life are not sufficient to historical reality.

Political dreams and hopes have their own energy. And much of the Islamic world seems driven by desires to overcome the legacy of colonialism, to reestablish past glories, not to be shamed by tiny Israel or manipulated by the superpowers in the Mid-East, and to find an honorable way to order the common life after the fall of the Ottoman Empire, the divisive struggles of Afghanistan, the fragility of the North African states, and the painful struggles in Pakistan, Bangladesh, and Indonesia, as well as the harsh viciousness of Iran, Iraq, and Syria. Further, no democratic regime exists in an Islamic country and no substantive movements toward constitutional democracy with guarantees of human rights are visible, although they are being advocated by a few contemporary scholars.[10] Still, something deeper than oil money and politics or psychology is at stake.

The problem is this: every civilization depends upon the vitality and the intrinsic reliability of a metaphysical-moral vision that stands at its core. That is what gives it an inner guidance system, that is what allows a society to correct its own course when it goes wrong. That is what legitimates its regimes as they rise, trying to to link power and justice. And that is what legitimates the oppositions when they fall after separating power from both truth and justice. That is what makes the people honor them generations on end in spite of ignorance and error, or conspire against them on short notice in the midst of technical competence.

Islam, which is obviously the greatest religion of this region, is in difficulty. A number of Islamic societies have, I fear, contracted a metaphysical disease and a moral senility, of which the painful incapacity to cope with modernization is the primary symptom, and for which fundamentalism — to which it has ever been disposed — is a desperate treatment.[11]

The recent Gulf Crisis is, I believe, simply the most recent, but surely not the last, episode of a much greater crisis in one of the world's great religions. It is no less true today than it has always been, that in order for a civilization to stand, the metaphysical-moral vision, usually religious, that it hosts must be capable of guiding the ethical and spiritual life as it is lived out in a larger context over the course of time. When the vision is constituted on a narrow basis, or grows cold, or rests on foundations that are untrue or unjust, as we have already seen with fascism and communism in this century, not only the religion but the civilization begins to lose its inner vitality. People in positions to make a difference do not believe it anymore. If they mouth its words, they do so to keep appearances or because they have nothing else to say, or to whip up the simple believers who cling to it with unknowing certainty. But it can no longer influence the sectors

10. This is most clearly stated in Abdullahi Ahmed An-Na'im, *Toward an Islamic Reformation: Civil Liberties, Human Rights, and International Law* (Syracuse: Syracuse Univ. Press, 1990).

11. The question as to whether the term *fundamentalism* can properly be applied to Islam, since it is a term that was newly developed in American Christianity in the first decades of the twentieth century, is widely debated. I intend the term to mean: an extremely high doctrine of the nature and authority of Scripture, a tendency to legalistic rigidity in morals, and a militant triumphalism in cross-cultural encounter.

of society that sustain the fabric of modern civilization — association, marriage, music, poetry, law, business, technology, industry, politics, medicine, and learning.

To be sure, very large dimensions of any faith are those having to do with personal devotion, with the ways in which we relate to family, and with the way we show regard for the neighbor, the stranger, the needy, and the weak. We should not doubt that a great number of devout Muslims find a personal relationship to God in the traditions of Islam that cultivate the religious sensibilities in these ways.

But other dimensions of every profound faith have to do with how these relationships and insights are woven into a pattern that sustains the possibilities of a genuine civilization. Here theology interacts with jurisprudence, polity, the natural and social sciences, the fine arts, and international policy. That has been problematic in Islam for some time.

The idea that its expansion was stopped by the West at the time of the Crusades was contrary to a key tenet of Muslim faith — it had to manifest its truth by its historical victory.[12] Without a theory of crucifixion, it had to conquer. But it was stopped. That could have been seen as a temporary setback, for Islam continued to expand to the east and to the south. But in the twentieth century it has met other crises. From the beginning, the relationship between religion and the formation of imperial politics was intimate. The prophet Mohammed was both a founder of the religion and the leader of the army that established a political empire. No small number of the sects of Islam derive from questions of succession to the throne. But since the Ottoman Empire fell, the connection of faith and regime has been maintained only by awkward fictions.[13]

The Threat of Modernity

Further, the inner fabric of Islamic culture is in danger of being conquered from within by social and intellectual influences that it

12. This feature of Islam is treated in Kenneth Cragg, *The Call of the Minaret*, 2nd ed. (New York: Orbis, 1985); Wilfred Cantwell Smith, *On Understanding Islam* (The Hague: Mouton, 1981); and Joseph van Ess, "Islamic Perspectives," in *Christianity and the World Religions*, by Hans Küng, et al. (New York: Doubleday, 1986).

13. See John L. Esposito, *Islam: The Straight Path*, expanded ed. (New York: Oxford Univ. Press, 1991), especially chap. 5, "Contemporary Islam: Religion and Politics," for a very sympathetic treatment of these issues.

cannot easily contain. Anyone who has traveled abroad in the last three decades has surely noted the flood of books, cassettes, radios, VCRs, videos, CDs, and magazines that have been carried into the Islamic countries on the tides of oil money. These have had an effect among the brotherhoods and in the harems as well as among those educated on international standards. New attitudes, new technologies, new teachings, and images of new life-styles creep into the region. They are both desired and despised. Islam wants what they bring; it hates what that means. It thought it was the only true religion with the only valid culture and law; but it finds that its message is resisted abroad and its culture is quietly eroding at home.

It is a serious question whether Islam is capable of receiving and adapting the accoutrements of modernity, as Japan, Korea, Thailand, and India seem to be doing with various degrees of pain and conflict. As presently constituted, Islam does not appear to be capable of facing the dynamics of democracy, including human rights, women's equality, and the social and technological transformations, that subvert Islam from within.

Partly, this is because Islam has a constitutional tendency to fundamentalism. It is not a contradiction for fundamentalists to use modern technology, as some have argued. Anyone who has heard a fundamentalist preacher on television should know that. Rather, it is a deeper problem of whether something human could change the understanding of the basic faith itself. Like Judaism and Christianity, Islam is based on the idea that we humans can not, on our own, raise ourselves to God. We need God to come to us. Thus it is a religion of revelation. Islam agrees with Judaism and Christianity that God reveals a vision of truth and justice to humanity, and that this vision is at least partially expressed in the Bible. But Islam has, built into its doctrine of revelation, a specific theory of Scripture that gives it its special fundamentalist stamp.

The Qur'an is held to be the "uncreated" thoughts of God. It would be impossible to write an "Islamic Gospel" and title it "The Good News *according to Matthew.*" The Qur'an is according to no human; it is according to God. It is not to be translated, contextualized, or interpreted by historical or critical methods; it is to be applied to political and economic issues through law as well as to issues of faith and morals. Indeed, these issues are issues of faith and morals. Of course, there has been interpretation in Islam — the legal commentaries are many and subtle; but this interpretation is seen as the application of fixed truths to concrete situations, not the development of, or even the promise of, something new.

When the threat to this faith is experienced internally and becomes visible externally by the dominating presence of modernization based on presuppositions from another faith, the crisis is severe. The reaction is much like the response to the publication of Salman Rushdie's *Satanic Verses* — a powerful novel that does to the Islamic establishment what Dante did to the Christian establishment in his own time.[14]

It is not surprising that so many Muslims resent the West, for Christianity and its secularized offspring now threaten to swallow up Islam, as Bernard Lewis has noted.[15] Nor is it surprising that the Islamic world views Israel as but an agent of the West. In its relative success with regard to modernization, Israel is not only a military threat, it is an affront to the faith that was supposed to correct, and complete, both Christianity and Judaism. Now the latter, backed by civilizations borne of the womb of Christianity, maintains an outpost of modernity in the midst of premodern societies. This can be said without approving of many of the policies of Israel, which is another matter.

We may condemn our forebears for their behavior during the Crusades against Islam; but we can also understand why the Christians felt that they had to defend the West against Islam. The world would not have been a better place if Islam had conquered all of Europe, as it threatened to do.

Today, it is not at all clear how Islam will find a way to face the future. It may renew itself and its host cultures, as did Christianity in ancient Rome when old paganism fell apart, and again in Northern Europe, when both the faith and society had become stultified, although it is hard to see where the voices of renewal might be in Islam today. Or Islam may crumble as did the religious civilizations of the Fertile Crescent and the pre-Columbian civilizations of South America. This would be a human disaster that would make earthquakes and typhoons seem like minor tremors in historical experience. When a great religion crumbles, civilizations shatter, societies collapse, and people die through no fault of their own.

A crisis of faith is a sad thing. As personal lives lose their

14. See Salman Rushdie, *Is Nothing Sacred?*, the Herbert Read Memorial Lecture delivered by a friend at the Institute of Contemporary Arts in London in February 1990 and published as a special issue by the literary magazine *Granta*.

15. "The Roots of Muslim Rage," *The Atlantic*, Sept. 1990.

orientation, so cultures and civilizations lose their sense of purpose and hope. We need to keep in our prayers all those thousands and millions of people who have tried to follow Islam faithfully all their lives (perhaps especially all those who thought they were doing their religious duty to fight against Christian infidels from the rout at Medina to the Gulf War). We need also to pray that they do not again turn the propensity to fundamentalism into a new fanaticism. The death throes of a false faith call up the demons of destruction, as we witnessed already in this century in Germany.

In any case, this challenge will be long and hard, and it will stretch our souls and our minds as well as our capacity to love the enemy more than did the struggles against socialism.

The Challenge Within?

The struggles are, in one sense, objective. We have to contend with the economic and political failure of a secular, humanistic philosophy that tried to play the role of religion and found that it could not creatively shape a viable society. We shall have to continue to work with many peoples around the world as we all face the crises of Islam.

But the harder difficulties appear at another level. We are faced with the fact that the two greatest post-Christian movements that have influenced great civilizations are in disarray, even crumbling before us. Our question is whether we have anything better to offer than they had, whether we have any better warrants for following what we believe, and whether our civilization is about to face major crises because our faith is inadequate to the task. In the midst of the apparent triumph of pluralistic, constitutional democratic ways of living, it is not clear that, in the decisive areas of public theology and ecclesiology, the ecumenically oriented Protestant churches know *what* they have to offer and *why,* although in principle they are heirs of resources of inestimable depth and breadth.

The world of the future is a world that will involve global interactions and global systems. It will be a world of corporate capitalism working in mixed economies. It will be technological, trade oriented, and in need of principles of international law that can shape the prospects of justice across cultures. Its literature, its art, its music will be cosmopolitan.

It will do little good to offer this world the various "liberation theologies" as they have developed in the last few decades. The more one reads of them, the more one becomes aware of the fact that they are little more than a baptized version of the humanist ideology that has been discredited with the fall of socialism. It takes no profound depth of insight to recognize that what is often proposed as a fresh new vision in the liberation tradition is simply a secondhand amalgam of Feuerbach, Marx, Engels, and Lenin, mildly peppered with Mannheim, Gramsci, Block, the Frankfurt School, and a few sprinkles of abstracted Bible verses, imposed on the pious of the Third World, who needed a language of protest against real evils, by theologians alienated from modernity and incapable of aiding the people's situation.

Nor should we shrink from saying this directly any more. The cost of following this path has become all too clear. Any reserve that is exercised in order to hear what oppressed voices have to say, or in order to let the contributions of previously ignored people find expression, or in order to acknowledge just criticism against the arrogant paternalism of Eurocentric thought can be extended only insofar as those who claim to speak for the oppressed no longer attempt to make the humanistic assumptions of the French and Marxist revolutions the program for tomorrow. It is a dead end.

Nor can we turn to the absolutist claims of revelational fideism. This has been the other temptation of those opposed to modernity within, as well as beyond, Christianity. If Roman Catholicism restricts the capacity of church theologians to search openly and critically for the truth, and if denominations such as the Southern Baptists continue their plunge toward fundamentalism unabated and gain increased influence in the larger society, we shall experience such a division between faith and reason that we will soon follow the Muslim world into crisis.

But we shall have to think more deeply than we have about the nature and character of revelation. Where does it happen? How do we know? What is its relation to public modes of discourse, especially the shaping of a civilization? If we can make no case for the faith that is within us, then why should anyone pay any attention?

It is not enough to know that we are anticolonialist, anti-imperialist, antipatriarchal, anticommunist, anti-secular humanist, antifundamentalist, or antifanatic. The challenge is harder: we have to know what to be *for.* A world civilization is on the horizon, and it is a serious question as to whether contemporary theology and ethics have anything to say that is indispensable to it. Can Christian faith renew civilization as it has in the past? Can Christianity offer anything to the victims of fundamentalist religion and of secular humanism?

Perhaps there is some other alternative. The contemporary fascinations with meditation, new age, neo-pagan, creation spirituality, crystals, along with many gentle forms of Hinduism and Buddhism are growing rapidly. A good bit of personal healing may go on in these centers, but they seldom attempt to address the questions of civilization. Indeed, they are so focused on the manicuring of the soul that one might suggest that they are among the most organized and expensive forms of irrelevance to our question that could be found.

Nor are we likely to find much aid in the dominant forms of contemporary philosophical thought. Postmodern pragmatism with its borrowed skepticism, deconstruction with all its pretentious echoes of Nietzsche, process philosophy with all its residues of nineteenth-century evolutionism, and neoconservatism with its perennial program of return to the Greeks have mounted major offensives against modern attempts to think theologically.

Christianity will be tested throughout the next decades and century, as the world begins to work out the implications of the present transformations. The world may begin to turn to principles of human rights, democracy, and the incarnational consequences of the theology and ecclesiology of previous centuries; but what is not clear is whether we can renew the theological and ecclesiological resources to extend our greatest legacy into the cosmopolitan tomorrow.

We, our children, and our children's children will have to make profound decisions. Indeed, we have to decide whether we think that our faith has anything to offer to the peoples of the world. I think that it does. But I also believe that it must become an enlarged, a cosmopolitan faith, one opening wider, thinking deeper, and praying broader than we have yet done in recent social-ethical witness.

The Church's Role

What then is the task of the church if it is to have a public role today? It must be first of all a theological center. It must preach and teach, offer and interpret the sacraments so as to explore the public as well as the personal theological content of the faith, recognizing that the public is now global in scope and endangered by both secularism and fundamentalism.

In this regard, we can learn a great deal from earlier eras when similar perils were at hand. One was when Christianity confronted Greco-Roman culture on the one hand and militant Manichaeism and Arianism on the other, at the time of the early councils and of Augustine. Another was when Christianity confronted the new paganism of Machiavellianism and humanism on the one hand and the militant absolutism of Muentzer and the Anabaptists on the other, at the time of the Reformation. In both cases, the church reformed its theology and ethics, its ecclesiology and polity, over the course of a century or two on a more cosmopolitan basis.

What shall be the topics today for this theological reflection? The central social questions turn out to be doctrinal ones: What ought we believe?[16] Is there an orthodoxy? How does God want us to live? How do we know? What difference does it make? These are decisive questions that center especially on the nature of God, on epistemology, and on the role of divine authority in pluralistic societies.[17]

Such issues, I believe, must be approached apologetically. That is, they must be addressed by philosophical theology fully aware of the kinds of social analysis that transcend contextualism if they are to speak to our present cross-cultural situation. Even more, such a theology requires that we no longer rely on arguments from the Bible alone, since other religions have their own scriptures and their own interpretations of inspiration that, in claim, are stronger than Christian doctrines. Christians will have to show why their Bible should be taken seriously in public discourse.[18] New perspectives on the Bible will have to be explored, specifically to find out whether, and if so how, it can address our new situation in a compelling way. Commentaries will have to be developed using comparative religion studies and cross-cultural ethical analysis.[19]

16. See Mark Heim, ed., *On The Doctrine of the Trinity: Confessing our Faith Today.* A project of the Faith and Order Commission, WCC (forthcoming). See also, A. A. van Ruler, *Calvinist Trinitarianism and Theocentric Politics: Essays Toward a Public Theology* (Toronto: Edwin Mellen, 1989).

17. The most compelling, if diverse, answers to this question seem to me to be those of Richard J. Mouw, *The God Who Commands* (Notre Dame: Notre Dame Univ. Press, 1990); Oliver O'Donovan, *Resurrection and Moral Order* (Grand Rapids: Eerdmans, 1986); and Franklin I. Gamwell, *The Divine Good* (San Francisco: Harper, 1990).

18. See my *Apologia: Globalization, Contextualization, and Mission in Theological Education* (Grand Rapids: Eerdmans, 1988).

19. Prof. Pheme Perkins of Boston College and I have been team teaching in this area and have discovered how slender the resources still are.

But beyond these foundational questions, we also must take up the substantive questions that will have to be faced in the twenty-first century, such as how we should responsibly shape the economic systems of tomorrow in a world that will, as mentioned earlier, involve corporate capitalism operating in a global market for as long as we can see into the future.[20] These issues are intimately linked to issues of technology, for the capacity to transform nature presents us with new problems that demand deeper sacramental awareness and a theological ethic of stewardship.[21] Also related will be new issues of international law that can embody the moral and spiritual foundations of our medically, ecologically, and culturally interdependent world.[22] Still further, it will be necessary to develop an awareness of how the "Independent Sector" can play a role in the formation of civilizations when societies are not governed from the top down but from the center out.[23] It is doubtful whether such a perspective can be developed without recourse to theological questions, although theologies based on confessional, narrative, and fideist bases (which are currently very widespread) are likely to be inconsequential for this task.

Of course, to address the questions seriously, issues of family life, of education, of healing, and of the arts, about which there are many confusions today, will also have to be addressed. In these, as doubtless in many other areas requiring attention, the decisive question is whether contemporary Christianity can renew its metaphysical-moral vision and play a redemptive role in the transformations that providence has brought. Can it guide modern pluralistic democracies with a commitment to human rights and a humane form of mixed-economy capitalism in the paths of righteousness? Can it con-

20. Dennis McCann, Shirley Roels, Preston Williams, and I are preparing a two-volume resource book on this topic. See also Charles Strain, ed., *Prophetic Visions and Economic Realities: Protestants, Jews, and Catholics Confront the Bishops' Letter on the Economy* (Grand Rapids: Eerdmans, 1989); Richard Chewning, John Eby, and Shirley Roels, *Business Through the Eyes of Faith* (San Francisco: Harper & Row, 1990); Donald W. Shriver and James W. Kuhn, *Beyond Success: A Business Ethic for the Nineties* (forthcoming).

21. See my "Godly Cooking: Theological Bases for an Ethic of Modern Technology," *First Things* (Fall 1990).

22. This is an area that remains wide open, but which is being explored most creatively by Harold Berman and John Witte at the Center for Law and Religion, Emory University, and in quite another way by Daniel J. Elazar and others at the Center for the Study of Federalism, Temple University.

23. See Robert Wuthnow and Virginia Hodgkinson, eds., *Faith and Philanthropy in America* (San Francisco: Jossey-Bass, 1990).

tain the temptations to arrogance in the West, develop a deep compassion for those shattered by these changes, and draw people of all sectors of all societies into faithful, truth-seeking, and justice-doing communities of commitment and cooperation?

Tomorrow's church will have a public witness or it will not be the church at all. But the texture of that witness is likely to focus as much on matters of polity as on those of policy, and on issues of meaning as on those of advocacy, on questions of ecclesiology as on those of social change, and on theology more than on the social sciences. In other words, we enter a new day when the key questions of policy, advocacy, change, and the social sciences are, at their depths, revealed to be theological.

A Response

Lois Gehr Livezey

Max Stackhouse is always engaging and provocative, setting forth common ground persuasively and dismissing alternative points of view cavalierly, and this paper is true to form. He is ever the generalist, both in the sense of being wide-ranging in his exploration of the terrain and in the sense of being given to generalization.

I appreciate much in Stackhouse's argument here. First, his paper is a call to political seriousness and to religious or theological seriousness. His concern, religiously and politically, is for our common world. He calls us to think theologically about the springs of our knowledge and action, focusing on the importance of public discourse and the question of what are we *for.* Indeed, the heart of the matter is public discourse, and that is, of course, what integrates his commitment to religious and political seriousness.

Second, although I will later raise some questions about his understanding of democracy, I think he is insightful in his discussion of the religious grounds of democracy with respect to (a) the human capacity to transcend interests, (b) the acknowledgment of sin (for Stackhouse, this is one ground of human equality), and (c) the call for "communities of commitment and mutual discipline" (p. 66) that are the heart and heritage of ecclesiology (at least in the Reformed and Anabaptist traditions).

Indeed, third, he offers an argument for the normative importance of ecclesiology for modern social movements with respect to the idea of a universal moral law, with its emphasis on human rights; the experience of self-governing communities, with their noncoercive modes of governance; and the historical role of churches in democratic movements, old and new.

Finally, his call to think theologically about revelation and public discourse is born of his conviction that "civilization" is at stake. He is committed to a wider and deeper, more "cosmopolitan" faith and to the public role of the churches. This is no retreat to local churches and their neighborhoods or to purely confessional theologies. His method of apologia depends on a philosophical and social analysis that transcends local contexts — or seeks to.

That said, I have serious reservations about his argument. Let me first raise my questions in relation to the fourfold structure of his presentation.

Democracy

The assertion of a universal moral law belies a complex argument; such a universal morality is not self-evident. The claim must take seriously our plurality, the realities of multicontext and multicultural grounds of interpretation of law and justice, the dynamics of social location. Whatever commonalties and universalities of moral law we achieve may be more the fruit of dialogue and negotiation than the givens of the world's religions.

For example, Stackhouse emphasizes universal human rights, but he names only the rights of religious freedom, expression, and association, that is, rights according to the classical U.S. Bill of Rights — and only a few of them. The Universal Declaration of Human Rights has a broader focus that includes both civil and political rights of the sort he names, *and* social and economic rights about which he is silent. If the argument for universal human rights had acknowledged the full range of internationally recognized rights, perhaps his discussion of socialism might have been more nuanced.

Socialism

Stackhouse does not seem to recognize the diversities within the world of socialist theory and practice, nor does he take seriously the religious arguments, even the Christian theological arguments, for socialism, especially democratic socialism. This failure to make distinctions among the varieties of socialism leaves his discussion of socialism utterly untrustworthy and hence unpersuasive.

His enthusiastic triumphalism is without nuance: "great will be the crash of them." I expect most of us share his excitement and exultation as democratic passions and insights spark the protests against communist regimes. But as Stackhouse notes elsewhere, there is great distance between what we are *against* and what we are *for.* It may be difficult to develop a constructive, consensual vision, structure, and process for a common life. Indeed, we are already seeing, in the former Soviet Empire, the explosion of ancient ethnic hatreds. Stackhouse's triumphalism may be premature.

He speaks of corporate capitalism working in mixed economies. Is this a matter of fact or a judgment of value and virtue? If virtue, what is the evidence — and counterevidence? For instance, how do we evaluate the actual cases before us — including the hard ones, like the persistence of violent ethnic conflict and abject poverty in India?

Islam

Again, Stackhouse does not acknowledge the differences within the world of Islamic theory and practice, apparently not considering them important. Perhaps Islam, like socialism, falls outside his earlier claim that all profound religious and philosophical thought acknowledges a universal moral law (p. 65). This is curious because, in fact, the Islamic countries are parties to the U.N. Covenants on Human Rights.

To claim that the problem with Islam is that it cannot cope with modernization only recalls the history of the Christian struggles with modernization. Indeed, his own account of the matter leaves me with the sense that Islam is more like Christianity than not, at least in these struggles. We are all under siege from the lure of greed on the one hand and the weight of injustice on the other. Nor is it clear how the various faiths will respond, nor what difference it may make. But within each of these great traditions are diversities of interpretation and diversities of active response to modern conditions of existence.

But my fiercest and most fundamental criticism of his discussion of Islam, as of socialism, is that he makes *no call for dialogue.* In my view, we must include Muslims in our dialogue, that is, in our Jewish-Christian dialogue, and seek to understand a faith that, like ours, stands under the revelation and sovereignty of God. We must do no further harm and, indeed, we must stand against the anti-Arab sentiment and prejudice in this country.

His lack of interest in dialogue is astounding — and mystifying, in one whose plumbline is democracy, whether representative or participatory, with its ecclesiologically born conviction that the will of God is discerned in the discussion within a community of faith and mutual discipline. Or maybe public discourse, for Stackhouse, is a forum not for discernment but only for didactics. A chilling sentence toward the end of his paper suggests that we can be committed to hearing the voices of the oppressed, the long-silenced, "only insofar as those who claim to speak for the oppressed no longer attempt to [build on] the humanistic assumptions of the French and Marxist revolutions" (p. 79). This is a mind-boggling statement, calling for an ideological test as the prerequisite to any dialogue in Stackhouse's democracy: political correctness with a vengeance.

Conclusion

I edited these comments during an election season in which a recent Grand Wizard of the KKK and Nazi Party member, whose rhetoric, if not his membership, still evokes his roots, was a serious contender for the governorship of Louisiana (having won the Republican primary). "Moral legitimacy broken"? Would that it were so. Stackhouse is far more confident than I about the declining significance of domination, degradation, and unequal access; the declining significance of race, class, and sex.

"Underclass" economics and unemployment statistics are rising even as they mask the real extent of people excluded from the workplace altogether or from jobs of their choosing, training, and experience, and jobs paying a living wage. Stackhouse's claims about the capacities of corporate capitalism to produce a just, democratic, and sustainable society are simply not borne out by the contemporary facts of economic life.

In the face of the escalating violence of ethnic conflict in Eastern Europe, the disintegrating Soviet Union and the United States, Stackhouse is unaccountably silent on matters of cultural diversity and the means by which the multicultural realities of our life together find expression and resolution in the articulation of a cross-cultural vision of a common good and a strategy for getting there. The universality of "democracy" as a moral and political principle or, at least, a good or a goal (note Richard McKean, *Democracy in a World of Tensions*) founders on the rocks of our deeply conflictual pluralities.

As Stackhouse does acknowledge in his discussion of the human capacity to transcend interests, it is the joy and pain of being human that we have *eyes* to see, *ears* to hear, *minds* to imagine beyond the bounds of our immediate experience, and *bodies* to sit together around a table and discuss, from divergent vantage points, our common stake in a just world. We should have learned from our own history: the Civil War and the abolition of slavery, the civil rights movement and the abolition of "Jim Crow," that breaking down the dividing walls of hostility — although real occasions for joy and celebration — do not bring hostility to an end but rather reveal and even raise new walls of hostility. What is required of us is not triumphalism but discernment, perseverance, humility, hard work with others, courage, and ultimate confidence in the love of God, who will not let us go.

Christian Ethics in Latin America, 1970–90: Reflections on the Church's Public Role

Gonzalo Castillo-Cardenas

In Plato's *Republic* poets are expelled because their poems do not help build the good society. But in the Genesis story the *word* creates the *world:* word and actualization are one and the same act. Even though the human word does not have this same power, it does have the power to recreate reality by naming the objects of creation, that is, through interpretation. This task involves description, classification, and, fundamentally, imagination: dream, vision, utopia, metaphor, and poetry.

In dealing with theology and ethics in Latin America in the 1970s and 1980s, let me begin with description and classification, the naming of reality, before attempting to interpret the transcendent power of the word as lived by segments of the church during that crucial period.

The Naming of Reality

During the 1970s Latin America experienced levels of repression unparalleled in any other period of the continent's history. Social oppression and political repression had always been present, and military dictatorships had appeared episodically in some countries, chronically in others, as the easiest way of dealing with conflicts between the enlarged egos, estates, or interests of dominant personalities or ruling groups, or to put down insurgent popular movements. But during the 1970s such phenomena became established practice, legitimized by the ideology of national security developed principally in the United States.[1]

1. See Jose Comblin, *The Church and the National Security State* (New York: Orbis, 1979).

The global confrontation between the so-called superpowers that assumed the need to keep in check "Soviet expansionism" translated in Latin America into a determination of the United States and of the privileged groups of the area not to allow the emergence of "another Cuba" in the continent. This goal justified and even necessitated every sacrifice, and toward this end, democratic institutions began to be viewed at best as a luxury and at worst as a threat.[2] This perspective not only dominated U.S. foreign policy in the region; it also provided the strategy and justification for the domestic national security states in most countries of the hemisphere.[3]

By the beginning of the 1980s, the national security state had produced identifiable results, one of which was the destruction of all forms of liberal democracy in most of the region.[4] Another was the emergence of a new elite, with the characteristics of "a new social class," concentrating agricultural, industrial, commercial, and financial capital and, at least at the beginning, supporting the military, which now monopolized all political power. Still another paradoxical result was the strengthening of the historical project of popular democracy through the creativity of the popular sectors (i.e., "the poor"), who were able to devise strategies of resistance and to create political spaces in which to keep alive the expectation of the poor for a more just and participatory society. All these results are impor-

2. See Michel Crozier, et al., *The Crisis of Democracy* (New York: New York Univ. Press, 1976).

3. The role of the United States in paving the way and helping to create the conditions for these developments within the context of the Alliance for Progress was candidly confirmed but not seriously criticized by Niebuhr and Sigmund in their joint book *The Democratic Experience* (New York: Praeger, 1969), pp. 133-34. The book noted that with American encouragement and direct military assistance "civic-action teams from the military have attempted to win over the peasants through literacy, health and welfare programs," that the anticommunist ideology of the cold war made it more unlikely for democratic changes to take place because "the armed forces can get more American aid and strengthen their domestic power if at last they have an enemy to fight . . . and if democratic governments do not make what they consider a sufficient effort to suppress the unrest, the military can accuse them of pro-communist and stage a *coup d'etat*" (p. 134). The authors further observed that American interventionism in the Caribbean during "three quarters of a century," U.S. military assistance through the Rio Treaty since 1947, and the association of the U.S. with military dictators (p. 147) had "increased U.S. influence on a crucial power factor in Latin American politics" (p. 147). But the authors still concluded that "a realistic assessment" of the effects of American influence on the growth of democracy "is a mixed one" (p. 146).

4. See Comblin, *Church;* Julio de Santa Ana, "Problemas y Mediaciones en la Marcha hacia la Democracia en America Latina," *Cristianismo y Sociedad* 76 (1983): 49.

tant aspects of the reality that is unfolding throughout Latin America today.

Two aspects of this reality deserve special consideration: one has to do with the objective limitations to democracy, even to the carefully measured democratizing steps allowed recently by the weakened ruling elite; the other is about the nature and reality of the commitment to the democratic ideal, principally among the popular sectors.[5]

(1) The *barriers* standing in the way of the democratic ideal are of various kinds. The first kind arise from the strong tradition of imperialism that Europe and the United States imposed upon the entire region. The "imperial content" of this tradition is not purely economic but also geopolitical, ideological, and cultural in nature.[6] As such it contains an ideology of conquest that divides the world between "civilization" and "barbarism," justifying a permanent "just war" against "the other." The same "just causes" that were given by most Spanish theologians to justify the original conquest in the sixteenth century have been offered to justify all subsequent interventions.[7] Since 1970, U.S. policy toward Nicaragua has become one more — but unfortunately not the most recent — illustration of this problem. It demonstrates that the United States considers national projects of radical democracy such as Sandinismo contrary to U.S. interests to such an extent that it is ready to use all means available, legal and illegal, to stop or reverse them — showing for that purpose not only disregard but contempt for international law and institutions, which have proved powerless and ineffective.

Another kind of limitation is cultural in nature. The hegemonic ethos of the dominant sectors, including intellectual and educational institutions embodying the dark side of the European "Enlightenment," tends to be elitist, racist, Eurocentrist, and filled with contempt for the common people, especially the poor. This ethos has alienated the national leadership and the ecclesiastical hierarchies from the majority of the population, creating a wall of separation that resists any truly democratic project in church and society alike.

5. By "popular sectors" we mean both the rural poor, including peasants, rural workers, and Indian communities; and the urban poor, including the self-employed of the "informal economy," the student, and working-class organizations.

6. See Giulio Girardi, *La Conquista de America: Con que Derecho?* (San Jose, Costa Rica: DEI, 1988), p. 17.

7. See Juan G. de Sepulveda, *Tratado Sobre las Justas Causas* (Mexico: Fondo de Cultura, [1551] 1941).

Another set of limitations is economic. The international economic and financial institutions put in place at Bretton Woods in 1945 without the participation of the poor countries of the world set specific conditions for economic and social development. In practice this policy places an iron curtain around the Latin American countries from which there seems to be no "rational" escape. The embargo, blockade, and strangling of the Sandinista regime in Nicaragua, the hard line toward the Latin American debt problem, and the draconian measures required by the International Monetary Fund and the World Bank as conditions for more loans have effectively forced the new "democratizing regimes" of South America to submit to the seemingly all-powerful market economy. As Julio de Santa Ana has written:

> There is a clear contradiction between the economic order that requires a high social cost and is predicated upon the exploitation of the poor to accumulate wealth in the hands of the few, and the economic exigencies of popular democracy. . . . These [economic limitations] affect negatively the popular political organizations and their interests forcing them into compromises and concessions to oppression which put a brake to democracy.[8]

Social scientists have analyzed in detail many other barriers to the democratic ideal, including technological and political ones. Among these, militarism and militarization are particularly recalcitrant, in part because of their structural connection with characteristic patterns of Western development. Thus, while the demise of the international framework under which militarism achieved its most extreme forms has weakened its claims, abated its effects, and loosened to a certain extent its hold upon society, the militaristic project seems to be alert and watching for new opportunities and roles in the hemisphere.

(2) These realities notwithstanding, the popular sectors have demonstrated during the same period their capacity not only to survive but even to strengthen their historical project through the test of fire of the national security state. While we must be careful to avoid a triumphalist vision of popular movements, it is important not to overlook three aspects of their democratic struggle that carry particular weight in terms of prospects for significant change.

8. Santa Ana, "Problemas," p. 53.

The first has to do with the subjects of the social struggle and the nature of their claims. They are mostly peasants, but also Indian communities, landless rural workers, and hosts of rural migrants forming the *tugurios, favelas, pueblos nuevos, villas,* and *miseria* now swelling many an old seigneurial urban center into a bustling megalopolis. When considered carefully and emphatically, it is not difficult to see that their struggle is for democratic relations: accessibility to land, respect for cultural and ethnic identity, and the right to work, that is, to an economic space to develop their economic and business creativity in the immense, alien, and threatening urban world.[9]

The second aspect of this reality is the process of popular education, which from its beginnings with Paulo Freire's philosophy and experiences in Brazil in the 1950s has now become the working assumption of most social activism throughout the continent. It is expressed in different forms. One is the realization that illiteracy does not mean ignorance and therefore that in the educational process the masses must often educate the educators. A related idea is the belief that the popular sectors know best, or share basically correct intuitions about the nature of the problems affecting them most directly and the general direction where solutions are to be found. This knowledge of the people is not scientific (i.e., systematic, or comprehensive) but a kind of wisdom that social activists should not dare to do without.[10] These assumptions are behind the concept of a "historical project of the poor," a category that remains important in the social analysis of liberation theology.

The third and not the least important aspect of the popular struggle is the emergence of the "church of the poor," or the "popular church," or the "base Christian communities" — concepts that have been a source of controversy within the church. To the critics they

9. The question of an "economic space" for the poor is closely related to "the informal economy" issue, which has become a major subject of study thanks particularly to Hernando De Soto's analysis of the Peruvian case in his book *El Otro Sendero: La Revolucion Informal* (Lima: Instituto Libertad y Democracia, 1986; 8th ed. Bogota: Editorial Oveja Negra, 1989). Since its original publication, the book has gone through eight editions and sold over 100,000 copies throughout the continent. It contains a thorough analysis of the economic creativity of the poor realized on the margins of the formal economy, amounting in some cases to 60% of the total national economy, in spite of the barriers to its development that are common problems of most "underdeveloped" countries around the world. De Soto's ideas became an important factor in the political campaign that elected Alberto Fujimori to the presidency of Peru.

10. See Orlando Fals-Borda, *Conocimiento y Poder Popular* (Mexico: Siglo XXI; Bogota: Punta de Lanza, 1986).

have the capacity to be used within an ideology of class struggle that closely parallels the Marxist concept of "the proletariat," and ecclesiologically they would seem to imply a radical denial of the institutional church.[11] The church of the poor is a vital reality as a form of being the church, but it is not the only one. Pastoral agents and theologians insist that it is not a movement inside the church, but "the church in movement,"[12] pointing toward an ecclesiology in which "the poor" (all of the believing and oppressed people) are the historical subjects of the church as the people of God. Liberation theologians agree that this vision of the church has contributed to the revitalization of the Christian faith and also, as a consequence, played a fundamental political role by providing a democratic space for dialogue and participation, a foretaste of the ideal that motivates the social struggles of the popular sectors.[13]

Theology and Politics

The aim of theology is not to pronounce the last word about a situation, thus bringing a conversation to a close by the sheer weight of its supernatural authority, its self-evident truth, or its pretended finality; theology aims rather at beginning and carrying on a conversation between the Word of God and a certain reality: The Word of God addresses the situation and it addresses us as part of it. As we understand and experience the situation, we respond to the Word of God, clarifying it and making it pertinent and applicable, so that we are able to say that the Word of God is alive. When this happens the Word is endowed with the power of recreating reality through the medium of human interpretation.

This understanding of theology became alive to me in March 1990 while attending meetings of two base Christian communities in Managua, Nicaragua. The electoral defeat of the FSLN had taken place a few weeks before and the mood in the city was a mixture of relief and

11. See Paul VI, "Evangelii Nuntiandi" (1976).

12. Interview with Carlos Chavarria, of IPA, in Cuzco, Peru. See also Stephen Judd, "The Emergent Andean Church: Inculturation and Liberation in Southern Peru, 1968–1986" (Ph.D. diss., Graduate Theological Union, San Francisco, 1987).

13. Pablo Richard, lecture on "Base Christian Communities: lessons in Methodology," at the DEI headquarters in San Jose, Costa Rica, March 20, 1990.

sadness. In meetings of support groups whose members from many countries had collaborated for ten years with the Sandinista project, anxiety and frustration could be detected. Not so among the Christian poor of the base communities. Let me quote from my field diary.

> March 17, 1990, 4:00 P.M. meeting at La Merced Church, a poor neighborhood in the outskirts of Managua. Attendance: about 30, mostly women. The meeting was in two parts. The first was to study the National Constitution, as approved by the Constitutional Assembly of 1985. Each participant had a copy. The second part was to reflect on the biblical text for the week: Jesus' parable of the Good Samaritan. About the constitution the main idea emphasized many times by the participants was "the strength and power" of the document because it had been produced democratically with the participation of hundreds of peoples' organizations, at all levels, and how difficult would it be to destroy it or annul it, and how important it was for each one to have the constitution to stand on. The second part of the meeting became an improvised dramatization of the parable. A strong woman got up, walked across the room, grabbed and tossed to the floor another woman who was sitting close to me, kicked and abused her several times on the floor, saying: "You voted for UNO, despicable woman" *(mujer miserable);* and left her wounded and unconscious in the middle of the meeting. Several of the people present got up, one by one, and looked at the wounded woman, some with fear and others with suspicion. Finally an older, frail-looking woman came close and revived the wounded one, helped her to get up, found a seat for her, and asked help of others to take care of her until she got well. Several reflections followed from the participants about the meaning of the parable.
>
> — One said: "Jesus wants us to guard against vindictiveness" *(revanchismo).*
> — Another: "Yes, the Christian does not kick anybody."
> — Another: "And besides, we should always raise up the one that lies on the floor."
> — Another: "That is true, and Jesus meant also to teach us to forgive."
> — Another: "We might not be ready to turn the other cheek, but we must be ready to raise the one that lies on the floor."
> — Another: "What does turning the other cheek mean? It means to do justice!"

Prayers followed about the social and political situation in the country, about "the contras," about their sons and daughters in the army, about the need for peace.

March 18, 1990. Base community in another poor barrio. Attendance: about 80, both men and women. Since it was a Sunday afternoon the meeting included the celebration of the Eucharist and a short homily by a priest, a Dutch missionary who had lived 20 years in the country. The Bible study was on the dialogue between Jesus and the Samaritan woman. The priest posed the question: "What does it mean to worship God in spirit and in truth?" The following ideas came up in the discussion.

— A woman: "It means that love is not only words but actions for social change, commitment" *(Palabras no son amores, sino hechos, compromiso!)*.
— Another: "It means to work for peace in Nicaragua."
— Still another (this time a man): "God is with us anywhere, but we make our own history; it means that we need to struggle for justice, so that the one who has no house, no shoes, no food, no shirt, may have all of these."
— Another: "Yes. Well said. And also it means that we can never stop; that is the temptation: to stop once the revolution wins; or once the UNO wins; or any other political party wins; to stop and leave everything to the government."
— Another: " 'In spirit' means 'with your thoughts,' and 'in truth' means with your actions!"

After the meeting, which ended again with prayers, I overheard an adult man, with the signs of labor and pain all over his face, saying to a small group: "I shall continue struggling for the ideals of the revolution, not to attain any economic advantage for me, because during the ten years of the revolution nothing changed *for me personally,* I remain as I was before. But I shall continue struggling for others who have nothing."

These simple reflections on biblical texts, done in the midst of great poverty, uncertainty, and insecurity, made me realize something of the nature of the Christian ethics that began to develop in the 1970s and 1980s among poor Christian groups, not only in Nicaragua but in Colombia, Peru, and Argentina, to mention only those countries where I had the opportunity to attend similar meetings during the summer of 1990.

Religion and the church had always played an important political role in Latin America. The only question is, in the words of Miguez-Bonino, "how, from what perspective, in which direction and on what basis."[14] In the past, and to a large extent also in the 1970s and 1980s, the church was politically allied with the established order either as part of the state's mechanisms or, in conditions of formal separation, by providing moral criteria on key issues such as education, the family, and labor legislation, from the perspective of the ruling classes and their need for stability. Within this "Christendom" type of alliance,[15] the church's model of pastoral activity was one that utilized or claimed as its right to utilize as mediation for the realization of its mission the political power and hegemonic control of the dominant sectors. Assuming that the church performs a much greater role in society to the extent that its presence and power is greater in the whole organism of the dominant political and civil society, the church attempted to penetrate, to replicate, or to have control over the social, cultural, and political institutions, for which it entered into the most diverse kind of alliances and compromises with the dominant groups.

This traditional alliance and this pastoral model have been challenged in the 1970s and 1980s from the perspective of "the preferential option for the poor" by significant Christian practice and theological reflection that shed light and give direction regarding the nature and forms of the church's public role. Some points are of special significance in this challenge: first, the crucial question of "subjecthood," that is, the poor as the collective historical subject of change and transformation; second, the question about the ideological role of religious symbols themselves through which religion and the church exercise their most direct and pervasive political influence; and third, the question of the nature of the democratic ideal and its relation to the Christian faith.

Subjecthood

In their political ethics, liberation theologians pay a great deal of attention to the European conquest of "the new world."[16] In this

14. Jose Miguez-Bonino, "Theology and Peace in Latin America," in *Theology, Politics and Peace*, ed. T. Runyon (Maryknoll, N.Y.: Orbis, 1989), p. 45.

15. Pablo Richard, *Death of Christendom, Birth of the Church* (Maryknoll, N.Y.: Orbis, 1987).

16. Gustavo Gutierrez, *The Power of the Poor in History* (Maryknoll, N.Y.: Orbis,

momentous event of modern history they tend to discern not so much antecedents or precursors but paradigms and suggestions about the patterns of historical domination and liberation.[17] Like all other similar expansions, the sixteenth-century conquest denied the humanity of "the other" by regarding the native populations as inferior, not fully human, and by robbing them of their right to be subjects of their own history.

The church participated in this conquest and with few exceptions shared its assumptions of European superiority and divine destiny. The few exceptions, of which Las Casas has been the figure most closely studied,[18] plus the many forms and manners of Indian resistance, were unable to stop the engulfing and dehumanizing tide of European conquest. Since then the question of the human status and historical subjecthood of the Indians, who have become the paradigm par excellence of "the poor,"[19] has been the central ethical issue of the continent, confronting all social actors, political leaders, and movements, and especially the church with a life-or-death decision. The issue continues to occupy the same centrality today.[20] In this context "the preferential option for the poor" becomes a most significant statement, both theological and political, based on faith in a God who has not abandoned the world but is present in it with the powerless and suffering poor.

In liberation political ethics the subjecthood of the poor (i.e.,

1983), pp. 77ff.; Enrique Dussel, *Filosofia Etica Latinoamericana* (Bogota: USTA-CED, 1980), vol. 5.

17. Girardi, *Conquista.*

18. Gutierrez, *Dios o el Oro en Las Indias: Siglo XVI,* Coleccion Bartolome de Las Casas (Lima: Instituto Bartolome de Las Casas, CEP, 1989).

19. Dussel, *Filosofia Etica Latinoamericana* (Bogota: USTA-CED, 1979), 4.79-80.

20. This issue is behind all ideological and political movements that have questioned or proposed identity definitions such as *Latin* America, *Indo*-America, *Hispanic* America, *Ibero*-America, *Raza cosmica,* and others; see Ribeiro (1972); Leopoldo Zea, *America en la Historia* (Mexico, 1957). It reappeared in Peru during the run-off presidential elections of June 1990 between Fujimori and Vargas Llosa in which racial/ethnic identity became a major factor. During my visit to the country I witnessed aspects of the confrontation between those who understood the European blood and ancestry as defining the very essence of being "Peruvian" and those who supported Fujimori — including the bulk of Indian peasants of pre-European ancestry — who challenged such exclusive identification, claiming not only the Peruvian identity for themselves too but also their right to be protagonists of social and political change. The same fundamental tension of identity and historical "subjecthood" is common to Guatemala, Mexico, Ecuador, Bolivia, Paraguay, and in some degree to the entire continent.

"the poor" as the dynamic agent of historical transformation) is not only the starting point but also the issue that provides the clearest perspective for three reasons. First, it is the key to address correctly the ethical inquiry about the nature of the good, that is, the kind of society that is good and just for Latin America, not the one that the powerful classes and countries consider possible or desirable in answer to their question "how can we help the poor?"[21] Second, "the preferential option" provides the ground of historical identity — the geopolitical and geocultural location from which to look at history and its processes.[22] Third, "the preferential option" points to the historical vocation of "the peoples without history" to make history. The seedbed of this theology is the "church of the poor," in which it has developed in close connection with the pastoral model of "inculturation," quite distinct from the Christendom or New Christendom models of the Catholic tradition.[23] It is a form of being the church with two conscious goals: (a) a more critical practice of the Christian faith by the masses of the poor, and (b) a commitment to social transformation through resistance to domination and struggle for justice (i.e., "a space of hope").

From the point of view of the church's public role the model of "inculturation" is a new methodology for the church's relation to society at the grass-roots level. In southern Peru, for example, in the four dioceses that attend to the vast region between Ayachucho and Puno, the "inculturation" approach means that pastoral agents seek to get closer to the Indian peasants and their reality: to their forms of work, exchange and struggle, and also to their ways of expressing hope, solidarity, and feelings toward family and to the internal and external communities. This pastoral model does not necessarily create new organizations but favors the strengthening of the peasants' own organizations, thus transcending other pastoral models that spend themselves in assistantialism. Above all, it is a force for "democratization" of the church and of society. Most of the themes that occupy their reflection, such as "we are the people, we are the church," "the land: gift of God, right of the people," have become pastoral letters and also major subjects of the theology and ethics of liberation. I was told by Carlos Chavarria that Gustavo Gutierrez keeps in close touch

21. Miguez-Bonino, "Theology," p. 47.
22. Girardi, *Conquista*, p. 13.
23. Richard, *Death*.

with these pastoral experiences. This model or very similar ones based on the subjecthood of the poor are practiced with other names such as "insertion" or "accompaniment" by Protestant and Catholic base communities throughout Latin America.

The charges of sociological naivete, humanistic messianism, or optimistic humanism point more to potential dangers than to lack of awareness or to dogmatic one-sidedness. Liberation ethicists are careful to point out the sociological and ethical ambiguity of "the poor";[24] that God's option for the poor is not based on merit or virtue;[25] that God's transcendence is not denied but affirmed in the "otherness" of the poor, who confront the system standing on ethical grounds external to it,[26] and who, in spite of the reality and depth of sin, are called to the task of recreating and transforming history from beneath.[27]

The Power of Symbols

Sociology of religion has documented the intricate ways in which politics and religion penetrate each other in public life. This interpenetration has become clearer to liberation theologians as they focus attention on the reality of poverty and domination. On the one hand, it is clear that there is a religious commitment implicit in politics, since we cannot conceive of the political reality merely as the rational exercise of instrumental reason, ignoring the whole ensemble of representations, symbols, and utopias that are incorporated in political life.[28] The symbolic universe of political ideologies tends to sacralize or sacramentalize certain interpretations of reality, projects, programs, and promises, and to condemn others as impossible, destructive, or leading to "chaos." The slogan "property, family, and tradition" that characterizes the conservative end of the spectrum in Latin America elicits the religious utopia of the nation as an extended family, homogeneous and united around the preservation of its resources and

24. See Miguez-Bonino, *Toward a Christian Political Ethics* (Philadelphia: Fortress, 1983), pp. 103ff.; Dussel, *Metodo para Una Filosofia de la Liberacion* (Salamanca: Ed. Sigueme, 1974), p. 226.

25. Victorio Araya, *The God of the Poor: The Mystery of God in Latin American Liberation Theology* (Maryknoll, N.Y.: Orbis, 1987), p. 116.

26. Dussel, *Filosofia*, 4.79-80.

27. Araya, *God of the Poor*, p. 137.

28. Miguez-Bonino, "Theology."

traditions. Such political ideologies usually incorporate Christianity as one of the ingredients of "tradition," sometimes as the very core of the national identity, its soul.[29]

Religious symbols serve not only conservative political stands. Franz Hinkelammert has analyzed in detail "the utopian reason" inherent in the neoliberal project of democratic capitalism with its fantastic illusions about the capability of "the market" to achieve the social good, defined as "freedom."[30] Thus one cannot ignore the ideological commitments implicit in *religious* symbols, whether playing alienating or "conscienticizing" political roles. The 1970s and 1980s in Latin American life have extensively illustrated both of these roles and also shown what happens when the implicit ideologies are made explicit by interested political movements or parties.[31] Pinochet in Chile and Rios Montt in Guatemala were able to draw extensively on evangelical Protestant symbols and discourse to legitimize and gain support for their counterinsurgence ideology. More recently, Vargas Llosa and Fujimori were also able to manipulate Protestant and Catholic feelings and interpretations for their political projects. The alienating and repressive role of religion to which Marx called attention a century and a half ago is still very strong in Catholic and Protestant traditions.[32]

29. The traditional Catholic interpretation of Latin American identity postulates "the Catholic substratum" as the element that gives unity to the plurality of Latin American cultures, a conception that has crept into the preparatory document (par. 23) for the forthcoming IVth General Conference of Latin American Bishops to be held in Santo Domingo in 1992. This is one of the many paragraphs being questioned by liberation theology groups (Church and Society Symposium, at the Instituto Bartolome de Las Casas, May 21, 1990, Lima, Peru).

30. Franz J. Hinkelammert, *Critica de la Razon Utopica* (San Jose, Costa Rica: DEI, 1984), chap. 2.

31. Humberto Lagos Schuffeneger, *Crisis de la Esperanza: Religion y Autoritarismo en Chile* (Santiago, Chile: Ed. Literatura Americana Reunida, 1988); Jorge Pixley, "Algunas Lecciones de la Experiencia de Rios Montt," *Cristianismo y Sociedad* 76 (1983).

32. In the notebook of my trip to Peru there is the following entry that illustrates this point. "May 10, 1990. Today I received a strong religious admonition from a simple woman. I had gone to her little shop, on one of the sides of the Plaza de Armas in Cuzco, to buy a little guide book of the city. She was pushing a large, expensive one and I was resisting. So, half serious, half joking I said: 'I cannot spend that much because I am poor.' To which she responded briskly, looking me straight in the face: 'Never say "I am poor"! The only poor is the Devil because he doesn't have God. If you have God you are rich!' Three days later another Indian woman from Pisaq, fifty miles away in another town of the Sacred Valley of the Incas, told me exactly the same words in a similar incident. It became clear to me that religious symbols carried for these people the power of explaining material poverty and wealth without reference to the economic and political structures of the country."

On the other hand, religious symbols can also serve ideologies of transformation. Sixty years ago Mariategui criticized the communist parties for ignoring the power of "myth" evident in the social reality of Peru. Today liberation theology is listening to this critique more attentively than the original addressees. One of its major subjects of study and interest is the staying power of popular piety and faith.[33] The new reading *(relectura)* of the Bible that goes on in the base Christian communities cultivates the positive political role of such religious symbols as the identification of Jesus with the suffering poor and the eschatological image of the resurrection as appropriated by the popular sectors, cultures, and classes that had been sentenced to death by the Western model of development and who now rise up to claim their right to live.[34]

I have to agree with Miguez in his critique that much of the ethical reflection on politics that goes on in the Northern world has not been critical enough about its own ideological commitments.[35] In Christian realism, for example, the subjecthood of the middle classes is clearly assumed and therefore such key concepts as "balance of power" and "interest" seem to communicate symbolic messages addressed to the powerful of the world, who are seen as invested with the historical responsibility of saving the world from "chaos." The complaint that neoconservative or ultraconservative political positions have "misunderstood" the tradition of Christian realism[36] has not led to fundamental questioning of the Christian realist reading of "reality" that lends itself to easy manipulation by ultraconservative forces.

Democratization and the Christian Faith

Is it possible to go beyond the superpowers and the balance that they supposedly created, without going beyond history, that is, without leaving the real world and entering the world of dreams? Or, on the contrary, is it precisely at this juncture in world history when a deeper

33. Marzal, 1989.

34. Julia Esquivel, *Threatened with Resurrection: Prayers and Poems from an Exiled Guatemalan* (Elgin, Ill.: Brethren, 1982).

35. Miguez-Bonino, "Theology," p. 46.

36. Ronald Stone, *Christian Realism and Peacemaking: Issues in U.S. Foreign Policy* (Nashville: Abingdon, 1988), p. 13.

reality is suggesting itself as possible, one in which the imperialisms give way to the self-determination and self-development of peoples struggling to achieve the ideals of equity and democracy? The developments of 1989 in Eastern Europe as iron curtains crumbled under the pressure of peoples' hopes have kindled similar hopes in other parts of the world. The current Latin American situation shows how far off such expectations still are there. But it also shows that the struggle for democracy has broadened its base, clarified its priorities, and deepened its understanding of the real barriers to, and possibilities of, a democratic project in the Southern hemisphere.

The sectors that carry on this struggle understand that democracy is both a type of society and a political regime. As a type of society the democratic utopia has deep roots in Latin American utopian history: a "radical democratic project" has been the banner of most social protest and rebel movements and uprisings among the Indians, the blacks, the mestizos, and the poor whites of the continent. It has also been the dream of Latin America's most perceptive political leaders and philosophers. Bolivar, Hostos, Marti, Juarez, Sandino, and Haya de la Torre (in his early years) all have reiterated the deep-seated aspiration for popular democracy.[37] However, the ruling elites that took over the reins of the new republics in the early nineteenth century adopted the forms of bourgeois or liberal democracy from their allies in the wars against Spanish colonialism, but without the corresponding economic and cultural transformations that had taken place already in the North Atlantic countries. As a consequence most of the political constitutions of our countries are democratic, but most of the social, economic, and cultural institutions are elitist and authoritarian. This is the reason why "formal democracy" became more a denunciation than a project for the popular sectors struggling for the democratic ideal. It is also one of the reasons why there has been so little reflection on democracy as a political regime among the popular democratic leadership. Both in reflection and in activism "the democratic" was overshadowed by "the revolutionary," with precious little theoretical elaboration or understanding of the actual functioning of "the logic of the majority."[38]

It is well known that the Catholic Church has a long and estab-

37. By popular democracy I mean a system in which the sectors traditionally oppressed are guaranteed the participation in the decision-making process about the matters that concern them most directly.

38. Zorostiaga (1982).

lished antidemocratic tradition in Latin America. In contrast, the Protestant churches first entered the area with the sponsorship and under the protection of foreign "democratic" countries and at the invitation of liberal bourgeois political leaders, which was their original strength and their Achilles' heel. In the 1970s and 1980s major developments have taken place in both Catholic and Protestant churches regarding their attitude toward democracy. Three tendencies have appeared: first, the traditional one, which took for granted that "representative democracy" as practiced in the Western capitalist countries is the best political system possible; second, the "revolutionary" position, which emerged in the 1960s and saw "formal democracy" as one more ploy of the dominant sectors to maintain their oppression and effectively to stall all movements for radical change; and third, a position that appeared with unsuspected force during the 1970s and that showed a disposition to accept the military regimes as "the lesser evil" in view of the perceived threat (defined as "chaos") if revolutionary or even populist forces had their way.[39] This third tendency found easy theoretical support in the conservative theories about the nature of "reality" that were being developed in the North Atlantic countries on the premise that institutions have a natural tendency toward order and against the threat of "chaos."[40]

Today, pain and suffering are making people, including revolutionary Christians, realize that a formal democratic space is not the goal but a necessary condition for the democratic struggle to continue; that democracy as a political order with division of powers and representation is fundamental for "democratization," in the sense of participation of all in government and access by all to the basic necessities of life, to take place.[41] The lasting value of the revolutionary critique of the 1960s, in line with the "radical project" of Latin American utopian history, lies in the realization that a system of representative democracy can coexist with the most flagrant injustices and oppressive social and economic practices. It has become clear, however, that "a possible democracy" is the first level of hope, a "taste" that provokes

39. These positions were the subject of analysis, critique, and theological reflection at a symposium called by ISEDET in 1983. The materials of the symposium were published as *Democracia: Una Opcion Evangelica*, ed. Severino Croato, et al. (Buenos Aires: Ed. Aurora, 1983).

40. Peter L. Berger, *The Sacred Canopy* (Garden City, N.Y.: Doubleday, 1967); Hinkelammert, *Critica*.

41. Miguez-Bonino, "Theology," p. 52.

greater commitment to a fuller satisfaction of the human need.[42] As an ecumenical study concluded on Argentina in 1985:

> Six months into the new ("democratic") government have provided us with new confirmations that democracy does not produce miracles, does not dissolve conflicts, does not stop the voracity of the rich nor fill the stomachs of the poor; but it has provided us with an experience capable of opening the eyes of many and of making us, little by little, more protagonists of our own history.[43]

From the perspective of a commitment to the poor, the church's public role can be defined as "to be present in the world witnessing to Jesus Christ by denouncing the injustices, the abuses of power, the threats to the survival of cultures, taking the side of the poor who are under cultural, economic and political aggression, thus contributing to the edification of a human community in which there is more justice, more freedom, and better quality of life."[44]

The emphasis on "denunciation" in this definition of the church's public role springs from the experience of repression during the 1960s and 1970s, when the struggle for fundamental human rights, especially the right to live, became the number-one priority for the population, and the church in many cases was the only channel through which to protest violations of the dignity of persons, and to witness to the sanctity of life. Agencies of the church became well known internationally for this courageous witness, which was rendered ecumenically, with Catholic and Protestant participation. Through this experience the church of the poor has been shown with new clarity and urgency a permanent component of its prophetic role; it has also clarified the fact that "taking the side of the poor" already contains all the dimensions of the church's contribution to the human community, and that "democratization" as an ethical principle is closely related to the church's intrinsic mission, since, profoundly

42. Edelberto Torres-Rivas, *Centroamerica: La Democracia Posible* (San Jose, Costa Rica: Ed. Universidad Centroamericana, 1987).

43. Fundacio Ecumenica; de Cuyo-Mendoza, "Seis Meses de Gobierno Democratico," *Cristianismo y Sociedad* 83 (1985).

44. Mario Yutzis, "Identidad Nacional y Democracia," in Croato, et al., *Democracia,* p. 15. This paper was presented at the symposium on "Protestantism and Democracy," called by ISEDET, October 1983, with the participation of theologians from all the denominations participating in ISEDET: Methodist, Reformed, Lutheran, and Disciples.

understood, it must be a process of qualitative change that is at the same time personal, social, economic, and political. For this reason Yutzis went on to explain that democratization "requires a human being more attracted by *being* than by *having;* more preoccupied about the quality of life than about the quantity of goods; a human being that tolerates the reduction of a high level of consumption for the sake of greater harmony among peoples and greater possibility for the underprivileged to use their right to a better life."[45]

But is that not a utopian ideal that disregards "the realities" of history and the radical limits of human nature? Here emerges the classic controversy about the nature of reality, of human nature and its hope, so intimately linked to the history of the modern world and so central to Christian theology. On this question let me make two points as a Latin American Protestant attentive to the theological reflection of the 1970s and 1980s, mostly among the church of the poor.

(1) As is well known, the classical Protestant tradition has taken a "pessimist" (or realist?) position about human nature (basically Hobbesian) that leads to a political philosophy of accommodation to the modern world within the space allowed by the Western systems of liberal democracy and the capitalist market economies, hoping within those constraints to achieve "relative justice." In the Calvinist Reformed tradition this philosophy has produced, in the Anglo-Saxon experience, a staunch resistance to absolute power, to authoritarianism and tyranny. In the Latin American experience this same political philosophy is also important, but its effects have been mostly negative not only because of authoritarian and repressive aberrations perpetrated in its name,[46] but principally because it lacks the philosophical motivation and power for the construction of a new social order. This *dynamis* was provided in the Anglo-Saxon experience by "the spirit of capitalism" with the possible contribution of Reformation ideas about "vocation" that the Christian was expected to implement in the context provided and permitted by the same economic and cultural system.

Besides lacking an abstract positive concept of equality, Calvinism has failed to inspire a radical democratic thrust of inclusivity

45. Ibid., p. 16.

46. Pixley, "Algunas Lecciones"; Rubem Alves, *Protestantism and Repression: A Brazilian Case Study* (Maryknoll, N.Y.: Orbis, 1987); Lagos Schuffeneger, *Crisis.*

and solidarity with "the other." Historically it has tended rather to nurture an ethos of exclusive "covenanted" communities that in Anglo-Saxon experience have assumed ethnocentric characteristics intertwined with such concepts as "the chosen people" and "manifest destiny." Scottish Presbyterianism, which was born and developed in the context of an anti-imperialistic struggle against Rome and the Anglican Church, was not exempt from Anglo-Saxon attitudes of superiority, of which John A. Mackay, its most outstanding missionary figure in Latin America, is not an exception.[47]

In the 1970s and 1980s, the historical task of the transformation of the world has been deeply impressed in the church of the poor as a challenge coming directly from the gospel because, as Miguez-Bonino puts it, "The gospel is the acknowledgment of our limitation as sinners and [therefore] the search for approximate solutions to insoluble problems. . . . But [the gospel] is also and above all, the acknowledgment of our freedom as children [of God] and therefore of the possibility to build the world."[48] This is one of the reasons why the symbol of the kingdom of God has received so much attention in recent biblical scholarship in Latin America: there is the realization that the hope of the kingdom points to the ultimate context of our responsibility as cocreators with God, a view that presupposes a human being capable of responding to God's invitation and of engaging in the historical task of recreation of reality. This view tends to provide not only the theological ground but also the *dynamis* for a commitment to "democratization" as a human possibility, not to be confused with, or separated from, the politics of the kingdom.

(2) My second reflection comes back to the issue of "subjecthood." The classical Protestant tradition does not represent or assume the perspective of "the poor" as the historical subject of the transformation of the world. That tradition, historically speaking, addresses rather the emerging, expanding, and conquering bourgeoisie, "the citizens" (who initially in Geneva were only male and property owners), and by implication assumes that these classes are the historical subject for the building of the good society. Now, the history of the modern world and that of Latin America have shown that the Western bourgeoisie in its attempt to establish global hegemony has in fact created not only the affluent capitalist society but also the

47. Sinclair, 1991.
48. Miguez-Bonino, *Ethics*, p. 46.

world of the poor inside the capitalist society and the world of the poor on the periphery.[49]

Today, the new historical subjects are precisely these majorities, unknown to the classical Protestant tradition, which in Latin America are awakening to the reality of a new kind of power for the "democratization" of the world, residing in their conscience and in their conscious activity. As "a people of sorrows and acquainted with grief" these popular sectors seem to have assimilated two important lessons of history: first, the realization that democratization is not guaranteed either by electoral processes under bourgeois rule or by revolutionary forces holding political or military power, but by building a new kind of power from beneath through conscientization and popular self-organization; second, that democracy is a long-term ideal that demands sacrifice, sustainability, and perseverance. In my recent study trip to the area I found evidence that these lessons have been widely assimilated in most countries and that "the church of the poor" has contributed significantly to these developments.

49. Eric Wolf, *Europe and the People without History* (Berkeley: Univ. of California Press, 1982).

Christian Realism and Latin American Liberation Theology

Ronald H. Stone

Introduction

The purpose of this essay is to present an encounter between two approaches to Christian social philosophy. The North American approach studied is Christian realism, and its classical proponent is Reinhold Niebuhr. The Latin American approach studied is liberation theology, and its classical figure is Gustavo Gutierrez. Reinhold Niebuhr died in 1971 without having studied liberation theology. Gutierrez knows of Niebuhr and Christian realism through his teaching at Union Theological Seminary, conversations with me, and his own study, but he has not engaged Niebuhr's thought or Christian realism in a systematic way.

Christian realism exerted a great deal of influence in the World Council of Churches and the National Council of Churches and in some mainline denominations like the Presbyterian Church and the United Church of Christ. It is one among other approaches to Christian social thought that contributes to present church discussions of social policy. More and more frequently insights and paradigms from liberation theology are being heard in church social policy discussions. Sometimes the insights from Latin American liberation theology and Christian realism clash and sometimes they reinforce each other.

This paper is an attempt to contribute to the dialogue between two approaches. My perspective is that of a Christian realist appreciative of liberation theology who is committed to an ongoing discussion between the two. In 1990, a sabbatical afforded the opportunity of carrying on the dialogue with my colleague Gonzalo Castillo-Cardenas in Latin America as we talked with many liberation theologians, visited their projects, institutes, educational institutions, and homes, and then returned to teach courses on this topic.

Christian Realism

Christian realism evolved out of the social gospel movement, the political expression of Woodrow Wilson's "New Freedoms" social reform program, and Robert La Follette's progressive reforming populism. Confronted by social evils of war, economic exploitation in the emerging mass-production industrialism, and the stubborn persistence of racism, Christian realism attempted to express a social reform agenda for the United States that would combine the social hopes of Christian reformers and the realism of Christian orthodoxy's symbols about human historical nature. Reinhold Niebuhr's *Moral Man and Immoral Society* (1932) may be regarded as the first significant publication of this method of synthesizing the North American, ecumenical, liberal reform agenda with an analysis of the difficulties of reforming society. Robert M. Lovett used the term "Christian Realist" to describe Niebuhr in a book review in 1934. In 1941 John C. Bennett published a book entitled *Christian Realism* that outlined the emerging social thought. During the 1940s and 1950s Niebuhr, Bennett, and other Christian thinkers expanded their influence in church and society, encouraging domestic reform legislation that moved from their earlier socialism to the mixed-economy, welfare-oriented democratic policies advocated by liberal groups, including the Liberal party and Americans for Democratic Action (ADA).

Niebuhr, Bennett, and others who joined them in the Fellowship of Socialist Christians and in the social action programs of the churches emphasized persuasion as the major method of social reform. They were fundamentally teachers of the churches from seminary positions in various fields. They taught students, wrote books, published essays, and gave countless sermons and lectures in worship services, church meetings, and also in nonchurch settings, including universities, labor meetings, voluntary associations, rallies; occasionally they also addressed government bodies.

The major vehicles for social change that they supported were labor unions, democratic politics (preferring in turn socialism, liberalism, and the Democratic party), political voluntary associations like ADA and its predecessor Union for Democratic Action, civil rights organizations, church and social action agencies and local church projects, and journalism through editorial boards, founding of publications, and frequent contributions. Various social experiments like the Delta Cooperative Farm, the Fellowship of Socialist Christians, and many short-lived organizations were attempted to contribute to social reform. The vehicles of their practical theology were numerous. The single greatest influence was probably Niebuhr's writings. Significant political figures from Hubert Humphrey through Jimmy Carter acknowledged Niebuhr's helpfulness in relating faith to practical life.

Niebuhr's influence waned with poor health in the 1960s. Though he supported the critique of the Vietnam War, he was not able to lead it. His influence on people like William Sloane Coffin, Jr., and the organizational founders of Clergy and Laity Concerned about Vietnam was evident. A letter to me in jail caught his frustration at supporting the opposition to the war but being physically unable to participate deeply in it. The rise of a new left caught Niebuhr unprepared and generally unsympathetic, and his thought became less fashionable, particularly so at Union Theological Seminary and in *Christianity and Crisis,* centers of his former influence. In uneasiness about Christian realism, Christian social activists have in some cases been drawn toward liberation theology.

Beginnings of Dialogue

The emergence of liberation theology, first in the policies of the 1968 Bishop's Conference at Medellin and in the writings of Father Gustavo Gutierrez, pushed a new social theology into the ecumenical discussions. It was predictable that the power of liberation theology would produce encounters with Christian realism. Conservatives who had never accepted the social reform demands of Christian realism resisted the voices of liberation theology in North American churches. But by the mid-1970s, textbooks by liberation theologians were being read in North American seminaries and the Presbyterian Church's task force on peacemaking and international relations was listening to liberation theology. Gustavo Gutierrez and Richard Shaull brought the liberation perspective to North Americans celebrating their own revolution at the bicentennial in 1976. Their dialogue, *Liberation and Change,* was published in 1977.

Christianity and Crisis joined the dialogue in 1973 by publishing an article by Thomas G. Sanders identifying Latin American liberation theology with the soft utopianism that Niebuhr had attacked decades earlier.[1] Sanders, a journalist-scholar who has written extensively on Latin America, was a 1959 graduate of Union Theological Seminary who knew something of Niebuhr's thought. He respected some of the cautionary insights of expecting too much success in social reform, warnings about moralism, the potential dangers of utopian politics, and overly direct theologizing about politics without adequate reflection on political realities. But he missed the passion for social reform, the arguments for the acceptability of revolution as a strategy for social change, and the necessity of moral critique as part of the social struggle. John C. Bennett, who had become very sympathetic to liberation theology, found strengths in Gutierrez's writing that Sanders had neglected, and affirmed it as the theology best expressing the misery of the majority of humanity and their cries for justice.[2] Bennett could accept the wisdom of the realist tradition, but he refrained from turning it against liberation theology.

Thomas Quigley, from the Latin American Division of the United States Catholic Conference, found the liberationists' social models of conflict to be a long way from the soft utopian reformists Niebuhr had criticized.[3] Robert McAfee Brown found liberation theology important in helping him see the world realistically.[4] Some among the half-dozen authors who responded found Sanders's cautions about what was realizable in Latin America helpful, but they rejected as inappropriate his attempt to squash liberation theology in the name of Christian realism.

Rubem A. Alves, who was asked to provide a response to Sanders, admitted that he was unable to produce "a cool and, hopefully, scholarly reply."[5] Commenting on an unidentified author's paper furnished him by *Christianity and Crisis,* Alves seems to have assumed that the paper represented Christian realism. So he countered with an attack on Christian realism, identifying it with "the basic axioms

1. Thomas G. Sanders, "The Theology of Liberation = Christian Utopianism," *Christianity and Crisis* (Sept. 17, 1973): 167-73.

2. John C. Bennett, "Liberation Theology and Christian Realism," *Christianity and Crisis* (Oct. 15, 1973): 197-98.

3. Thomas Quigley, ibid., pp. 200-202.

4. Robert McAfee Brown, ibid., pp. 199-200.

5. Rubem A. Alves, "Christian Realism: Ideology of the Establishment," *Christianity and Crisis* (Sept. 17, 1973): 173-76.

of positivism," Mannheim's critique of pragmatism, and the ideology of the American establishment, a system that excludes morality. Moreover, he identified its proponents at Union Theological Seminary with John Foster Dulles. A reader of the debate would conclude that Princeton Seminary–educated Alves could have learned a little more about Christian realism from that faculty. Union Seminary graduate Sanders seems to have turned his education into a dangerous weapon to attack liberation theology. Sanders's superior, condescending tone must have contributed to Alves's unnuanced and outrageous caricature of the school he attacked.

Dennis McCann's study, published in 1981, returned the debate to scholarly channels.[6] But his study of the practical theologies of liberation theology and Christian realism suffers from two deficiencies. He did not then know Latin America or Spanish, and he did not know of Niebuhr's practical work. So his study remained at a rather abstract level.

McCann's major reservation about the liberation theology of Gutierrez and Segundo was that it would be forced into deeper politicalization to avoid trivialization, eclipsing the essential religious message and consequent reservation about politics. In his opinion Christian realism protected transcendence better than liberation theology. Liberation theology, he feared, led to reducing religious transcendence to "revolutionary enthusiasm."[7] I do not know Segundo personally, but this is a danger I would not ascribe to Father Gutierrez. He is a loyal parish priest serving his parishioner's spiritual needs, as Robert McAfee Brown described him in his biography.[8] If there ever were such a danger, the pressure of Vatican politics reversed it. Gutierrez is a loyal Catholic priest before he is a liberation theologian. His recent writings should persuade even the hardened critic that though he is politicized, his religious vision is intact.[9]

McCann's critique of Niebuhr is less severe than his rejection of liberation theology. His criticism is that the later Niebuhr was subject to ideological drift and that he failed "to develop a fully explicit model for

6. Dennis McCann, *Christian Realism and Liberation Theology: Practical Theologies in Creative Conflict* (Maryknoll, N.Y.: Orbis, 1981).

7. Ibid., pp. 236-37.

8. Robert McAfee Brown, *Gustavo Gutierrez* (Maryknoll, N.Y.: Orbis, 1990).

9. Gustavo Gutierrez, *We Drink from Our Wells: The Spiritual Journey of a People* (Maryknoll, N.Y.: Orbis, 1984); idem, *On Job: God-Talk and the Suffering of the Innocent* (Maryknoll, N.Y.: Orbis, 1987).

practical theology," weakening the necessary critical perspective.[10] The "ideological drift" must refer to Niebuhr's abandonment of Marxism and socialism before communist societies did. But this is not "drift." Niebuhr changed his mind and came to regard communism as bad politics, bad economics, and bad religion. His ongoing advocacy of mixed economic models and farther-reaching welfare policies than this nation has ever achieved is part of the published record. If McCann's criticism has meaning, it is that McCann the critic has more severely criticized North American failures than Niebuhr, at least during the period they were both students and writers in social ethics. I cannot find in McCann's published works any critical comments on Western society that are more severe than Niebuhr's: "The Negro Minority and Its Fate in a Self-Righteous Nation" or "The King's Chapel and the King's Court."[11]

McCann's book does highlight the powerful way in which Niebuhr uses symbol and myth. He is very appreciative of this use and calls it "a Mythical Method of Interpretation." A recent study has followed McCann in this approach to interpreting Niebuhr,[12] providing an important insight if it is not overdrawn. McCann is tempted to interpret Niebuhr as a systematic theologian rather than as a philosopher of religion and a social ethicist. The use of myth, which is important in understanding Niebuhr, is grounded in his early student work at Yale University in philosophy of religion. But McCann errs in attempting to derive Niebuhr's social ethic from what he says about myth in politics and religion.

Niebuhr's public ethic comes from the public ethic tradition of the history of Western philosophy. His understandings of justice and principles of social order depend on his analysis of the history of ideas. These resources of his thought are perhaps best appropriated from the tape recordings of his history of Christian ethics course or his writings on public ethics. Here one sees clearly the persuasive influence of Augustine and other thinkers.

Moving beyond McCann, one can see that an alliance between Christian realism and liberation theology is possible because neither one of them has quite the errors frequently ascribed to them. Before moving ahead to investigate that alliance, a review of the later Niebuhr's perspectives on Latin America is in order.

10. McCann, *Christian Realism*, p. 237.

11. Published respectively in *Social Action* (October 1968): 53-64; *Christianity and Crisis* (Aug. 4, 1969): 211-13.

12. Kenneth Durkin, *Reinhold Niebuhr* (Harrisburg: Morehouse, 1990).

Niebuhr on Latin America

Christian realism was originally Eurocentric in its view of the world. Niebuhr never visited or studied Latin America seriously, nor did any of the major figures associated with the origins of Christian realism. In a letter to his closest friend, Bishop William Scarlett, he confessed that he knew very little about Latin America. Except for a chapter in the book he coauthored with Paul E. Sigmund, *The Democratic Experience,*[13] he published no sustained reflection on Latin America. Students of Niebuhr's thought are uncertain as to how much of chapter 8, "Latin America: Democracy Imposed on Feudalism," is Niebuhr's and how much is Sigmund's. Niebuhr at least agreed with the content of the chapter, and he made many of the points of the chapter in his lectures at Barnard College in 1963. The book itself was based on a course taught jointly by the two authors at Harvard in 1962.

The chapter anticipates little success through widespread social revolution in Latin America. Niebuhrian preferences for democratic, efficient, progressive governments were clear, but the roads to achieving such governments were difficult. The authors saw the influence of the United States ambiguously. Some developments, like contributions toward programs of land reform or tax reform, were hopeful, but the authors recognized that U.S. economic presence was often regarded as exploitative. Economic growth was necessary to any social justice program they could envisage. Prospects for progress in democratization seemed better for Latin America than for most of the developing world, but the poverty in rural and urban areas threatened to rise up in attempted revolutions to throw off the misery. Preferences for Christian democratic parties rather than socialist parties is clear in the chapter, but the focus of the chapter is not on the cold war but on possible democratic and economic developments in Latin America. Third ways were sought between "restrictive exploitative and foreign dominated capitalism" and "inefficient socialism." In this chapter the authors found U.S. intervention generally a block against democratic development, but they detailed some cases where in their judgment the United States had aided liberal democracy in Latin America.[14]

Niebuhr's articles on Latin America in *Christianity and Crisis* and

13. Reinhold Niebuhr and Paul E. Sigmund, *The Democratic Experience: Past and Prospects* (New York: Praeger, 1969).

14. Ibid., p. 147.

The New Leader from the time of Kennedy's inauguration until Niebuhr's death in 1971 are less than ten short pieces. In them he castigates Kennedy for the U.S. Bay of Pigs intervention in Cuba, praises Kennedy and is grateful for the avoidance of war over the missiles, criticizes the U. S. presence in Panama in 1964 and urges renegotiation of the canal treaty, and condemns the 1965 military action in the Dominican Republic. Also in the 1960s, Niebuhr told me that he had advised President Kennedy to appoint James Loeb from ADA as ambassador to Peru. The 1969 publication noted the changes in the Latin American ecclesiastical scene, but since it was written even before Medellin it did not pick up the emerging theology of liberation. In any case, Niebuhr would not have regarded the church as the central player in the Latin American drama. Sympathetic Christians in North America need to avoid regarding published liberation theology as *the* reality of Latin America.

Dialogue in Latin America

An Argentine theologian of culture, Gerardo Viviers, suggests that the dialogue between Christian realism and the liberation theology of the mid-1980s is no longer relevant.[15] As a supporting argument he offers this statement: "Liberation theology is in a process of change." But more central to his refusal to interest himself in the conversation is his expressed conviction that both liberation theology and Christian realism were too captured by the rational categories of the Enlightenment. The future theologies of Latin America will be more open to myth, symbol, story, and the experiences of indigenous religious expressions. Much of Viviers's work in the Department of Communication of ISEDET (Instituto Superior Evangelico de Estudios Teologicos) is directed at protecting cultural resources from economic shock policies of the International Monetary Fund, and trying to develop alternative channels of public communication, particularly radio. He is also developing a major conference on culture and ecology for which the principal speakers are all liberation theologians. While welcoming a dialogue with North American theologians that will move away from classical theological paradigms into emerging forms of speech and consciousness, he finds the possibility difficult.

15. Interview with Dr. Gerardo Viviers at Instituto Superior Evangelico de Estudios Teologicos in Buenos Aires (June 29, 1990).

Viviers emphasized four factors affecting the relationship between North and South America. (1) The language differences are a substantial barrier. (2) The economic relationship is one of a dominant economy to dependent and exploited economies. (3) The political relationship is one of North American democracy encouraging Latin American dictators and rendering U.S. advocacy of democracy suspect. (4) Only in faith, Bible, and church is there common ground for relationship. But in many ways church practice adds one more division to a badly divided world, as liberation theologian Beatriz Melano Couch reminds us.[16]

The older liberation theologian Jose Miguez-Bonino, who could be regarded as the dean of this generation's Latin American Protestant political ethicists, saw more possibility in the dialogue.[17] He has discussed Christian realism in two of his recent books on political ethics. He encourages reading Niebuhr from the perspective of the younger, progressive Niebuhr and recommends reading Paul Tillich the same way. He thinks Niebuhr became less useful after his commitment to the cold war. As a Latin American he finds Niebuhr overemphasizing the Apollonian tendencies at the expense of the Dionysian realities of much of life. Miguez's printed critique of Christian realism objects to its pragmatic acceptance of the status quo and its critique of utopianism. Interestingly, however, he does not explicitly critique either Niebuhr or John C. Bennett, whom he mentions as the pioneers of Christian realism. Instead he criticizes Herbert W. Richardson's acquiescence to the "sociotechnical intellectus" and journalist Thomas G. Sanders's attack on liberation theology as utopianism[18] (neither of whom would I identify with Christian realism). This leaves open for debate the question that perplexes Miguez: "Who are the Christian realists?"[19]

Reporting on an informal gathering of liberation theologians in 1990, Miguez outlined what he considered the major emphases of contemporary liberation theology. First, he thought liberation theology would soon deepen its pastoral work among the poor and strengthen

16. Unpublished manuscript entitled "God's Word and World." Referred to in Robert McAfee Brown, *Gustavo Gutierrez* (Maryknoll, N.Y.: Orbis, 1990), p. 200, as *Towards a New Humanity.*

17. Interview with Jose Miguez-Bonino at ISEDET (June 29, 1990).

18. Jose Miguez-Bonino, *Toward a Christian Political Ethics* (Philadelphia: Fortress, 1983), pp. 87-90.

19. Interview with Jose Miguez-Bonino.

its sense of solidarity with the poor. This original commitment of liberation theology remains unchanged, but the pastoral connections could be strengthened and emphasized more in the writing of liberation theologians. Second, he expected the work of anthropology and research into popular culture to be deepened. The work of exploring the inculturation of the Christian faith would be expanded. Third, he expected to see more work on the relationship of the democratization process to liberation. Fourth, the emphasis on how to strengthen the frail economies of Latin America would continue. The parallel or informal economy has always been part of the Latin American process. But he expected further investigations into how to strengthen it and how to make life more bearable in the marginalized economy. Finally, in response to a question, he indicated a fifth continuing emphasis on doing theology from the perspective of suffering. Gutierrez's *Job* is an example, but as the economic suffering increases more expressions of theology from the context of suffering may be expected.

Obviously, a Christian realism seeking an alliance with liberation theology can more easily engage in dialogue and discussion on the question of democratization than it can on the subject of world-economic structural impact on frail economies. Christian realists, in imagination and by action, can stand in solidarity with the suffering and the poor. As a liberation academic in Chile said, "There is for us Chilian Methodists no question of an option for the poor; we are simply poor, almost all of our churches are poor." For Christian realists, most of their churches, people, acquaintances, supporters, and coactivists are North American middle class, and their social ethics will reflect critically that ethos. But the gaps of language, economic policies, and power politics described by Viviers will remain.

On the question of the relation among realism, liberation, and utopia a little relaxation of the debate is in order. Miguez resents writers who condemn liberation theologians as utopian; both he and Gutierrez are rather careful in their use of the term. They are able to treat it as a hopeful social projection distinguishable both from the kingdom of God and from the realizable programs of existing political parties.[20] Niebuhr may have overdone his critique of utopianism in the social gospel and in communism, but certainly both programs had in them grand illusions. Niebuhr also critiqued the pretensions of laissez-faire capitalism and the utopian fantasies of contemporary

20. See Miguez's discussion of utopianism in *Christian Political Ethic,* pp. 87-94.

American presidents. While Miguez's warning against leading Christians into dubious historical commitments may be less strident than Niebuhr's, he too wants to avoid sacralizing or clericalizing historical projects.[21]

From private conversations with Miguez, Gutierrez, and Niebuhr I can detect no reason to regard any one of them as less concerned than the others for what can actually be accomplished in a given historical moment. Catalina Romero, who administers Instituto Bartolome de Las Casas in Lima, said: "Our reality is so dark that we must look to our hopes."[22] Certainly ministry or social action in the barrios of Rimac or the much more desperate lower-class barrio of Grande Canto in Lima requires hope grounded in resources beyond the observable phenomena. But criticism of the United States' optimistic illusions may have a role in reducing the pretensions of U.S. policy vis-à-vis the world. The critical work of raising utopian hopes for a better place may be part of the work of the kingdom in the poor barrios of Lima, and at the same time the explanation that utopia also means "no place" needs to be heard to keep fanatic Americans from trying to impose their ideals on foreign cultures.

A visit to the Centro Ecumenico de Accion Social in Buenos Aires produces reflections on how community, solidarity, and hope are nurtured among pregnant teenage servant girls from the countryside. The center can provide community and teach solidarity and hope as it helps the young single mothers to build relationships, learn skills, and organize. A little utopian thought there about building a new world and a new form of life while they anticipate the birth of their child is in order. The words of Paul are offered as the conclusion to the orientation pamphlet shared with the young women: "Donde hay un cristiano, hay humanidad nueva; lo viejo ha pasado; miren existe algo nuevo."[23] The new life seen in the cribs evokes hope, but the economic recession presses in upon those young lives even as they sleep. The North Americans and *los portenos* discuss in the next room the reduced funding of the center and their church's responsibility in the face of increasing need.

Liberation theology had caught my attention in the early 1970s

21. Ibid., p. 94.

22. Interview with Catalina Romero, May 8, 1990, in Lima.

23. *La Felicitamos y le Damos la Bienvenida* (Buenos Aires: Centro Ecumenico de Accion Social, 1990), p. 6.

because of its engagement with revolutionary struggle. My first essay on liberation theology discussed it as a form of revolutionary theology that was seen as having honorable precedents in Gregory VII, Luther, Calvin, Knox, Witherspoon, etc.[24] Gustavo Gutierrez was invited to Pittsburgh Theological Seminary in 1976 to celebrate the bicentenary of the North American revolution and to discuss the promise and ambiguities of theology and revolution with Richard Shaull.

Liberation theology was always more than a theology of revolution. It was always a form of practical theology for society. Revolution might or might not be a possibility in a given society to consider theologically. Now the emphasis on social revolution has been minimized by world events and local changes. A parallel shift, in some aspects, is evident in the distance between Niebuhr's *Moral Man and Immoral Society* (1932) and *Christian Realism and Political Problems* (1953).

Liberation theology was always as broad as critical reflection on the social praxis of the church with and for the liberation of the poor. In this meaning it is encountered throughout Latin America as one of the motivations and reflections on church social action. It is part of the theory of Christian social action of Latin America. In this broader sense it starts to lose specificity, as both the Vatican and Protestants begin to accept it and recognize it as a contribution to Christian theology.

Some of the vocabulary, concepts, and spirit of liberation theology surface for me in efforts of Mexico City Christians to utilize the resources of their base community to shelter refugees fleeing the Central American wars. It appears again in the research center of Gustavo Gutierrez in Rimac, Lima, Peru. Finally, out of the city center it characterizes the work of the pastoral team laboring in the barrio of Canto Grande. The work of the IPA (Andean Pastoral Institute) in the South Andes reflects the spirit of the theology of liberation while suffering from the attacks of the conservative bishops. Both the Protestant Centers of Seminario Biblico in Costa Rica and ISEDET in Buenos Aires are working out the implications of liberation theology for theological education and pastoral work. Still, students complain that most of the pedagogy is standard. At ISEDET Beatriz Couch launches stinging attacks against cruel male chauvinism and the shortsighted disruption of community by the decision to have students live off campus.

24. Ronald H. Stone, *Realism and Hope* (Lanham, Md.: Univ. Press of America, 1977).

It is easy to observe that much of the daily work of social action projects visited in Cuzco, Peru, Buenos Aires, Rio de Janiero, and Lima is carried out by women. Most of the theological posts are filled by men. Elsa Tamez's books have provided gentle prodding to liberation theologians, and some male writers have taken the liberation of women seriously. But it is still possible to encounter relatively unreformed "macho theologians" in the institutions and individuals influenced by liberation theology.

Whether in projects related to evangelization, inculturation of the church, drinking water, flood control, manual education, sheltering of refugees, or the election of a moderate in Peru, it is not possible to think of this work of liberation theology as contributing to a violent revolution or as being dependent upon Marxist analysis. The charges that are still directed against liberation theology do not fit the daily work of base communities as I experienced it, nor do they fit the theologians' recent analysis and publications. To attack the current work of Instituto Bartolome de Las Casas or Gustavo Gutierrez as Marxist is as wide of the mark as J. Edgar Hoover's pursuit of accusations that Reinhold Niebuhr was a communist.

Recent Christian Realist Response

In an earlier book on *Christian Realism and Peacemaking* (1988), I identified Christian realism with the political thought of Reinhold Niebuhr and George Kennan, and I regarded Hans J. Morgenthau as closely related in philosophy to the school. I assumed the position as my own, and I think of John C. Bennett and Roger L. Shinn as two who have developed the tradition within Christian ethics. Many in the younger generation of Christian ethicists owe a considerable debt to Niebuhr. In discussions within North American church social action circles and papers and conversations in the Society of Christian Ethics, his work still exerts a great influence. A recent work *Realism and Hope in a Nuclear Age* by Kermit D. Johnson who, succeeding George Chauncey, led the Presbyterian Church's Washington office in its critique of U.S. policy in Central America, is typical of the ongoing Christian realist tradition.[25] The borders of the tradition are quite

25. Kermit D. Johnson, *Realism and Hope in a Nuclear Age* (Atlanta: John Knox, 1988). After discovering my book with a similar title, General Johnson phoned and

fluid; my expansive descriptions of the perspective would include the later Martin Luther King, Jr., and Paul Tillich's faithful realism. In this essay, however, I am using Christian realism as descriptive of socially engaged, reformist Christians who are economically left of the center of the Democratic party. The U.S. president who most identified himself with Niebuhr's thought was Jimmy Carter, but generally speaking most of the scholars of this group would be more comfortable to the left of Carter.

Two studies appeared in 1990 that are related to Niebuhr and liberation theology. Paul E. Sigmund, who coauthored a book with Niebuhr on democracy and its prospects, published *Liberation Theology at the Crossroads,* which contains a section on "The Niebuhrian Critique."[26] Robert McAfee Brown, a student, friend, and colleague of Niebuhr, who recently edited a book of his essays, published *Gustavo Gutierrez: An Introduction to Liberation Theology,* which covers some of the same critics as Sigmund in a section "Lesser Critiques."[27] Brown notes how Gutierrez has changed his emphases, but brushes the critics McCann and Novak aside. Brown has moved into the liberation theology paradigms himself and is inviting other North American Christians to join him there. The move involves recognizing one's complicity in oppression, becoming a traitor to one's class, and broadening one's base. While Brown's book retains its academic integrity, it enters the polemics and defends the side of the liberation theologians, particularly Gutierrez.[28]

Sigmund writes about liberation theology without identifying with it. He sees liberation theology having made several gains and exhibiting some failures. The Latin American church has become more committed "to the defense of the poor," the biblical criticism of wealth has been reasserted, the Bible is read locally, and thousands of poor have won a sense of dignity. Particularly in Brazil, it has encouraged democracy and in many places it has promoted "grass-roots community action" and pressed for policies to "support the

---

apologized. We both laughed at the fact that I had a forthcoming book with a similar title.

26. See Niebuhr and Sigmund, *Democratic Experience;* Sigmund, *Liberation Theology at the Crossroads* (New York: Oxford Univ. Press, 1990), pp. 139-42.

27. See Brown, ed., *The Essential Reinhold Niebuhr* (New Haven: Yale Univ. Press, 1986); "Lesser Critiques," in Brown, *Gustavo Gutierrez* (Maryknoll, N.Y.: Orbis, 1990), pp. 132-36.

28. Ibid., pp. 178-82.

struggle of the poor." He finds on the negative side "a mindless revolutionism." He thinks liberation theology is "ignorant of contemporary liberal thought" and too negative on the market system and possibilities of reforming capitalism. He does not see it transforming base communities into active political forces except in Brazil and possibly Central America.[29]

As a social scientist committed to Christianity and to "modern reformist liberalism," he would like to see dialogue with liberation theologians concerned with social science on six issues.

1. Must capitalism be replaced by socialism? If so, what kind?
2. What is the relation of private property and liberation?
3. How are human rights to be understood?
4. How will liberation theology relate to democratization?
5. How is the role of prophetic religion to be exercised? How specific should it become?
6. Should revolution be abandoned for investigation of the weaknesses and cures for democracy?[30]

He concludes his careful study: "liberation theology will have to choose which it is to represent — democracy or revolution."[31] It appears to me that liberation theology in 1990 continued to affirm solidarity with the poor and pastoral work among them. The question of revolution or democracy is now a secondary question. Encouragement and work will be given to the democratization process, not to revolution. But listening to the cries of the poor for life has the priority. Northern liberals have still to hear these cries.

Proposals for the Church

Through seven months of travel in Latin America and dialogue with my friend and colleague Gonzalo Castillo-Cardenas, a few things have become clearer. Much of the difference between Christian liberation and realist theologians is social location. Dr. Castillo and I attended the same seminary, the same university, and teach in the same insti-

29. Sigmund, *Liberation Theology*, p. 195.
30. Ibid., p. 198.
31. Ibid.

tution. We agree on many things and normally operate in alliance on social issues, but our perspectives are different and we disagree vehemently on some issues. His perspectives are also in debt to his origins in Colombia and the impact of North American power there, and my perspectives are indebted to my origins in the center of the North American empire. His work in Latin American churches and church social projects affects him, and my work in North American churches and church social agencies affects me — and divides us. It is too simple to say with Viviers, as suggested at the beginning of this essay, that the church unites us. This difference became clearer to me in Lima, Peru, late at night in conversation with my friend. No synthesis of Christian realism and liberation theology is possible. But dialogue and alliances are possible and desirable.

To promote dialogue and alliance between theologians of liberation and realist church leaders and theologians in North America, I suggest the following:

(1) Church agencies should sponsor a major theological consultation between liberation theologians and Reformed theologians of several denominations (Bonhoeffer, Barth, Lehmann, and even Brunner seem better known in Latin America than Reinhold Niebuhr). The consultation should be held in a Spanish-speaking culture, perhaps at a seminary in Latin America.

(2) Church policy against armed intervention and "low-intensity conflict" in any Latin American country needs to be developed, along with evaluation of recent U.S. interventions. The policy posture needs to be developed with churchwide discussion of the issue.

(3) As it begins to study the justice of world economic structures, the church needs to listen to and dialogue with Latin American theologians and political economists. This dialogue may have more significance if it is focused on Latin–North American economic relationships (trade, aid, debt, multinationals, financial structures, poverty, and dependency theory evaluation).

(4) The church ecumenical needs to clarify its thinking about the worldwide democratization process and its relationship to Christian faith. Studies of the process, policy, and educational materials should involve both North American theologians and Latin American theologians who are close to the poor.

The American Churches and U.S. Interventionism

James Hudnut-Beumler

William Appleman Williams published his classic text *The Tragedy of American Diplomacy* in 1959. In this book he made the by-now familiar charge that Americans believed their nation, unlike any other, acted altruistically in foreign affairs, on the basis of the needs of others rather than to promote self-interest. They further believed that their programs of assistance were gifts of charity, and that their use of armed force and economic coercion were part of a selfless plan to bring American democracy to the less fortunate people of the world. That other nations acted on the basis of self-interest, but not the United States, was the pervasive myth.

In fact, Williams charged, the United States usually acted on the basis of self-interest, though the overwhelming belief in the purity of American motives in foreign affairs served to cloak self-interests in the mantle of charity, imbuing it with a religious sense of mission — witness America's many "crusades" and the recurrent theme of manifest destiny. Simultaneously, this inflated sense of national virtue made the acts committed in the name of spreading democracy and the American way of life much worse than the acts of self-consciously self-seeking countries, rendering unintelligible the rebuffs of foreign governments and people of other nations.

Religious Ideals and the Tragedy of American Diplomacy

This essay is about religion, the churches, and the tragedy — as Williams styled it — of American foreign diplomacy. This topic is, I believe, especially well suited to the goal of this volume, which is to see what historians and ethicists have to say to one another about the phenomenon of the public church in the twentieth century. If we are looking at the public church and asking what has happened and what should happen in the future — the questions of retrospect and prospect — we need to go beneath the surface perceptions of past analysts and examine the roots of Williams's tragedy. In doing so we will be concerned with two principal lines of inquiry: (1) why the American people think about foreign affairs as they do; and (2) what the churches have done to influence this area of the nation's life.

I have tipped my hand already by my choice of title and indicated that I believe that the religious communities of the United States do share a large burden for the interventionist nature of much of twentieth-century American activity in international relations. Thus I reject from the very start any depiction of the churches as the one force holding the government back from even more Grenadas and Vietnams. The story is much more complex than that. I also must insist, however, that any version of the history of American foreign policy that lays all of the blame at the doorstep of religious bodies and people for their promotion of moral objectives in international relations is too facile, and even dangerous. Thus, after examining how the people and their churches have thought and acted in this century on issues of public affairs, I will venture an opinion based on the historical record about what the public testimony of the churches on international affairs has looked like in its best moments. (A caveat is in order. Examining the actions — past and present — of the churches in relation to major issues of foreign policy may lead to false conclusions if done without sensitivity to how religion actually functions in the lives of its adherents and in cultural context.)

One of the classic texts on the domestic context of American foreign policy devotes a scant four pages to religious groups and notes that "Religious organizations, like women's groups, are often liberal and internationalist, with a touch of religious pacifism. This is, of course, a source of weakness, since it often misrepresents church members."[1] This observation is true, but insufficiently deep. For religious persons are affected not only by the positions that their church bodies take on specific foreign policy issues, but also by the other things their churches teach them regarding the requirements of the

1. Barry Hughes, *The Domestic Context of American Foreign Policy* (San Francisco: W. H. Freeman, 1978), pp. 45-47, 178-80.

faith, not to mention the other messages they receive and accept in other parts of the culture.

Therefore, it might well be the case that a given church takes a stand against American involvement in a particular conflict and a majority of its members favor involvement on *religious* grounds. When pressed as to their reasons for supporting the cold war, many individuals explained their positions in terms of opposing "godless communism," or standing firm against an ideology that denied the value and dignity of the individual over against the collective. Human dignity and worth and the recognition of the sovereignty of God are indeed taught in the churches of this country, and it is the multitude of levels at which religious belief and practice can be at work within a culture that makes "the religious factor" so difficult for social scientists to assess.

The value of William Appleman Williams's analysis that distinguishes it to this day from those others who have sought to study the roots of interventionism is that he was able to see the *ideological* dimension of American foreign policy. He traced the essential problematic of American relations with the rest of the world to three key ideas:

> In the realm of ideas and ideals, American policy is guided by three conceptions. One is the warm, generous, humanitarian impulse to help other people solve their problems. A second is the principle of self-determination applied at the international level, which asserts the right of every society to establish its own goals or objectives, and to realize them internally through the means it decides are appropriate. These two ideas can be reconciled; indeed, they complement each other to an extensive degree. But the third idea entertained by many Americans is one which insists that other people cannot really solve their problems and improve their lives unless they go about it in the same way as the United States.[2]

Since we are interested in examining the source of American intentions in foreign affairs, the importance of exploring these notions further is obvious. But less apparent are the religious underpinnings of the three key ideas. I submit that Williams's three guiding conceptions are the secular manifestations of religious ideals present in the

2. William Appleman Williams, *The Tragedy of American Diplomacy* (New York: Dell, 1959, 1962), p. 9.

American character from the beginnings of the Puritan experience. The humanitarian impulse is easy to understand as emanating from religious sources. For example, the principle of love motivates the actions of the good Samaritan. Self-determination is the secular analog of several Protestant principles: that no one can or should stand between a human being and his or her creator; that churches in an imperfect world should be gathered, not imposed; and the great principle of the Second Great Awakening, that people could effect their own salvation.

The final idea in Williams's trinity is American exceptionalism. Ever since John Winthrop had said to the Massachusetts Bay colonists, "Wee shall be like a City upon a Hill," Americans have imbued their politics with a note of religious-based exceptionalism.[3] They have been convinced that they were God's new Israel, a new chosen people, and God's last great hope of the earth, and have talked about themselves as the new Jerusalem and pictured this nation as bearing the "apocalyptic candle" westward. This third idea was the most problematic so far as Williams was concerned. For when it encountered the other two it inevitably fostered failed international relations characterized by American smugness at best, and at worst by an utter denial of the American impulses for humanitarianism and self-determination.

For the historian of American religion, the myth of a special American purpose is doubly problematic, for it has proved to be a two-edged sword and responsible not only for many of the bad, but also many of the good, things about American life. Exceptionalism sometimes functions in positive ways, by challenging Americans not to settle for the mixed moral results of their own culture but to seek reform and improvement. John Winthrop used the idea of the special errand in the wilderness to inspire an idealistic performance in the new land. More than three centuries later the speech of Martin Luther King, Jr., "I Have a Dream," played on similar themes, using the myth of America's higher moral calling to summon its people to honor with action the promise of their rhetoric. But when American exceptionalism was applied abroad, it could not help being comparative and definitionally insulting to other nations and people.

Accepting Williams's characterization of the American mind-set,

3. John Winthrop, "A Model of Christian Charity," *Winthrop Papers*, vol. 2 (Boston: Massachusetts Historical Society, 1931), pp. 292-95.

we can begin to understand why the American people in the twentieth century have shown a great proclivity for getting into trouble abroad. By comprehending the ideological, and particularly the religious, sources of the underlying thinking we can understand how deeply seated the tendency toward intervention is. We thus derive a partial answer to our first line of inquiry — why American people think about international affairs as they do — and develop an appreciation of the importance of the basic teachings of the churches in forming the moral thought of the people and in turn their nation's behavior beyond their borders. As for the second line of inquiry, we now turn to ask what the churches have done to promote, retard, prevent, or correct the spirit of interventionism that has reigned in American foreign policy during this century.

The Public Church and International Interventionism

To talk about the history of the public church in relation to international intervention is to raise two questions: What is meant by "the public church," and why limit discussion to international intervention. Here "public church" denotes organized religion operating at a supracongregational level, within either an ecumenical or a specific ecclesiastical tradition, and concerned with issues of public, social, and political importance. The public church thus defined includes nondenominational religious social movements like the Fellowship of Reconciliation, the National Conference of Catholic Bishops, as well as the General Synod of the United Church of Christ and other denominational bodies. Analysis of the public church so defined also need not be limited to the explicit statements made by its entities. This latter qualifier is important, for the historian's first observation about the public church and international intervention endorses the old maxim, "Actions speak louder than words."

The American churches' words and deeds involving international interventionism are the focus of this discussion because international intervention is the international-relations issue before which all others pale. Persons can believe a great number of things and affect no other persons. Attitudes toward intervention in the affairs of other nations, however, have a way of bearing fruit in foreign policies that affect the lives of other people. The attitudes and actions of the public church in the twentieth century lead to three historical observations.

Historical Observation One: The American churches have a record of almost a century of public statements making the moral case against intervening in the affairs of other nations. Despite this record, the churches have acted in their own material interests from time to time in foreign affairs, and throughout the century they have supported in deed what they have opposed in words and in principle.

The current century opened with the first great episode of U.S. foreign intervention in progress. Prior to 1898 and the beginning of the Spanish-American War, our national history had been remarkably free of direct military involvement with other nations.[4] The United States was a great sea power and trading nation, but had no colonies of its own. Now the prospect of the United States fighting another nation, either to "free" Cubans from the Spanish or to gain colonies of its own, was disturbing to representatives of the public church. The Roman Catholic Archbishop of Peoria, John Lancaster Spalding, wrote in 1899:

> We have never looked upon ourselves as predestined to subdue the earth, to compel other nations, with sword and shell, to accept our rule; we have always believed in human rights, in freedom and opportunity, in education and religion, and we have invited all men to come to enjoy these blessings in this half a world which God has given us; but we have never dreamed that they were articles to be exported and thrust down unwilling throats at the point of the bayonet.[5]

Presbyterian Henry Van Dyke asked pointedly, "Have we set the Cubans free or have we lost our faith in freedom?"[6]

Not all representatives of the public church agreed with Spalding and Van Dyke about the immorality of the Spanish-American War. The influential editor of the *Christian Union* and the *Outlook*, Lyman

4. The War of 1812, the Mexican War of the 1840s, and the internal wars of conquest against American Indians, though involving American armies, did not involve the pursuit of American foreign policy objectives through coercion outside the continental land mass and are therefore different in kind from those interventions that followed 1898. Intervention in Nicaraguan affairs in the nineteenth century was the small exception that would become the rule after the Spanish-American War.

5. John Lancaster Spalding, *Opportunity and Other Essays and Addresses* (Freeport, N.Y.: Books for Libraries, 1900, 1968), p. 215.

6. Edwin Scott Gaustad, *A Documentary History of Religion in America Since 1865* (Grand Rapids: Eerdmans, 1983), p. 100.

Abbot, addressed an audience of mainline evangelicals at a session of the Lake Mohonk Conference with these words:

> I believe the proudest chapter in our history is that written by the statesmanship of McKinley, the guns of Dewey, and the administration of Taft. There is nothing to repent, nothing to retract; our duty is to go on and complete the work already so well begun. I do not defend or apologize for what we have done in the Philippines. I glory in it.[7]

The Spanish-American War deeply divided the religious community in the United States. For some, like Abbot, it was a war fought "to free a people to whom we owed no other duty than that of a big nation to an oppressed neighbor."[8] To others, like Spalding and Van Dyke, it was the very pinnacle of oppression. None of these men, nor the rest of the religious community at the time, would have quarreled with the proposition that the United States should not impose itself on other unwilling peoples. Nor would the religious community have argued against the claim that American foreign policy ought to be conducted on the basis of humanitarian interests in which self-interest played no part. The public church at the turn of the century, then, could be said to have been of one mind that self-interest was to play no role in international affairs. In reality, however, the public church was up to its neck in self-interested international intervention.

By 1900, the public church had long established a tradition of violating its general principle against unsolicited interventionism. Before there were American imperialists, there were American missionaries. The one experience of foreign affairs most American had prior to the Spanish-American War was secondhand reports of the experience of distant lands and peoples conveyed to them by their churches' missionaries. Paul Varg was one of the first historians to probe the connection between missions and international intervention. In the 1950s he queried why the American people should have accepted "the christianization of far-off lands as one of the most laudable of all human enterprises."[9] Why should Christians have been so willing to intervene in another culture, to insist upon the need to forcibly change other persons' religion, customs, and behaviors if

7. Lyman Abbott, *Reminiscences* (Boston: Houghton Mifflin, 1915), pp. 436-38.

8. Ibid.

9. Paul A. Varg, "Motives in Protestant Missions, 1890–1917," *Church History* 23 (1954): 68-82.

those in the other culture were unwilling to do so simply upon being shown the option?

William Hutchison believes that the answer to these questions lies in the expressed intent of the turn-of-the-century liberals and revivalists to conquer the world not only for Christ but also for "Christian Civilization."[10] Thus intervention was labeled as something quite different. The actual experience of China, the Philippines, and Puerto Rico demonstrates that missionaries ended up functioning as an advance guard for American imperialism. But the public church thought its actions were consistent with its opposition to colonialism, interventionism, and the use of armed force to open and to protect markets.

Another historian, Kenneth M. MacKenzie, has tracked the relationship of what he calls "the robe and the sword" from the perspective of the Methodist Church. He concludes that Methodists believed their own self-contradictory doublethink. With the highest of ideals, they opposed European-style imperialism but supported American expansionism. Why was American intervention different? Because it was benevolent and exercised only for the "brotherhood" of all nations. Ironically, MacKenzie claims, the expansionist missionaries who called in the troops to protect their schools and hospitals may have actually softened the use of force because of their long association with and understanding of foreign people and their cultures. MacKenzie credits the Methodist Church with helping "to make American imperialism benevolent in fact as in word."[11]

Whether one agrees with MacKenzie's assessment depends on one's acceptance of his belief that American external aggression was inevitable. If one believes that the "inevitable" was brought on in part by a "missionary" view of the world, then MacKenzie's thesis becomes less tenable.

However one decides the issue of missionary benevolence, the fact remains that the very churches that decried the use of force in world affairs as meddling were simultaneously engaged in meddling of their own, and on a grand scale. In the case of Puerto Rico, this use of intervention for religious purposes was extremely pronounced. Emilio Pantojas Garcia makes a persuasive case that the reason this

10. William R. Hutchison, "A Moral Equivalent For Imperialism; Americans and the Promotion of 'Christian Civilization,' 1880–1910," *Indian Journal of American Studies* 13 (1983): 55-68.

11. Kenneth M. MacKenzie, *The Robe and the Sword: The Methodist Church and the Rise of American Imperialism* (Washington, D.C.: Public Affairs Press, 1961), p. 116.

accidental colony was held on to so long and subjected to an extreme campaign of forced Americanization was the direct result of missionary intentions to de-Hispanicize and de-Catholicize the island's inhabitants.[12] Reeducation camps are one of the marks of the unsuccessful regime that must resort to force. Puerto Rico was in effect turned into such a camp for the purposes of imposing the unwanted standard of Protestant Christian civilization.

My historical observation would have little ethical punch if it were only that — an historical observation about church intervention in foreign affairs now safely in the distant past. Yet the public church, as we have styled it, continues to this day to be an international interventionist. Conservative right-wing Protestant churches have taken over the role played by mainline churches at the turn of the century in supporting armed intervention and surrogate wars to combat communist insurgencies and topple left-wing governments. Additionally, as a study by Bruce Nichols makes abundantly clear, religious bodies of the right and left still work hand in glove with the state in the promotion of American foreign policy abroad.

Though the nature of missionary activity changed after World War I, with an increasing emphasis being placed by the churches upon humanitarian aid of various forms, the sheer scale of American religious action abroad remained intense. Herbert Hoover, the American Friends Service Committee, and the American Red Cross as they cleaned up after the carnage of World War I established a model for relief activity that most other agencies began to follow. During the period of 1939 to 1945 nearly six hundred private voluntary organizations (PVOs), most of them religious, operated overseas. After World War II these groups were sought out to help implement the Marshall Plan and address the problem of displaced persons. The public church, acting abroad, thus became bit by bit an extension of the U.S. government's Department of State and the Agency for International Development (U.S.A.I.D.). By the early 1980s the level of grants made by U.S.A.I.D. through PVOs with religious origins and purposes had reached $600 million annually. This kind of funding in many cases exceeds mission giving from strictly religious sources. Even more importantly, it comes with strings attached.[13]

12. Emilio Pantojas Garcia, "La Iglesia Protestante y La Americanizacion de Puerto Rico: 1898–1917," *Revista de Ciencias Sociales* 18 (1974): 97-122.

13. J. Bruce Nichols, *The Uneasy Alliance* (New York: Oxford Univ. Press, 1988), p. 8.

Since 1945, the federal government and the religious relief societies have worked closely to promote the humanitarian objectives of U.S. foreign policy. Not all these actions of intervention were the benign supply of provision of surplus rice to starving children. The religious relief agencies of the early postwar period were instrumental in encouraging those in the "captive nations" of Eastern Europe to become refugees.[14] In China, in the late 1940s, Christian missionaries sided with Chiang Kai-shek and helped the Truman administration persist in its refusal to accept the loss of the mainland. Later, after the Vietnam War, Laotian refugees in Thailand received food ration cards only after they accepted baptism from the American Catholic missionary order administering the relief for the U.S. government. In numerous cases, right down to the war in Afghanistan, the public church has implicated itself in the exercise of U.S. interventionist foreign policy abroad. Today the army of American citizens working abroad for Protestant and Catholic agencies numbers more than 50,000. About 85,000 U.S. citizens work in Israel. Meanwhile, the State Department and U.S.A.I.D. employ only fifteen thousand, one-third of whom are in the United States at any given moment.[15] Given these facts, the urge to accomplish foreign policy goals through the use of religious workers is as irresistible to the government as the lure of government money is to the religious groups.

Historical Observation Two: As much as the public church, when gathered in national convocations and discussing interventionism, resembles liberal pacifists, the church often asks the government to engage in various forms of international intervention that are irreconcilable with strict religious pacifism.

Here a litany of past American church actions will illustrate the point without further analysis.

> In the 1910s, the American churches lined up behind President Woodrow Wilson, a former ethics professor, who argued that the United States must fight in Europe to make the world safe for democracy. Disgusted with the war as it turned out, many churchmen and churchwomen swore allegiance to pacifism as the Christian way of life.

14. Ibid., p. 10.
15. Ibid., p. 21.

In the 1930s, as Japan took over Manchuria, Richard Niebuhr wrote in the *Christian Century* that this action was evil, but sometimes one must have the Christian patience to do nothing. His brother Reinhold disagreed in writing a few weeks later in the same magazine. Most of those writing letters to this flagship journal of the public church agreed with Reinhold that evil should be actively opposed, though they stopped short of endorsing war.

In the 1940s, Hitler and the Nazi project called forth a military response from the American people and their churches. Though church attitudes toward the war were much more subdued than those expressed during the previous war, the United States emerged from World War II with pride in the role it had played as global policeman.

In the 1950s, the American churches decried totalitarianism in Eastern Europe, the Soviet Union, and China, and almost universally supported the use of armed force by a U.S.-dominated United Nations peacekeeping force to contain the spread of communism in Korea.

In the 1960s, most denominations finally came out against the war in Vietnam at the end of the decade; but earlier they had endorsed it and Lyndon Johnson's 1965 invasion of the Dominican Republic as democracy-promoting actions. Church support for Israel during the 1967 Six Day War was also remarkably high. American churches also often endorsed international development efforts and organizations enthusiastically, with no awareness of the ways development fostered dependence and despotism in the Third World.

In the 1970s, the public church provided some of the most visible leadership of the movement to end armed intervention in Southeast Asia. But the churches also endorsed a different kind of international intervention when they actively supported President Jimmy Carter's human rights agenda, which called for U.S. foreign aid and trading-status decisions to be linked to the human rights practices of other nations.

In the 1980s, American church leaders called for the use of economic sanctions to isolate and cripple the economy of South Africa until such time as it eliminated its policy of racial apartheid. American churches — Protestant and Catholic — also provided the primary leadership in the sanctuary movement, whose objective was to defeat the inhumane policy of their own government toward Central American refugees seeking political asylum by challenging the harsh behavior of the Immigration and Naturalization Service and by transporting or giving hospitality to undocumented refugees.

In short, the American churches have, throughout the century, often endorsed U.S. governmental coercion — in its greater and lesser forms — to achieve greater goods or to stop evil abroad. They have also been willing to use direct methods of resistance to counter the effects of a military campaign of low-intensity conflict they opposed. After viewing the church's twentieth-century behaviors, one would clearly have difficulty demonstrating that international intervention per se has been opposed by the public church, even if the church's rhetorical record would seem to indicate otherwise.

Historical Observation Three: The American churches in the twentieth century have displayed a tendency to waver between utopian views of American foreign policy and what has been called "realism." In ironic ways both of these have fed the basic tragedy.

From what has been said already it should be obvious that claims to the effect that the church does not support intervention in the affairs of other nations are false if not further qualified. How and to what extent these claims are and can be qualified is the subject to which we now turn.

As we have seen, the public church in the twentieth century has often engaged in interventionist activities of its own. It has also asked the government to do many things in the name of morality that must fall under the rubric of intervention. Therefore to clarify under what conditions and to what extent the church is willing to see the United States intervene in direct and indirect ways is critically important. It is one thing to say that you will allow intervention to the extent of providing food aid and contraceptive devices to other nations without further conditions. It would be another thing to condition further hunger relief upon zero population growth, and quite another thing to threaten a country with nuclear annihilation unless it achieved the same objective.

What the public church has not done is to provide a consistent ethic of intervention or nonintervention that could clarify the church's vision of the acceptable use and limits of military force or economic coercion, *and* be an ethic that the church could actually implement. In the absence of a consistent ethic of intervention, the church has produced a variety of positions that, because inconsistently applied, have made the basic tragedy of American diplomacy worse.

I would venture a guess that the high regard in which American Mennonites are held for their international relief work is in part because they have a consistent ethic of engaged pacifism by which they are willing to live. They will intervene to provide food, clothing, shelter, wells, roads, and sanitary conditions, but will not engage in plotting to overthrow even the most despicable host government.

Alas, most American churches do not have the record of consistency in the twentieth century that the Mennonites hold. Consider the case of the Methodists. In 1936 the General Conference of the Methodist Episcopal Church declared:

> War as we now know it is utterly destructive. It is the greatest social sin of modern times; a denial of the ideals of Christ, a violation of human personality and a threat to civilization. Therefore, we declare that the Methodist Episcopal Church as an institution does not endorse, support or propose to participate in war.[16]

Given World War I's outcome, and even avoidability, who could blame the church for resolving never to fight again. The Northern Methodists were not alone. A year earlier the College of Bishops of the Methodist Episcopal Church, South, had issued a similar statement:

> We shall hold in contempt this entire nefarious war business. War as a method of settling international disputes has not one single defensible argument in its behalf. We reiterate what we said a year ago to the General Conference: "it is archaic, belongs to the jungle period of human development and should be branded as an iniquitous and inhuman procedure."[17]

The peace movement spread like Pentecost itself through American churches in the 1930s. The General Convention of the Episcopal Church foreswore war forever, as did the Northern Baptist Convention, the Disciples of Christ, the Universalist Convention of California,

16. Quoted in Kirby Page, *Must We Go to War?* (New York: Farrar and Rinehart, 1937), pp. 182-86.
17. Ibid.

the General Council of Congregational and Christian Churches, and both of the major Presbyterian churches. All these churches did so within the two-year period 1934–36. The Disciples' leading pacifist, Kirby Page, reported that in 1934 complete questionnaires were received from 20,780 members of the clergy who were asked, among other questions, "Do you believe that the churches of America should now go on record as refusing to sanction or support any future war?" A total of 13,997 respondents (70%) said yes.

Thus convinced and in good company, the Methodist Church made its commitment never to go to war again, to be a peace church like the Mennonites or the Quakers. How long did this pacifism last? Only until Pearl Harbor. Then the preachers and their churches, virtually everyone in the peace camp except the few courageous leaders like Kirby Page and Harry Emerson Fosdick and the conscientious objectors of the time, succumbed either to the martial spirit or to the logic of the conflict: that while the last war was not worth supporting, this one was different. Therefore Methodist laypersons were encouraged in 1941 and for the duration to serve in the Armed Forces or to do their parts at home, and Methodist clergy were not only permitted but encouraged to serve as military chaplains.

When principles can be discarded so easily, what credence should they be given? When principles are not applied in practice, but are still given lip service, the standard charge is that the moral actor is a hypocrite. The reversal of the churches may have contributed something to the low esteem in which their social teachings are held. Worse yet, sufficient evidence suggests that by deceiving a generation into believing that the church would never again sanction war, the fair-weather pacifists made the eventual armed conflict worse. By creating an ethos in which dictators thought they would be unopposed in their aggression and in which the international community failed to take adequate preparations, the churches and other pacifists allowed the international situation to get beyond the control of more limited uses of force. Having noticed only after 1940 that the situation had become intolerable, the churches demonized opponents and swung from pacifism to the excesses of unlimited warfare, eventuating in Dresden and Hiroshima.

Following World War II, one would have thought that the Methodists, like other peace churches of the 1930s that deserted their positions to oppose Hitler, had demonstrated to themselves that they lacked the constitution to be a peace church, that some things were worth fighting for and others not. Such was not to be the case, however. In 1972, when the Social Principles of the United Methodist Church were revised and adopted to replace the Social Creed developed in the social gospel era, the following passage became that church's stand on the limits of intervention:

> We believe war is incompatible with the teachings and example of Christ. We therefore reject war as an instrument of national foreign policy and insist that the first moral duty of all nations is resolve by peaceful means every dispute that arises between or among them.[18]

That position too would have been fine, if the rest of the church's teaching had followed suit. But the church's Social Principles, while opposing the draft, vowed to "support those persons who choose to serve in the armed forces or to accept alternate service."[19] Thus within the same document the Methodist Church taught that all war was wrong but that serving in a war-making army and by extension in a war was morally acceptable behavior for its members. Which of these things does the church really believe? Is it a selective just war ethic? Neither the Social Principles nor the United Methodist Bishops' pastoral letter, *In Defense of Creation,* is clear on this point.

Meanwhile, the other churches that had been caught up in the pacifist movement of the 1930s took a more restrained postwar posture and endorsed some version of the realist position on what was then called "power politics." Or so they thought, for it was difficult at times to determine what the realist position involved.

The theologian Reinhold Niebuhr had been one of the earliest advocates of rejecting the pacifist position as overly sentimentalized Christianity having nothing whatsoever to do with the gospel. In its place he proposed that Christians and their churches were called to respond realistically to the gospel in the sinful world of power politics, including Adolf Hitlers, nuclear bombs, nation-states, armies, and the will to power. In short, they were called to respond to sin. In an essay entitled "Why the Christian Church is Not Pacifist," Niebuhr dealt directly with the risks of intervention and nonintervention:

18. Quoted in *In Defense of Creation: The Nuclear Crisis and a Just Peace: Foundation Document* (Nashville: Graded Press, 1986), p. 20.

19. Quoted in Paul Ramsey and Stanley Hauerwas, *Speak Up for Just War or Pacifism* (State College, Penn.: Pennsylvania State Univ. Press, 1988), p. 12.

> The refusal to recognize that sin introduces an element of conflict into the world invariably means that a morally perverse preference is given to tyranny over anarchy (war). If we are told that tyranny would destroy itself, if only we would not challenge it, the obvious answer is that tyranny continues to grow if it is not resisted. If it is to be resisted, the risk of overt conflict must be taken. The thesis that German tyranny must not be challenged by other nations because Germany will throw off this yoke in due time, merely means that an unjustified moral preference is given to civil war over international war, for internal resistance runs the risk of conflict as much as external resistance.[20]

Niebuhr had a gift for aphorisms and for a quick turn of an argument. Without rejecting the special witness of the historic peace churches, he made a clear case that any church which did care about living in this world must deal with the world on its terms. Such a church must also accept relative justice, for no other kind would be found.

Niebuhr, however, did not have a copyright on the concept of Christian realism. In the popular mind, John Foster Dulles was just as likely to be associated with the name Christian realism, for his brand of faith was as tinged with power politics as was Niebuhr's. This association is unfortunate, for Dulles was more a Christian idealist who talked tough and threateningly than he was a realist. Still, he remains the only example I know of parlaying church committee work into a cabinet post. During World War II, Dulles chaired the Federal Council of Churches' Commission on a Just and Durable Peace, which was notable for its realistic treatment of possible postwar problems and its suggestion of workable solutions, many of which, including the United Nations, were later adopted in some form. After this service, Dulles began to be mentioned in Republican circles as the most likely candidate for secretary of state in a Republican administration. Though he had to wait for that distinction until 1953, once in office he proceeded to demonstrate how quickly Christian positions on international affairs could degenerate into the kind of moralism associated with his fellow Princetonian, Woodrow Wilson. He also showed how interventionist politics might be played as a dangerous game when, in the pursuit of power and national interest, he was

20. Reinhold Niebuhr, *Christianity and Power Politics* (New York: Scribner's, 1940), p. 15.

willing to threaten massive nuclear retaliation in response to minor Soviet acts of aggression.[21]

More recently Michael Novak and other neoconservatives have claimed the realist mantle for themselves. They argue that the only moral question to ask about international politicians is "did they pursue the vital interests of the people whose nation they represented?"

What passes for Christian realism under a Dulles or a Novak has also worked to deepen the tragedy of American diplomacy.[22] The public church is not prepared to accept the claims of neorealists who deny that human rights, international justice, fair trade, development, and the prevention of war as independent categories are of moral worth in international relations. The liberal public church thus continues to support interventionist policies based on humanitarian and self-determinist impulses, blind to the issue of self-interest, while Reaganite neorealists pursue the international relations of national interest, deaf to the cries of human rights victims and democracies in decay. To top it all off, right-wing Christians, seeking the defense of Western Christian civilization, make common cause with the neorealists to mount surrogate wars in the Third World.

Just Peace — An Interventionist Ethic for American Churches

Where does this discussion of the history of American international intervention and the public church leave or lead us? Precisely back to where we started, with the tragedy of American diplomacy and the urgent need for the church to do more than contribute further to the tragedy.

The history of American religion and interventionism in this century shows that a public church ethic of absolute nonintervention has not worked to date. For a mix of theological and practical reasons, most American Christians are unwilling to tolerate Hitlers and Pol

21. John Foster Dulles, "A Policy of Boldness," *Life*, May 19, 1952, pp. 146, 151, 154.

22. I accept Ronald Stone's recent defense of the concept of Christian realism in its purer forms from those who would apply the title too widely to all who, like Dulles, would favor force in given situations and link their reasoning to faith claims. But my emphasis here is on how Christian realists have been perceived rather than what they have thought at their best. See Ronald Stone, *Christian Realism and Peacemaking* (Nashville: Abingdon, 1988).

Pots, concentration camps and killing fields, or the starvation of their fellow Christians in the southern Sudan. An ethic that the church cannot live by and commend to the people of God and their government(s) is worse than useless. It diminishes the church's authority in matters where a moral voice is most needed.

At the same time, the persistent attraction of the public church to pacifism as a social teaching suggests that American Christians in their best moments are also unwilling to endorse governments that go to war to preserve access to cheap supplies of oil, to prop up friendly authoritarian regimes that abuse the rights of their people, or to force "free trade" on unequal partners. The public church has often taken a pacifist position on intervention for fear of giving ideological ammunition to a government bent on pursuing an unjust crusade or of sending the wrong signal to the people. Yet an on-again, off-again ethic also diminishes the church's authority, for it hides the truth in the name of giving people only what it is thought they can handle. That kind of intellectual sham has a way of being discovered when people face hard choices.

Tragic situations deserve tragic interpretations. That is, the history of the public church in the twentieth century teaches that we need an ethic which does justice to the complex relationships between differing moral goods sought in international relations as well as the real evils present in human affairs. We began the 1990s in the midst of yet another crisis in international affairs, the Iraq-Kuwait conflict, in which we needed more than ever a public church able to help Americans sort out self-interest and altruism in foreign affairs. To paraphrase Niebuhr, the church should help the society develop the courage to intervene on the side of a just peace, the serenity to refrain from unjust and selfish acts of intervention, and the wisdom to disentangle the two.

Recovery of the justifiable war tradition in the Catholic Bishops' Pastoral Letter of 1983 and the Presbyterian Church's social statement on Christian Obedience in a Nuclear Age (1988) are gratifying recent signs. Both of these ethical guides speak clearly for peace but also acknowledge that conflict, sometimes even war, is a fact of human existence. Because of candor on this and other points, these churches' positions on the ethics of nuclear deterrence are credible. An ethic of just peace offered in these social teachings advances a corrective to the exceptionalism inherent in American thought about the rest of the world. But behavior counts as well as rhetoric. Will these churches and the public church be willing to stand by their ethic? Let us hope so.

Changes in Ecumenical Public Witness, 1967–90

Christian T. Iosso

Introduction

Public witness is the savor in ecumenical salt. Ecumenical organizations, preeminently the National and World Councils of Churches (NCC, WCC), are certainly founded on the conviction that there is but one, holy, catholic, and apostolic church, whose unity is God's will. Yet these councils, and their predecessor and cognate bodies, were also organized to accomplish specific purposes better achieved in concert. Ecumenical public policy and education efforts aimed at reforming the social order were key purposes for such joint work. But if the two preeminent interdenominational bodies are losing their capacity for public impact directed by the gospel, are they not losing their savor — and should they not then be trampled underfoot, as Jesus suggests of the worthless salt?

This chapter is an attempt to assess the saltiness of the public witness of the two main ecumenical bodies supported by U.S. Protestant denominations and Orthodox churches: the NCC and the WCC. It links a review of ecumenical social policy with an assessment of the public effectiveness of these councils as vehicles for that witness. It asks, How well do the message and the medium fit together? My review benefits from several excellent studies of ecumenical social thought and analyses of specific issues.[1]

1. Three issues of the *Ecumenical Review* are particularly relevant: "Church and Society: Ecumenical Perspectives" (Jan. 1985); "Fifty Years of Ecumenical Social Thought" (April 1988); and "Commemorating Amsterdam 1948: 40 Years of the World Council of Churches" (July-Oct. 1988). Volumes from particular conferences and con-

In part, an assessment of public impact means focusing on those elements of structure and program in the ecumenical bodies directed specifically toward social witness. How effective have they been in key areas of engagement: peace, civil rights, economic and social justice, equality for women, ecological concerns, and the liberation of the poor and oppressed, broadly conceived? I will compare certain efforts at earlier periods with public witness emphases in the 1970s and 1980s, and I will suggest changes in the degree and kind of attention to issues.

A more comprehensive assessment of ecumenical public witness also means looking at the role of the ecumenical bodies within different cultural, political, and economic contexts. Here we can only suggest some of the changes that affect the position of the churches and ecumenical bodies, even limiting our attention mainly to the United States. How seriously such societal changes are to be taken is an ecclesiological question, as the importance of church public witness is itself a theological matter.

My own position can be summed up as, "more public, more witness." I count efforts to build "social righteousness" among the works of "spiritual administration" that, with preaching and the proper administration of the sacraments, are among the basic functions of the church in Reformed perspective. Public support for order, freedom, and justice (to cite Robin Lovin's formulation)[2] is among the responsibilities of religious communities, though the churches' emphasis needs to vary with "the signs of the times." I do in fact support most of the public policy positions of the NCC and WCC, and wish they were backed by the more comprehensive approach I propose in the third section of this chapter.

---

sultations (the WCC has held more than 600), as well as the major assembly series, all offer material for a comprehensive review. Robert S. Bilheimer's *Breakthrough: The Emergence of the Ecumenical Tradition* (Grand Rapids: Eerdmans, 1989) lists the major items in the "Official Ecumenical Corpus" at the end of his narrative of the WCC's history. On the NCC side, there is a wide range of material, including the official version, *Church Cooperation and Unity in America: A Historical Review: 1900–1970,* by Samuel McCrea Cavert, et al. (New York: Association Press, 1970).

2. See Robin W. Lovin, "Religion and American Public Life: Three Relationships," in *Religion and American Public Life: Interpretations and Explorations,* ed. Robin W. Lovin (Mahwah, N.J.: Paulist, 1986). Max L. Stackhouse's *Public Theology and Political Economy* (Grand Rapids: Eerdmans, 1987), part of a strong series initiated by the NCC's Commission on Stewardship, provides a longer and more classical list of elements for "public theology" and a helpful emphasis on institutions as carriers of values.

At the same time I would affirm that the church's strong public role should be understood as a form of witness to the gospel, with a sharp awareness of Christian distinctives. The church itself needs to sustain its own communities and culture with some separation, even in necessary coalitions, lest it identify itself inauthentically with groups representing narrower interests than its own. I believe we need better theological grounding in some ecumenical witness efforts, and would generally favor more integration of a Faith and Order perspective in the NCC's social justice work, aware that the greater Faith and Order component in the WCC has not benefited some of its strategies.

Two Dynamics in the 1967–90 Period: Liberation and Marginalization

Two factors give impetus to this review of recent ecumenical public witness. One is the impact of the newer social movements and theologies of the 1970s, or of the "second sixties," from 1967 to 1975.[3] Both ecumenical bodies have often championed liberation approaches since that time, and have utilized liberation thought to guide strategies of solidarity and inclusiveness. The second factor, at least as important to ecumenical self-understanding today, is a sense of marginalization, seen in the backlash and retrenchment of the 1980s. Conservative and neoconservative groups have directed particular fire at the councils and at liberation thought, but some criticism has come from within the ecumenical movement, contrasting the neoorthodox and *liberal* "church and society" approaches of the 1940s–early 1960s with *liberation* praxis.

Paul Abrecht, the WCC's Church and Society director from 1949

3. The concept of a "second sixties" is summarized by Leonard I. Sweet in "The Modernization of Protestant Religion in America," in *Altered Landscapes: Christianity in America, 1935–85*, ed. David W. Lotz, Donald W. Shriver, Jr., and John F. Wilson (Grand Rapids: Eerdmans, 1989), pp. 25-27. Sweet argues that the change in mood (more polarized), forgetfulness of the past (absorbed in changing trends), and strength of social movements distinguished the "second sixties" from the first, and from the end of Protestant "modernism" that followed. His argument for the significance of architectural changes in reflecting these changes would be strengthened by the data on mainline demographic and institutional decline, starting around 1966, that have been assembled in William McKinney and Wade Clark Roof's *American Mainline Religion* (New Brunswick: Rutgers Univ. Press, 1987) and Robert Wuthnow's *The Restructuring of American Religion* (Princeton: Princeton Univ. Press, 1988).

to 1983, made this contrast strongly, claiming that the various liberation theologies have contributed to a virtual standstill in ecumenical work on social issues. Writing in early 1988, Abrecht pointed to the Vancouver Assembly's inability to develop a consensus report on "Justice and Human Dignity." He saw this difficulty also reflected in the WCC's inability to find someone balanced or pansympathetic enough to survey its social-ethical initiatives of the period since 1969, which Abrecht called "the period of liberation ecumenism."[4] As Abrecht described the impasse,

> After the Nairobi Assembly [1975] . . . WCC staff were increasingly divided about the substance of Christian ethics. The emphasis on identification with the poor and the oppressed as the sole criterion for Christian action in society, the attempt to focus all ecumenical action on the struggle against classism, racism and sexism, seemed to many to oversimplify the problem of Christian action in society. . . . The fate of the World Student Christian Federation . . . [moribund by 1975] . . . was seen by some ecumenists as an omen of the dangers of a one-sided approach to world social issues.[5]

4. Paul Abrecht, "From Oxford to Vancouver: Lessons from Fifty Years of Ecumenical Work for Economic and Social Justice," *Ecumenical Review* 40, no. 2 (April 1988): 148, 159-60. Abrecht also notes that while the liberation emphasis grew within the WCC, "by hindsight we now know that various developments in the period 1975–80 had begun to weaken liberation theology's diagnosis of the world political-economic situation and its remedies" (p. 164).

5. Ibid., p. 162. Abrecht continues his criticism in "The Predicament of Christian Social Thought after the Cold War," *Ecumenical Review* 43, no. 3 (July 1991). Abrecht is by no means alone in his view of the late-sixties move away from the "responsible society" methodology and content. A number of younger ecumenists joined Abrecht and other veterans in an open letter of July 27, 1990, to WCC General Secretary Emilio Castro, criticizing the JPIC process.

Charles West's "Ecumenical Social Ethic Beyond Socialism and Capitalism," ibid., maintains that "a new and more complex form of social alienation has developed and has found in ecumenical Christianity a vehicle" (p. 336), using a hermeneutic of suspicion, making partisanship a test of faith, valorizing the poor without criticism, and stressing immanent human achievements of liberation. He proposes a theological-ethical "retrieval" (not his term) based on mutual dependence within the *oikoumene* and a new, post-Marxist period.

A third similar account can be found in Thomas Sieger Derr's "The Economic Thought of the World Council of Churches," *This World* 1, no. 1 (Winter/Spring, 1982). Derr moderates charges of one-sided anticapitalism, anti-Americanism, and focus on white racism, but does see some "inconsistency in ethical judgement," "loss of realism," and an "invasion . . . by the dynamics of anger, blame, and guilt . . . overlooking the complexities and ambiguities of both human nature and the social order" (p. 32).

While Abrecht argued that the WCC has resisted many emphases in the liberation perspective, particularly Marxist and overly optimistic versions, and has continued to pay attention to the scientific-technological-environmental issues sometimes seen as First World, he saw no successor to the moderate, pragmatic (realistic?) social ethical tradition of "Oxford-Amsterdam-Geneva." Further, after his own forceful criticisms of the liberation ecumenism period, which he saw almost at an end, Abrecht underlined the difficulties of developing a coherent theological-ethical basis for ecumenical social thought and action.

Unity, or at least general consensus, is a key goal of ecumenical social witness in Abrecht's view. Whether one sees the current situation as a standstill, creative ferment, or necessary self-critique in the light of praxis, the realities of cultural diversity among and theological pluralism within the churches are challenging. Does the impact of the churches' social witness depend upon reasonable unity of voice as well as accuracy of position? This is a question posed dramatically by South Korean Hyun-Kyung Chung at the Canberra WCC Assembly in 1991, in an address that integrated liberation, earth- or life-centered, and traditional Korean understandings of life energy and compassion. Her cultural contextualism appealed to "my gut feeling deep in my people's collective unconsciousness that comes from thousands of years of spirituality," an approach that was literally foreign to some from other cultures.[6]

Put differently, does the public witness of the churches embodied ecumenically depend upon an internal "public sphere" of shared values, views, and communication? My sympathies are with Abrecht and the traditional aspiration of solidarity within the ecumenical movement, but the questions are then: (1) what theological basis of unity? and (2) does this understanding of unified witness presume a unified public for the church to address, much less transform? We will return to these questions in the concluding section. At the same time, ecumenical acceptance of the power of liberation thought to unmask other ideologies, and the enrichment of "the banquet of ecumenical theology" by contextual contributions, have made the witness

6. Hyun-Kyung Chung, "Come Holy Spirit, Renew the Whole Creation," WCC Seventh Assembly Document PL 3.3, Feb. 8, 1991, p. 7. Some reactions made her paper sound like an Asian version of *Foucault's Pendulum* (1990), a novel by Umberto Eco that received much criticism from the Roman Catholic Church in Italy for its "syncretism."

of the councils more credible in many non–Euro-American communities — whatever the internal conflicts and weaknesses.[7]

Turning now to those weaknesses, the second major factor affecting ecumenical public witness, one can immediately see institutional decay in the ecumenical movement, most notably in the NCC, emerging in 1990 from its second reorganization (and downsizing) in seven years. Many countries have certainly felt less of the antiecumenical winds that swept the United States since the late 1970s, and the WCC has remained proportionately healthier than the NCC. But at least in the United States, the situation seems quite serious.

Indeed, more threatening than opposition is the weakening of support among the denominations that have been the wheelhorses of the ecumenical movement, the seven mainline denominations that have lost over 25 percent of their membership since 1975. It would be surprising if the "ethos of decline," disorientation, and loss of initiative within these basic constituency groups had not carried over to their chief ecumenical vehicles.[8] Any initial assessment of ecumenical health must note the declining proportion of funds going beyond the local congregation for denominational as well as ecumenical mission purposes. The morale and quality of leadership within the organization is also a good indicator of problems.

Further, since 1983 organized conservative factions prompted a number of denominations to study their relationships with the councils. The resulting denominational findings and membership surveys suggest that the ecumenical movement has lost much of its franchise among mainline communicants. This is not to say that the Presbyterians, American Baptists, and Disciples have bought the position of right-wing and neoconservative critics; the mainline bodies without exception have held to their formal ecumenical commitments.[9] Yet

7. The quoted phrase is from Dale T. Irwin's article by that title in *Ecumenical Review* 42, no. 1 (Jan. 1991), which celebrates the WCC as a table where pluralism and de-Europeanization are moving the church forward. In that same issue, however, John Deschner's article, "More than Inclusiveness," criticizes several reductionistic kinds of inclusiveness and suggests a helpful combination of pluralism and intercontextualism with koinonia, convergence, and the cross as a preeminent sign transcending divisions.

8. My Ph.D. dissertation, "A Church for the Lean Years: Toward an Economic Ethic for the Future Life and Witness of Mainline Protestantism," Union Theological Seminary, New York, 1991, surveys the literature on church decline.

9. These studies deserve separate treatment, which is not possible here. Trust relationships needed to be established in the study processes, which also revealed how little interpretation had been given the NCC and WCC in recent years. Reports of the

the membership has little positive sense of what the ecumenical bodies do, is unwilling to pay much for them, and has taken major symbolic and actual steps to distance itself from them.

Of greater practical and symbolic significance are the consequences of the debates over location of national offices in the 1980s, which were body blows to the NCC's everyday operation.[10] In no case was a major chunk of denominational administration put into the NCC's New York City location, and in two major cases, the Presbyterian Church and the United Church of Christ, most of their offices were moved out. The merged Evangelical Lutheran Church put its new offices in Chicago; the Christian Church (Disciples of Christ) built new offices in its previous location, Indianapolis, as did the National Baptist Convention, in Knoxville. While these actions were taken mainly for intradenominational reasons, it is hard to see any significant concern for practical ecumenical cooperation in them. For the Presbyterians and United Church of Christ, the study processes and decisions were in part votes against staff leadership perceived as left-leaning and ecumenically oriented. With little financial justification, the symbols and values attached to New York as an ecumenical, interracial, international, and cultural center became decisive factors to be opposed in almost arbitrary decisions for Louisville, Kentucky, and Cleveland, Ohio. Recurrent debates within the United Methodist Church also challenge the presence of its Global Division in New York, although that denomination wisely maintains several major office locations.

This is not to denigrate as unecumenical any church with offices not in New York, or to make of that city a sacred space or idol. But in addition to acting out institutional weaknesses and preferences for more heartland locations, the denominational office-site decisions raise a number of questions about the location of public witness. In

---

Christian Church (Disciples of Christ) and Presbyterian Church (U.S.A.) study processes can be found in their General Assembly minutes (1986–88, with progress reports). William F. Keucher's "American Baptist Churches, USA, Review Ecumenical Ties," *Ecumenical Trends* 17, no. 9 (Oct. 1988), reports on that denomination's study and careful recommendation: "To broaden American Baptist ecumenical commitments, we reaffirm our present memberships in the . . . NCC and . . . WCC and will seek to become an official observer in the National Association of Evangelicals (NAE)" (p. 133).

10. The analysis that follows was presented in part in a series of articles I wrote during 1985–86 in *Presbyterian Outlook, Presbyterian Survey,* and *Christian Century.* It also reflects my own experience of daily ecumenical contact as a staff person in the United Church of Christ and in the Presbyterian Church, 1979–84.

his theological reflections on the Presbyterians' "fresh beginning" in Louisville, Walter Brueggemann seems to suggest that the geographical move from New York and Atlanta parallels a spiritual movement into exile, a "daring break with all things imperial . . . and the embrace of an alternative vocation."[11] Brueggemann distinguishes the departure out of Babylonian exile, which is also a "homecoming," from the departure from Egypt, which led into wilderness, but implies that Louisville provides some distance from idolatrous power centers and cultural fleshpots. The question, then, is whether a symbolic location in the heartland or hinterland is more appropriate to public witness than a more culturally cosmopolitan or imperial setting, a New York, a Washington, a Rome, a Chicago, an Atlanta, or a Jerusalem. If some kind of "margin" is chosen, does the witnessing body also choose nonimperial methods and media, perhaps a way of dispossession in solidarity with those on the underside of power?[12]

These location-prompted questions also relate to whether the churches are in a fully post-Constantinian period, bereft of significant influence or power.[13] Alan Geyer's words on the power of pronouncements and the limits of secularization in politics are helpful here: "Beware of claiming too much for religious influence — but beware, equally, of underestimating its influence."[14] The four-part definition of public witness below is designed to assess more of the councils' influence than that found simply in written statements, acknowl-

11. Walter Brueggemann, "Disciplines of Readiness," a paper of the Theology and Worship Unit, Presbyterian Church (U.S.A.), 1990, p. 7. A similar argument was made in a letter to *Presbyterian Outlook*, comparing the move to Louisville to a congregation's move from main street to a side street. Brueggemann's application of exile themes is persuasive to me generally.

12. Thus the location issue relates to how the church should oppose both cultural captivity and a host of social oppressions. Does public witness imply compromise with the dominant cultural elements, and is some kind of positive withdrawal or contrast church strategy most effective? How much cognitive minority status is sustainable for mainline churches in actual minority settings? And how much is the disestablished, minority, or exile status embraced by some in the ecumenical and mainline church leadership more a reflection of their theological views than those of their churches, at least in Canada and the United States?

13. I allude here to the debates over the Third Disestablishment and arguments that it is best to abandon the cultural suppositions of previous, supposedly Christian eras, which no longer provide the church much support anyway. The question here, ultimately, is whether it is God's will or the world's will that the church shrink, in numbers, influence, or presence otherwise conceived.

14. Alan Geyer, "The Power of Pronouncements," *Christianity and Crisis* (Feb. 20, 1989): 27.

edging the complexity of comparing the councils and relating their influence to that of their member communions.[15] The assumption governing the joint treatment, however, is that these bodies live in the same theological currents, share similar purposes, and will experience a similar future.[16]

A Four-Part Definition of Public Witness

Not all public witness is intentional. The effectiveness of a particular campaign is dependent on the image, influence, and economic and political power that an organization itself holds on a continuous basis. While dedicated and enthusiastic campaigners are crucial, a group's pull is related to the loyalty and shared identity of its constituents, a kind of capital in the marketplace of ideas, or a kind of franchise on consumer loyalty to particular brands. This residual strength translates into an ability to deliver — or resist — a given impact at the right time. Without this element of support that can be counted up as well as counted on, the institutional agents of the churches cannot claim to be representatives. They may try to walk loudly, but they carry a only a little stick.

Thus the public witness task cannot be defined too narrowly. It reflects the institutional strength of the bodies involved, the quality of their internal relations and activities, and, to be effective, requires a range of strategies that reflect the full nature of the church's commitments. For example, church advocacy for economic justice gains from the investment of members and money in serving the poor directly, from perceived fairness in the compensation of ministers and other church personnel, and from the voting patterns of church mem-

15. A thoughtful comparison of the NCC and WCC from an ecumenical Roman Catholic perspective can be found in Brother Jeffrey Gros, "The Vision of Christian Unity: Some Aspects of Faith and Order in the Context of United States Culture," *Mid-Stream* 30, no. 1 (Jan. 1991). His paper is a guide to the NCC debates over "cooperative agency" or "community of communions" and to their practical consequences, in the light of WCC advances in ecumenical understanding.

16. Other presuppositions of this chapter are: that the church context is of primary importance to the ecumenical movement — whatever else God is doing in the world; that history moves through a conjunction of forces and meanings, both of which are reflected in and sometimes influenced by the church's own life; that particular leaders are as important as groups; and that the ecumenical vision and movement ought to be strengthened institutionally.

bership. That almost two-thirds of middle-class white Protestants voted for Ronald Reagan certainly hurt official church lobbying against Reaganomics — even without business-supported lobbies trumpeting this fact.

At the same time, it is not enough to focus on changing government policies. Some appeal must be made to public opinion (a mixture of images and responses), a related appeal must be made to the faith and values of individuals, and a further part of the overall strategy must connect with specialized constituencies concerned with the given issue. In the passage of civil rights legislation in 1964 and 1965, for example, church support was felt in a range of ways, including the participation of pastors in communicating with their legislators, the civil disobedience of members and ministers (such as Eugene Carson Blake), and some coordination with the black organizations leading the campaigns. Public opinion was also influenced — in part by televised images — and individuals were asked to repent of racism. Later racial justice efforts by mainline churches illustrate some of the limits of lobbying and staff integration without much organic link to predominantly white congregations. Further, the churches can lift up few successful interracial enterprises of any sort as exemplary alternatives to our society's failures in race relations.

These considerations suggest that public witness can and should try to shape or influence the larger society through four related means:

1. Influencing public opinion, by presenting persuasive ethical apologetics.
2. Appeals to the faith and values of individuals, particularly in their church life.
3. Efforts to achieve specific policies, involving informed constituencies.
4. Exemplifying viable alternatives through church-based social relations and organizations which show that some courageous experiments work.

This approach retains a responsibility to contribute to the common good, but recognizes that each effort to change the world leads back to Christian faith claims and actual church efforts. Particularly when it comes to the efforts of the mainline churches acting ecumenically to achieve policy goals of racial justice, economic fairness, equality for women, full civil rights for lesbian and gay citizens, and so forth, the churches' own practices have indeed become the first arena for struggle.

An Application of the Four-Part Definition to the Two Councils

Each council has certain characteristic strengths and many well-designed programs as well as weak points, some of which mirror current dilemmas of liberal or mainline Protestant theology and mission, and others of which indicate even broader societal problems. An initial schematic application of the four-part definition will help identify some of the elements that may be influenced by the councils, and others that reflect broader forces.

Influencing Public Opinion

NCC: This element seems to have largely dropped out of social policy aspiration, at least on domestic concerns. Compared with the massive, lay-expert-studded economic ethics series from 1952 to 1965, which supported public welfare policies, regulation, and limited economic planning, even the well-written 1983 NCC broadside against Reagan's policies, "The Remaking of America?" is a defensive effort that has to start from scratch at certain points.[17] Many resolutions assume division within the churches; a concern to be right rather than effective is present in a self-conscious minority.

17. A good example of the broader 1950s and early 1960s strategy can be found in Howard Bowen's volume in that Cameron Hall-inspired series, *Social Responsibilities of the Businessman* (New York: Harper Brothers, 1953). In addition to an awareness of public policy issues (an FCC concern going back to the Social Creed), and a then more recent awareness of power dynamics and the "organizational revolution," Bowen's work emphasizes vocation as the link between personal faith and community, and uses an explicit public opinion strategy. In his words, "This implies that, under pressure of public opinion, businessmen can be persuaded to accept new duties and obligations. . . . The means of achieving higher morality in business behavior is to create public attitudes which enlarge the moral reponsibilities of business" (p. 68). Bowen assumes the business world is still part of the usual moral universe and wants to encourage professionalism in management, while also pushing a "social audit" and countervailing powers. The public opinion approach is also explicit in Marquis W. Childs and Douglass Cater, *Ethics in a Business Society* (New York: Harper, 1954), which popularizes the study's work. All of this is in considerable contrast to the more narrow foci of the corporate social responsibility movement and much business ethics guidance that assumes professionalism.

It is also helpful to recall the series of study conferences and high-profile reports on international affairs from 1940 to 1958, reprinted recently in Harold Lunger's *Facing War, Waging Peace,* though some of those efforts also included specific policy recommendations.[18] More activity seems most called for in relation to the United Nations, in a broad effort to revive some of the internationalism so crucial to earlier ecumenical periods. The early 1991 statements and strategy of the NCC in opposition to the military intervention in Kuwait-Iraq represent a step in the right direction, despite initial concern that the council and church leadership had been too noninterventionist and, of course, unpatriotic.[19]

WCC: Good general concepts have been developed, serviceable in an international and cross-cultural context, orienting member communions and framing debates. Publication strategy is noteworthy, if perhaps too academic. In the United States, layers of denominational structure and concentration on the NCC prevent most members and ministers from a clear view of the WCC, which has a little-known office in the Interchurch Center. In an analysis of the arguments offered in *Church and Society* social ethical writings, James Gustafson identified four varieties: prophetic (annunciation and denunciation), narrative, ethical issues, and policy discourse, and suggested that the policy arguments need to offer more ethical justification.[20] To the degree that these arguments are presented to the public, people should hear the positive, hopeful side of the prophetic as well as the denunciation side.

Appeal to, or Coherence with, the Beliefs and Church Life of Church Members

NCC: The denominational studies reveal erosion in identification with the NCC by members, though the NCC suffers from the general faith crisis of the "liberal" or "moderate" churches, their fuzzy identity, and lack of leadership. Do the NCC's strategies assume an educated, theologically literate, politically liberal church member — who is quite

18. Harold Lunger, ed., *Facing War, Waging Peace* (New York: Friendship, 1988).

19. A booklet, "Pressing for Peace: The Churches Act in the Gulf Crisis," contains the NCCCUSA's record of statements on the Gulf Crisis from August 1990 to January 1991. It is available from the council's Middle East Office.

20. See James Gustafson, "An Analysis of Church and Society Social Ethical Writings," *Ecumenical Review* 40, no. 2 (April 1988): 268-70.

rare? Fear of offending more members and member communions appears to lie behind the refusal to admit Metropolitan Fellowship of Community Churches: suspension of the prophetic role here left the NCC on the defensive with many supporters.[21] The issue here is the relation of ethos to ethics; church members should be able to make faith-sense of a position's moral and theological claims, even if they disagree with the specific policies recommended.

By contrast, many churchgoers see no relation of the NCC to their struggles with church growth, youth ministry, twelve-step programs, new age threats, etc.; instead they associate the NCC with issues like the *Inclusive Language Lectionary* that may force a rethinking of the faith.[22] New ventures of this kind arouse controversy that obscures a stewardship emphasis and relief appeals well targeted to congregations. Other problems related to the liberal or modernist faith position are: few personal models of progressive piety, and emphasis on critique rather than construction, on diversity rather than connectedness, and on process over content. Along with the importance of distinguishable leaders as models — if not heroes — there seems to be a need for more narrative communication to form identity, illustrate virtues, and perhaps to provide "an organizing perspective, metaphor, analogy or principle."[23]

WCC: Generally WCC work has a higher theological quotient. There is a major cross-cultural issue in the Dialogue with People of Other Faiths, since this program works with universal and pluralist elements at the boundary of Christian self-definition. It contrasts with the WCC's primary cross-cultural approaches of solidarity with other churches and the oppressed.[24] The WCC Baptism, Eucharist, and

21. As in the case of the WCC study of the Community of Women and Men in the Church, the NCC study of MCC membership involved its Faith and Order unit and dealt extensively with ecclesiological questions. To some, it appeared to raise heterosexism to confessional status; opponents of full membership status challenged "the narrowness of its organizing principle, the new biblical insights it claims, and the challenge they raise to biblical ecclesiology." See Jeffrey Gros, "A Gay Church in the NCC?" *Christianity and Crisis* (May 2, 1983): 167-171, from which the above quote is taken.

22. It should be noted that the NCC's communication strategy at the publication of the three-volume *Inclusive Language Lectionary* was excellent, as was its fanfare for the New Revised Standard Version.

23. Gustafson, "Analysis," p. 268.

24. To the extent that the WCC works with those beyond the Christian community, it may lessen its chances at joint work and mutual recognition with either the self-defined evangelical community or the Roman Catholic community, at least as

Ministry document was broadly successful in expressing (and helping create) a "convergence" and "mutual recognition," but the new theological work and ethical investigation reaches few people in the United States (e.g., the covenanting process on Justice, Peace and the Integrity of Creation [JPIC], and the Ecumenical Decade for Churches in Solidarity with Women, 1988–98, are little known here). The lack of ecumenical youth or university groups may be more serious for the WCC than, say, any weakness of state councils of churches may be for the NCC. The ecumenical movement's confessional groupings, such as the World Alliance of Reformed Churches (WARC) and the Lutheran World Federation (LWF), complement WCC efforts by lifting up some leaders, enriching ecumenical relations with bilateral linkages, and treating similar global concerns in the idioms of confessional theology and tradition.

Efforts to Achieve Specific Policy Objectives, with Involved Constituencies

NCC: It often exhibits very effective staff work on targeted issues. Work with sponsored, related movements and coalitions focused on specific issues gives some feet to policy recommendations. In Washington, staff helps coordinate the Interfaith Staff Cabinet. In general, however, the constituency of the NCC is denominational staff who populate its committees, leaving out significant bodies of lay experts in given fields and ministerial representatives from local congregations.[25] The denominations have largely come to run their own study committees, usually choosing from a more limited pool of interested talent and attracting little public notice.

officially authorized. A good study of cross-cultural issues is found in *ATS: Theological Education*, Supplement 1, 1990, "Fundamental Issues in Globalization." Mark Kline Taylor and Gary J. Bekker's paper, "Engaging the Other in the Global Village," provides seven helpful models for cross-cultural relationship including the three close to the three used here, the "universal," the "ecclesial," and the "political."

25. John Bennett notes this significant difference between the NCC of the 1950s, with its widely respected expert panels, and the NCC of the 1980s, scrambling for allies. John Howard Yoder is more critical of the NCC, seeing it simply as a clearinghouse of like-minded bureaucrats. Their remarks are among comments (Jan. 15, 1979) by a number of informed church leaders in Tracy Early, "The State of the Council," *Christianity and Crisis* (Dec. 11, 1978). Ten years later, *Christianity and Crisis* (Jan. 9, 1989) featured articles by William McKinney and Linda-Marie Delloff on the NCC, which again elicited a set of informed comments.

WCC: Retains more of a stable of lay and clergy experts in various areas of perennial debate, working in some technical areas but not on many country-specific issues. For example, the WCC's ability to assimilate First, Second, and Third World technical materials for all three parts of its program on JPIC has been widely questioned.[26] Of all the WCC constituency groups efforts to interpret that triad, so far the process (not program) seems most inadequate from the point of view of women.[27]

Exemplifying Viable, Church-Related Alternatives to Society's Practices

NCC: Assuming that the mainline churches and the ecumenical bodies themselves are not constituted on a "believer's church" basis, the examples intended here are on a smaller scale — alternative communities, social relations, programs, and enterprises that with God's help "make and keep life human." While "viability" may seem a concession to the world's terms, I think it reflects accurately the way an institution like the NCC, struggling for viability, is discounted if it cannot practice what it would preach. Reaching into the churches, however, can yield

26. Alan Geyer's report on the JPIC consultation in Seoul, March 1990, notes its poor organization and complains that East-West peace issues get short shrift. A perennial scientific contributor, Charles Birch, suggests two good meanings for Integrity of Creation, relating to the interdependence and intrinsic value of all species in "The Scientific-Environmental Crisis," *Ecumenical Review* 40, no. 2 (April 1988): 191-92, although he sees the creation side largely ignored. Certainly the preparatory "Letter of Faith" on JPIC, "A Covenant for Life," seems more substantial than the laundry-list style "Now is the Time: Final Document and Other Texts," coming out of the Seoul World Convocation. One of the leaders of the JPIC process, Jan Love, provides a remarkably self-critical assessment in *Ecumenical Review* 43, no. 2 (Jan. 1991).

27. In "JPIC: a Critique from a Feminist Perspective," the late Jane Cary Peck and Jeanne Gallo point to the weakness in conception so far, and suggest the thinking to be done in relating the exploitation, objectification, and violation of women to that of nature. They underline the concerns of women for "right relationship" and "embodiment" that affect the relation of justice and creation, and the impact of more equal participation of women on peace and militarization issues. Elsewhere in that issue of *Ecumenical Review* 41, no. 4 (Oct. 1989), dedicated to "Issues of Justice, Peace and the Integrity of Creation," creative work on the theme is done by George Tinker and Harvey Sindima, and Ronald Preston points to the work left undone on "Participatory" and "Sustainable" from a previous WCC triad. To my mind, the work of cosmologists and others on the theology of nature and creation theology should receive a growing hearing; the relation of women and nature has been less examined from a theological perspective, and this would have a bearing on the nature of gender relations that (still) pose questions for the churches.

many good examples that would be enhanced through publicity and reinforcement. For example, advocates of genetic diversity in plants — related to the integrity of creation — might be strengthened with findings from the high-altitude seed farm run by the Ghost Ranch Presbyterian conference center in New Mexico.

WCC: Some WCC units communicate examples and stories better than others (Urban Rural Mission comes to mind), but most do provide a forum in which to share the actual practices of churches with other churches. Some programs of the WCC also have high symbolic value: for example, the Programme to Combat Racism (PCR) is a valued sign of antiapartheid solidarity in Africa, even if it has received controversial treatment in the West.[28] In terms of global relationships, the WARC and the LWF provide models of the application of moral sanctions in their suspension of member churches that do not repudiate apartheid. The concept of *status confessionis,* so explicitly a matter of faith, might have analogues in the areas of setting and enforcing global human rights standards. At the same time, Ulrich Duchrow's proposal to make global capitalism a matter of *status confessionis* has been largely rejected as unworkable.[29] The example of the Ecumenical Development Cooperative Society (EDCS), a Third World development bank linked to the WCC, has considerably more power as a church-based alternative, especially in a global debt crisis that continues to grind Third World economies.[30]

Nor can one ignore the witness made in the churches' own life by its treatment of women, both lay and ordained. Although Roman Catholic efforts at a pastoral letter on women recently foundered, a WCC (or NCC) statement might be more difficult than expected, and not simply because of the Eastern Orthodox viewpoint.

28. A recent study of the PCR is Zolile Mbali, *The Churches and Racism: A Black South African Perspective* (London: SCM, 1987).

29. See Ronald Preston's review of Duchrow, *Global Economy: A Confessional Issue for the Churches?* (Geneva: WCC, 1986) in *Ecumenical Review* 40, no. 2 (April 1988): 279-86, and that by H. B. de Lange and B. Goudzwaard, ibid., pp. 293-94.

30. The Uppsala Assembly began the organization of the Ecumenical Development Cooperative Society (EDCS), a creative economic enterprise designed to (1) loan money to poor communities neglected by conventional banks and development projects, (2) provide an investment vehicle for church endowment monies to assist in this grass-roots economic empowerment, and (3) provide a viable model of an organization able to do this without being itself dependent on the grant/aid model. Though this is still a small venture relative to need and total amount of First World church investments, I see it as a good example of the kind of church-linked transformative enterprises or alternatives the ecumenical movement should develop.

Changes in WCC Social Ethics and Witness Strategy

The WCC developed a number of remarkably creative and durable concepts with which to challenge Western societies and the divided world over which they have had great influence. Progressive and neoconservative interpreters differ on how adequate the council's attention has been to the responsibilities of poorer nations and regions for their own self-development, and on the degree that freedom and democratic change can or should be prerequisites for East-West cooperation. Here we review some of the leading concepts and corresponding roles of the church.

Chief interpreters of the WCC's social thought agree that its genesis lies in the Life and Work Conference of 1937, which asserted the priority of social ends over economic means. J. H. Oldham, chief organizer of that Oxford gathering and its still-impressive study literature, developed the concept of "the responsible society," irreducible to either capitalism or socialism, which was explicitly carried into the work of the Third Section of the 1948 Amsterdam Assembly. The church needs critical distance from the society around it and must beware of embracing even victorious ideologies, while rejecting nostalgic fixation on a civilization that, Reinhold Niebuhr noted in addressing the 1948 Assembly, "was never Christian in achievement."

Labor and capital needed to cooperate, and enlightened societies needed to establish ground rules for their productive interaction. At the same time, it was clear that power needed to be balanced, and the social ethic involved needed to recognize the group selfishness of unions and business corporations. Did the WCC go easier on labor in its analysis? Did the church itself escape scrutiny for its labor or employment practices? Certainly the WCC's work cannot be compared to that of the NCC's series on Economics and Ethics under Cameron Hall's guidance, although that series did little exploring of the international situation. For those nations on the way to industrialization, the WCC favored the organization of unions and what would now be called workers' rights, and offered some encouragement for indigenous strategies of economic development. The emphasis on "human development" was an effort to broaden the understanding of economic growth.[31]

31. In some contrast to the work of Thomas S. Derr noted above (n. 5), John C. Bennett provides overviews of ecumenical economic thought in *The Radical Imperative:*

In the mid-1950s, after Evanston, Paul Abrecht supervised the production of a series on the Church and Changing Societies. The economic element here encouraged the growing initiative of the "Two-Thirds" world in establishing its priorities and determining its destiny in a "responsible world society." The study examined the economic concomitants of the decolonialization process, and the responsibilities of the churches in nation building. This role, at least for churches in the emerging economies, was less independent than the role of churches in more industrialized economies.

In the 1960s, the preparatory materials for the Geneva conference on Church and Society reflect the shift from "changing" to "revolutionary" societies. Social and economic inequities were so serious that nothing short of revolutionary reversal was needed. The technologists of development were challenged, but the conceptual alternatives leaned toward political solutions and dialogue with Marxist alternatives. Although the Geneva conference was explicitly designed to speak *to* rather than *for* the churches, the public role of the First World, Western, or now Northern church was to affirm the alternatives to business as usual in their societies and in the international economic order. A New International Economic Order (NIEO) was beginning to take conceptual form, with its repudiation of debt, improved terms of trade, domestic import substitution, etc. The shift discussed at economic consultations in Beirut and Montreal was from aid to trade, although the churches' own programs continued to be mainly in the aid category.

The Uppsala Assembly began to put a number of the ideas of the Geneva Conference into institutional form. The Commission of the Churches on Participation in Development (CCPD) and the PCR are well-known additions to the WCC's own structure, and EDCS, the Third World development banking cooperative, less well known. Sodepax (1968–75) was a venturesome joint project of the Council and the Roman Catholic Church that hosted the conference in 1970 at which Gustavo Gutierrez first proposed the shift from development

---

From Theology to Social Ethics (Philadelphia: Westminster, 1975), and in "Protestantism and Corporations," in *The Judeo-Christian Vision and the Modern Corporation*, ed. Oliver Williams and John Houck (Notre Dame: Univ. of Notre Dame Press, 1982). David A. Krueger relates ecumenical economic ethics to the thought of major Protestant theologians in "Capitalism, Christianity and Economic Ethics: An Illustrative Survey of Twentieth Century Protestant Social Ethics," in *Christianity and Capitalism*, ed. Bruce Grelle and David Krueger (Chicago: CSSR, 1986).

to liberation. Though obviously frustrated in its broader ecumenical vision, Sodepax proposed alternatives to the "development apocalypse," and necessarily included some treatment of ecclesiological issues.

At Nairobi in 1975, the WCC took a major step to link its economic witness with its ecclesiological self-understanding. Although not directly related to the Faith and Order stream within the council that would soon originate the Baptism, Eucharist, and Ministry document at the Lima Conference, the concept of a "church of the poor" developed by CCPD under the leadership of Julio de Santa Ana was affirmed by the assembly and led to widespread debate on the nature of the church in both poor and rich countries. This was a fairly explicit embrace of the ecclesiology of the theology of liberation, with a strong emphasis on solidarity, dispossession, and the rights of self-determination. I think the council was careful to avoid much use of Marxian categories or "metaphysics of collective ownership," as shown in a fine collection of background papers, *Separation Without Hope?* (1978) that provides the church an understanding of its own history (or lack of it) with the poor and modern industrial and economic forces.[32] Nairobi also authorized a study program on transnational corporations, which produced a series of small books generally critical of their unaccountable power and limited vision, especially in the Third World.[33] It should be noted that the 1979 MIT Conference on Faith, Science and the Future represented the traditional concerns of Church and Society even during this period, although contrasting views on the church's role were expressed there.

Richard Dickenson's fine review of the recent debates over the church of the poor, *Poor, Yet Making Many Rich,* notes that those who emphasize dependency may put undue responsibility on the rich nations for internal societal disorganization and oppression, while those who encourage others to pull themselves up sometimes seem to "blame the victim." Part of the JPSS concept (a just, participating,

32. I would note especially the initial essay by André Bieler covering Christian understandings of social and economic problems in the late eighteenth and nineteenth centuries, a very important history he treats more fully in *Chrétiens et socialistes avant Marx* (Geneva: Labor et Fides, 1982). The more policy-shaping book, edited by Julio de Santa Ana, was *Towards a Church of the Poor: The Work of an Ecumenical Group on the Church and the Poor* (Geneva: WCC, 1979).

33. See the summary volume, *Churches and the Transnational Corporations: An Ecumenical Programme,* ed. Marcos Arruda (1983).

and sustainable society), when applied to the development debate, was to emphasize the distinctiveness of each national or regional economy and the limits of imported models, despite the homogenizing nature of global economic forces.[34]

The WCC's public witness changed and ecclesiological issues became more explicit when, in Edward L. Long's terms, "the protest against oppression broadened" in the 1970s and 1980s.[35] The narrative up to Nairobi is one of increasing Third World participation: by the time of Vancouver's less-focused gathering in 1983, the agendas are multiple and we come to the analysis represented by Paul Abrecht in the second section of this chapter. Certainly environmental concern gained at the assembly, and concerns for international peace were well represented. The Community of Women and Men within the Church, leading up to the Sheffield conference, won some acceptance, in principle, of equal participation by women, but women's numbers and roles remained an area of tension at Vancouver and at the 1991 Canberra Assembly. In areas relating to representation of women, youth, and others, the WCC's leadership needs to weigh carefully how prophetic or challenging an intrachurch posture it may adopt.

The Canberra Assembly's contribution was modest. Little from the Seoul convocation on JPIC was actually acted upon, although ecumenical participation in an Earth Summit was authorized and could be fruitful. The preoccupation of much of the gathering with the Gulf War revealed a general trend toward pacifism among delegates, though this was not formally endorsed. The relation of the council to indigenous peoples and religions in Australia attracted attention and prompted more theological reflection than some similar elements (including a totem-pole raising) at Vancouver.

34. Dickenson is quite perceptive in identifying the threats to the traditions and selfhood of other nations posed by the cultural forces of TV, film, music, and marketing from the North. These forces replicate modernity and disenchantment with a vengeance. If not an acid bath, this exposure is at least an automated carwash for which a local culture's windows should be rolled up, even if its wheels remained locked on the forward conveyor. Looking at the Marxian framework of much Latin American liberation theology from an Asian angle, Aloysius Pieris criticizes it for neglecting the distinctive spirituality of poverty, which he associates with the need for renunciation and dispossession. See his *Asian Theology of Liberation* (Maryknoll, N.Y.: Orbis, 1987). Hyun-Kyung Chung, in her work noted above (n. 6), picks up on this point.

35. See Edward L. Long, "Christian Ethics as Responses to Social Conditions," in *Altered Landscapes*, pp. 305-6.

Public Witness in a Reorganized National Council of Churches

Rather than examine in a strictly chronological way the public witness of the National Council of Churches of Christ in the U.S.A. (NCC), this section will focus on three council operations most necessary for public witness: the Division of Church and Society (DCS; now: Prophetic Justice), the Washington Office, and the Division of Studies and Planning (now vestigial, but representative of a needed function). Certainly other parts of the council structure are also part of its public witness, such as the overseas area offices in the preparation of statements on international affairs. But until the early 1980s, the international affairs office was part of the DCS. Now it and the human rights office are part of the Church World Service and Witness unit, which also has its own presence in Washington.

This functional approach to the NCC is due partly to the significance of its shrinkage and turmoil during the late 1980s, including the resignation of a president (James Armstrong, 1985) and a general secretary (Arie Brouwer, 1989). The reality of declining finances and struggles over centralization and relations to member communions is a far cry from the confident, establishment organization begun in 1950, able to resist McCarthyism, support internationalism, and muster support for an impressive Interchurch Center in Manhattan. The reorganizations of the NCC in 1972 and in the late 1980s have now become a significant part of the history of the council, but our focus is on the council's capacity for future witness.[36]

In the "second sixties" and the 1970s, the DCS and sponsored-related movements linked to it initiated and encouraged a range of influential witness efforts. Working first for the passage of landmark civil rights legislation through an emergency Commission on Religion and Race, and then after 1968 in a major "Crisis in the Nation"

36. A brief history produced by the council itself on its fortieth anniversary, "Sketches From the Journey," by Sarah J. Vilankulu, is helpful in providing an overview. A good digest of the early 1980s reconceptualization is contained in *Journal of Ecumenical Studies* 22, no. 2 (Spring 1985). A more strategic review of the NCC's learnings during the 1980s is contained in Arie R. Brouwer's address to the 1987 Governing Board meeting, "Eight Essential Elements of Ecumenical Credibility," repr. in *Ecumenical Review* 40, no. 1 (Jan. 1988): 79-86. The tensions between Brouwer and Richard Butler, director of Church World Service, leading to both their resignations, show tragic misjudgments and weak leadership in the member communions. From a public witness point of view, it may have looked as if ecumenical "revolutionaries" were eating their children.

program, the NCC played a key role in support of greater racial justice. In conjunction with the efforts of the National Committee of Black Churchmen (NCBC) and the campaigns of the Southern Christian Leadership Conference, the DCS coordinated member-church participation in and support for the civil rights movement. The Delta Ministry in Mississippi was given strong support. Black church leaders within the NCC and mainline denominations helped make the concept of "black power" more understandable and more influential to the white community. The National Black Economic Development Conference, which sponsored the call for reparations in 1969, was partly encouraged by the Inter-religious Foundation for Community Organization (IFCO), at that time lodged in the DCS. Although the reparations controversy and its reverberations raised hackles in some quarters, the mainline churches did contribute approximately $20 million to minority economic development operations and, more importantly, took steps to recruit and advance blacks within their own administrative structures. At the same time, particularly after the occupation of certain churches and church offices, the NCC distanced itself from the strategies and leadership of the reparations effort, which lost momentum within a year.

In the 1970s, the DCS continued its racial justice commitment, including advocacy for women of color, and also housed offices for an ecumenical minority bail fund, a domestic hunger and poverty effort, an energy and environment program, an international affairs component (concentrating on Vietnam, and then on nuclear arms), and the Corporate Information Center (CIC), which began in the same offices that earlier housed the Study Commission on the Church and Economic Life. In 1974 the CIC became part of the Interfaith Center on Corporate Responsibility (ICCR), a sponsored-related movement that has now become almost totally independent.

Notable efforts of the 1970s included support for the antiwar movement (beginning in 1965), with a targeting of church military investments, advocacy for selective conscientious objection, and a top-level panel on U.S. war crimes in Indochina. There was a very strong energy statement (in 1979), in many ways more coherent (and more antinuclear) than that of the WCC. This policy statement on "Ethical Implications of Energy Production and Use," developed in a five-year study process cochaired by Margaret Mead and René Dubos, had the visibility and specialist knowledge for significant impact, and the program produced many items (e.g., on energy conservation) for internal church benefit. This program was opening onto a range of environmental concerns in the early 1980s but was not adequately staffed from 1985 to 1991, after its organizing staff person died, leaving the initiative to grass-roots groups.[37] The NCC and Union Theological Seminary also cosponsored a "Task Force on the Future of Mankind and the Role of the Christian Churches in a World of Science-Based Technology," which brought together creative thinkers and produced two influential books, *To Love or To Perish* and *To Create a Different Future.*[38]

The DCS staff organized collaborative support for the development of hunger programs in some denominations to address development failures abroad and at home, and coordinated advocacy for the Equal Rights Amendment, for pay equity, and for women in ministry. The well-respected work of the religious liberties office continued throughout this period, sparking internal debate at one point over efforts to counter official Roman Catholic involvement in court cases on abortion rights. That office early recognized the dangers of "governmental intervention in religious affairs" and worked creatively across the whole religious spectrum to address the threat.[39]

Questions about the leadership of the DCS came to the fore in the late 1970s and early 1980s in relation to the participation of IFCO in the defense of blacks and others apparently targeted by racist public authorities. Though a close account of the transition is beyond the scope of this overview, leadership on some racial justice issues was shifted to a small "fifth commission" on Justice, Liberation and Human Fulfillment (later, Justice and Liberation), and IFCO was removed from direct sponsorship by the council.

37. The Eco-Justice Project, developed by Cornell campus minister William Gibson, publishes a quarterly journal, *The Egg,* which is cosponsored by the NCC Eco-Justice Working Group. The energy study included a book, *Energy Ethics,* ed. Dieter Hessel (New York: Friendship, 1979), as well as a succinct policy statement and energy study resource packet.

38. See *To Love or To Perish,* ed. J. Edward Carothers, Margaret Mead, Daniel D. McCracken, and Roger Shinn (New York: Friendship, 1972); and *To Create a Different Future,* ed. Kenneth Vaux (New York: Friendship, 1972). A third book, Norman Faramelli, *Technethics: Christian Mission in an Age of Technology* (New York: Friendship, 1971), received less attention. This joint NCC-UTS venture built on an earlier study by the NCC, *Human Values and Advancing Technology: A New Agenda for the Church in Mission* (New York: Friendship, 1967), which was compiled by the longtime director of the Department of the Church and Economic Life, Cameron P. Hall.

39. This church-state emphasis contrasted strongly with the ACLU's near-exclusive effort to eradicate all religious symbolism or activity on governmental property.

The current leadership for church and society work has been considerably more cautious. Throughout the 1980s the DCS sometimes seemed to be less than the sum of its parts. A new emphasis was added in the area of Child Advocacy, which encouraged and supported churches active in childcare as well. Certain efforts still captured public attention, such as the very effective campaign to end infant-formula marketing abuses (the Nestlé Boycott and pressure on U.S. manufacturers), which was coordinated by the ICCR. Although that effort, which gained widespread public and denominational support, was owned by the NCC, as was ICCR's focus on South Africa, other divestment, boycott, and union-related efforts were kept at arm's length.

Increasingly in the 1980s, right-wing critics focused on indirect NCC and member-church involvement in various progressive campaigns or organizations, often putting NCC leadership in a reactive posture to defend its positions and associations. Would better leadership have owned more of these efforts directly, taken the lead in framing the issues in public debate, or forged a clearer strategy or set of positions? In the reorganization of 1988–89, the DCS was renamed the Unit on Prophetic Justice. Racial justice remains a major concern, along with efforts to be devoted to issues of JPIC. Certainly the number of combined portfolios will mean less ability to initiate plans and to produce substantive materials — a councilwide problem.

The second arm of public witness, the Washington Office, was designed to represent the position of the Governing (now, the General) Board, and not to be a lobbying agency similar to those of the denominations. Though in the past some desired a kind of official Protestant outpost on issues that would directly concern churches to facilitate expression of as unified a voice as possible, this office has been criticized as being in a holding pattern since the early '80s. In part, this criticism reflects the broader reality that mainline churches have been on the losing side in many recent policy debates. Though certain issue-coordinating functions have been performed and a newsletter produced, the office's staff has been heavily involved in internal council affairs in New York. During the 1980s, few NCC staff had significant access to the nation's executive branch, and denominational staff have organized and participated in a wide variety of specialized organizations, often in coalitions with non-Christian groups that are not members of the councils. Many of these issue- or region-focused groups have performed brilliantly, and without the lag time and moderation that ecumenical coordination might have involved. At the same time, the unified Christian witness represented by the NCC in the past — and performed in relation to public opinion and the appeal to the faith and self-understanding of individuals — has been lacking. This lack helped leave the ecumenical organizations open to broadsides from right-wing organizations, prompting further distrust and retrenchment.

Without a thematic self-understanding, much less an orchestrated concept of the day,[40] the NCC Washington Office was reduced to serving as little more than a functionary to the denominations. While many do not want the church's major leaders to be involved in overly specific policy statements, the NCC's idea of Governing Board representation might have guided the churches to involve their recognizable leaders in major public debates, assuming that the churches have recognizable leaders — whether official clergy or laypersons of acknowledged expertise and public credibility. Yet the personnel appointments and budgets of most denominations have indicated that they do not wish to compete with lobbies and political action committees that use celebrities and power brokers, people who can attract media attention and get access. The churches, then, utilize networks of specialized constituencies to make a social policy witness, sometimes with influence commensurate with their knowledge (e.g., on hunger, or Korea policy), but more often in fairly powerless opposition.[41] An effective strategy must back the aggressive policy work of countless little centers and coalitions with the broader appeals to public and Christian opinion.

It is a mistake to think that the churches and the NCC's witness in Washington is weak by necessity. The desire not to play with any Washington insiders, or with the imperial realm's coins, is a matter of choice or of political location. Even the strategies available to an oppositional minority seem underused, and in a government environment of widespread confusion and lack of leadership, it is not clear that the positions of the churches need be so unknown or given little weight. Real prophets, like the leaders of the Sanctuary Movement, could have

40. The enormously effective daily coordination of government press relations during the Reagan period has been analyzed by Mark Hertsgaard in *On Bended Knee* (New York: Atheneum, 1988). It suggests the need for a coordinated church strategy with clearly repeated goals.

41. The role of the specialized bodies disproves, to a large degree, the contention of Paul Ramsey and others that the churches should not be too specific.

been given more support, leveraging their symbolic power. Denominational staffers can still call on advisory boards with "name" figures of credibility and clout, heavy hitters who would not be on the church's payroll. The NCC's communication staff could learn something from Washington's progressive public relations firms, though the Roman Catholic bishops' efforts on abortion show that hired guns sometimes backfire. Educational efforts and seminars, such as that of a single congregation, the Chevy Chase Presbyterian Church, show that access and serious dialogue can be developed using constituency at multiple levels. And the chief ecumenical think tank of Washington, the Churches' Center for Theology and Public Policy (CCTPP), shows the value of intellectual throw weight in a think-tank environment.[42]

This last enterprise points up the lack of significant study and research capacity in the redesigned NCC. Certainly the NCC's Office of Research, Evaluation and Planning was never large, nor as proportionately important as the study function in the WCC. But the track record of this office was good: the indispensable *Yearbook of American and Canadian Churches* is still produced, important studies of evangelicalism and televangelism were published, and staff took a leadership role in the Religious Research Association and in working with denominational and interfaith counterparts on the future of religion in American society. Some of the most generally informative articles from the *Review of Religious Research* are reprinted in the *Yearbook*.

Alan Geyer, former director of the CCTPP, argues for a strong continued research function in an essay, "A Ten-Part Dream for the NCC." For Geyer, it is not simply that Washington (and New York) is a think-tank environment; we live in "what has become a think-tank society. The manipulation of social data, the rewriting of political history, and the generation of public myths and dogmas are increasingly the distinctive functions of think tanks, too many of which are appendages to special economic interests." The NCC needs a capacity for "serious research" in order to be a player in this context, which is not possible "through a proliferation of ad hoc committees and short-term task forces — many of which have pleaded for help from the Center for Theology and Public Policy."[43] This problem reflects the

42. The center has in the past produced helpful short studies of debated public issues in its Shalom Paper series, and since fall 1989 has been publishing a new ecumenical journal, *Theology and Public Policy.*

43. Alan Geyer, "A Ten Part Dream for the NCC," *Christianity and Crisis* (March 3, 1983): 83. The other nine elements here would also be very helpful.

lack of significant involvement by laity with specialized knowledge in development of church social thought and witness. This vacuum tends to be filled by further moves toward "actionism" with whatever program monies are available to the council.

The prospect for NCC public witness looks daunting, in the light of this brief overview of the Church and Society or Prophetic Justice Unit and Washington Office. The two successful policies celebrated at the 1990 Governing Board meeting, those on Child Care (a domestic issue) and the Middle East, are indeed fine pieces of work and have been influential, even beyond specialist circles. Yet both of these are in need of broader ownership within the churches (not simply duplication in denominational dress), and both will need updating by financially weakened departments. Further, while NCC staff turnover will provide some opportunity for new directions, denominational representatives are often drawn from the same group of denominational staff and other insiders long involved with the NCC — new constituencies are needed.[44] It also remains to be seen whether the NCC's international affairs and human rights offices will be able to continue to broaden church support for their efforts for more foreign policy morality and less militarism. This emphasis requires more strategies of education, solidarity work, and field visits beyond specific campaigns.

Right-Wing Criticism of the Two Ecumenical Bodies

Most informed churchgoers are aware of the attacks on the councils in 1983 by *Reader's Digest* and the "60 Minutes" television program. They are also aware of the repetitive nature of some of this criticism, going back to the Federal Council and, early in the NCC's history, to the efforts of J. Howard Pew and other conservative business figures to silence the NCC's public voice. Although the more recent period of the late 1970s and early 1980s differed from the earlier periods due to the role of neoconservatives and to the greater political involvement of right-wing Christian televangelists, the hard-line business base and fundamentalist theological animation of the critics are fairly constant. The neoconservatives generally maintained the nationalist anticom-

44. The loyalty and tenacity of many ecumenical and denominational staff members is praiseworthy, especially through years of attrition.

munism of the traditional right, adding to it a particular animus against affirmative action and feminism, and a strategy for dividing the leadership of the mainline churches.[45] The televangelists, long at home attributing personal corruption to liberal social ideas and vice versa, focused more strongly on abortion and homosexuality than the neoconservatives, but added civic corruption to their scripts. They were also more concerned to split off part of the Democratic party than simply to neutralize the mainline churches.

In fact, the right-wing criticism of the councils in the United States follows debates in secular politics fairly closely, and is stimulated in part by the churches entering those debates. While the media effectiveness of the right wing in the Reagan period heightened the impact of their critiques far beyond that of the ecumenical bodies' initial activities, their criticism of the councils remained reactive as well as reactionary. In *Who Speaks for the Church?* (a book directed at the 1966 Conference on Church and Society), Paul Ramsey first sounded many themes. He challenged the overly specific nature of some pronouncements and policy statements, but he also challenged the movement toward corporate witness by the churches — deliberating and acting as corporate bodies — speaking "for" as well as speaking "to," although the Geneva Conference (and the WCC generally) specified that it spoke "to" the churches.[46] Considerable argument was also generated by assertions that this and later books had a subtext of discomfort over the allegedly disproportionate number of Third World and minority delegates at ecumenical conferences. This trend did begin with that conference's substantial Third World (developing nation) contingent — well represented in Chair M. M. Thomas of India and others in the WCC's "curia" — though the criticisms of

45. Some have seen considerable resentment at work in the positions of neoconservative leaders, who may have had or hoped for greater leadership roles in the mainline bodies, were it not for liberal and liberation trends. The spirit, then, would be "rule or ruin." The neoconservatives were often close to Jewish neoconservatives and to the position of Israel, among the positions leading to the May 1990 split between Richard Neuhaus and his more traditional Rockford Institute patrons. See Richard Bernstein, "Magazine Dispute Reflects Rift on U.S. Right," *New York Times*, May 8, 1990, p. 1. The contributor lists to magazines edited by Neuhaus or Michael Novak remain the most convenient ways to chart the influence of neoconservativism in the churches (as *Commentary* is in Judaism), though of course not all contributors fit this designation.

46. Paul Ramsey, *Who Speaks for the Church?* (Nashville: Abingdon, 1967). John C. Bennett, "The Geneva Conference of 1966 as a Climactic Event," *Ecumenical Review* 37, no. 1 (Jan. 1985): 27-28, stresses that the "speaking to" function was quite clear then.

Vietnam and neocolonialism were later amplified in the statements of U.S. churches themselves.

The authority and legitimacy of ecumenical church pronouncements have been challenged through a number of techniques: using poll results against selected policies (showing a purported lack of democracy); challenging decision-making processes as well as individual and collective leadership styles (alleging lack of participation); claiming disproportionate influence by overseas or minority persons; and decrying faceless, insensitive, out-of-touch bureaucracies.[47] With glee, conservatives have lifted up embarrassing fund recipients or allies, claiming to find "Marxists marching under the banner of Christ," although such discoveries showed the church institutions to be less than monolithic. Actual polling of church members and ministers, such as that of the *Presbyterian Panel*, shows some polarization on the edges of the religiopolitical spectrum, but no overwhelming right-wing majority.[48]

Although probably the larger proportion of right-wing criticism has focused on the foreign policy positions of the councils — particularly the WCC's sometimes muted criticism of Eastern bloc and revolutionary nations — the effectiveness of this justified or unjustified wolf crying relates to more mundane factors. Sociologist Dean Hoge has argued that family, career, and white middle-class standard of living are the primary factors in mainline church membership, elements that I have argued any public witness strategy must address. In *Division in the Protestant House*, Hoge found that fear of communism, social action, and, in the Presbyterian Church, of Angela Davis had little impact on membership or giving.[49] Thus whatever the claims of *From Amsterdam to Nairobi* by Edward Norman or *From Mainline to Sideline* by K. Lloyd Billingsley regarding a left-wing tilt toward atheistic and terroristic regimes, most church members would react based on anxieties closer to home.[50]

47. An early effort critical of bureaucratic operations in the denominations — including mergers and the 1960s and 1970s locations of offices in New York — was Paul Mickey and Robert Wilson, *What New Creation? The Agony of Church Restructure* (Nashville: Abingdon, 1976).

48. See Dean R. Hoge, *Division in the Protestant House* (Philadelphia: Westminster, 1976), particularly pp. 77ff. for an analysis of *Presbyterian Panel* data and its relation to the public/private Protestant split identified by Martin Marty and David Moberg. Wade Clark Roof and William McKinney analyze more recent data in their *American Mainline Religion* (New Brunswick: Rutgers Univ. Press, 1987).

49. Ibid.

50. The two volumes cited are published in this country by the Ethics and Public

Some conservative criticisms are shared in part by those supportive of the councils, as I have suggested above. The charge of "actionism" seems to have actually begun among WCC staff who became uncomfortable during the transition to programs of various "action-reflection" kinds begun under General Secretary Eugene Carson Blake. They felt that such programs jeopardized the council's theological emphasis, and perhaps its unity.

There are certainly some social questions, especially involving women, feminist reinterpretation, and the status of the Universal Fellowship of Metropolitan Community Churches for the NCC, where unity or entente between churches has resulted in variable standards, strengthening conservative hands and perhaps limiting the progress of the whole. So long as the church's right and responsibility to speak are not circumscribed by the demands of national security or establishment powers, however, it seems wrong to put reasoned criticisms of particular council actions in the same category as the broadsides and caricatures coming from the neoconservative camp.[51] Edward L. Long's point that right-wing political conservatism "in its own way" shares the goal of "transformation of society in accord with God's will" should also be noted.[52]

Given the continuities in conservative criticism of the councils, the larger question is whether a "middle" must be reconstructed for the public voice of the councils to have influence among the churches and in the larger public. My argument would be that a strong conciliar voice — to challenge parochialism and xenophobic elements, to reconceive nationalism, and to revive a vision of the common good — is necessary to help recreate in theology, economics, and politics the middle that has indeed been eroded. In *Reconstructing the Common Good: Theology and the Social Order* (1990), Gary Dorrien argues that, like the middle class, the mainline churches are "schools of ambiguity, containing nearly the entire range of class interests and ideologies that exist in liberal societies," threatened by both growing inequality and

---

Policy Center, a neoconservative think tank headed by a one-time NCC study participant, Ernest Lefever, whose nomination to be Assistant Secretary of State for Human Rights was defeated in part by the NCC's efforts.

51. It is primarily the subordination of religion to a public purpose defined outside the church that prompts Martin M. McLaughlin to place A. James Reichley's *Religion in American Public Life* in the neoconservative camp; see "Agents or Instruments?" *Christianity and Crisis* (March 17, 1986): 94-95.

52. Long, "Christian Ethics," in *Altered Landscapes*, p. 309.

the rising demands of people of color, and experiencing a tension between pluralism or tolerance and moral coherence. For him, "the way out of this circle is to take the liberationist option seriously."[53]

But here we must put in perspective the experience of the NCC and WCC, to the extent that they have tried to do just that. Are these bodies, as the conservative opponents wish, headed on a collision course with their remaining constituency? Or is there an option for the NCC's public witness to help restore its purpose and viability? My answers are no and yes, respectively. My immediate response to Dorrien is that for his strategy to work, an embrace of the various liberation options by the ecumenical bodies and their member churches has to involve precisely the kind of inclusion of traditional ecumenical Christian and democratic concerns that his historical work reflects.

Witness in a Post-Public Society

If the councils' public witness on human rights, equitable development, nonviolent conflict resolution, and other matters has basically been on target, it would be unfair simply to blame them for ineffective communication or strategy, a "blame the church first" approach. A wide range of other egalitarian and public-minded organizations, even parties, have certainly not been doing very well either.[54] What points of contact do the public churches have with other mediating struc-

53. Gary J. Dorrien, *Reconstructing the Common Good: Theology and the Social Order* (Maryknoll, N.Y.: Orbis, 1990), p. 174. Dorrien is also a strong critic of Marxian elements in liberation theology, arguing in this and his earlier work, *The Democratic Socialist Vision* (Totowa: Rowman & Littlefield, 1986), that "To make concrete social gains in the political contexts of the first world, the Left needs to appropriate the religious tradition of socialism represented by Rauschenbusch, Temple, Tillich and others, which has insisted that the moral and political language of rights must be applied to the economic order" (p. 12). Dorrien's effort to restore the tradition of Christian socialism in the United States creatively connects the social gospel, socialist politics from Thomas to Harrington, European political theology, and liberation theology by emphasizing their democratic and decentralized elements, leaving his project only confirmed by the democratic revival in Eastern Europe.

54. One can point to the defeat of Jimmy Carter as the symbolic repudiation of values closer to those of the churches, or one can look at the surprising success of Jesse Jackson as a sign that more progressive values can attract substantial support. As for those not involved in the political system as voters (a limited avenue for activity in any event), Alan Geyer's "Political Ministry," *Christianity and Crisis,* describes the anarchy, alienation, and powerlessness, even in Congress.

tures or spheres of discourse in the larger society? This is not simply a problem of audience for the mainline churches and ecumenical organizations. In the present context, groups do not earn a hearing — they buy a hearing from an increasingly alienated and depoliticized American populace. The churches' lack of fit with a recognizable public says a lot about problems within the culture, not just within the churches.

A number of theorists have mourned the end of a public sphere in contemporary culture, differing as to the cultural, psychological, economic, and political reasons for the privatism or individualism they decry.[55] Gregory Baum sums up the situation in noting that "contemporary culture undermines all forms of social solidarity."[56] In this context, the institutional problems of the NCC and WCC should perhaps not be taken as indications of a fundamental disestablishment, because it is hard to argue for a coherent establishment, beyond certain network audiences and product markets. However fractious the divisions of WCC and NCC and contrasting theological approaches may appear, the community of discourse within does allow for some public claims and arguments before an even more divided society. A certain unity also appears in contrast to the culturally limited conservative understanding of the church's public responsibilities.

Space does not permit prescription here, beyond the argument that the unified, four-part approach would not only strengthen public witness but provide some reinforcement for the community of Christians represented by both ecumenical bodies. My rather retrospective view of the WCC's witness, and the more prospective view of the NCC's, both emphasize the internal, institutional factors over the

55. This position is expressed by Richard Sennett in *The Fall of Public Man* (1974), which charts the rise of psychological man and the process of having more and more of the valued elements of life take place in private. Christopher Lasch's *Culture of Narcissism* provides another view of the problem. Lasch's analysis of the current inability to make serious and compassionate commitments withstands much of Paul Wachtel's criticism in *The Poverty of Affluence* that he neglects the influence of economic inequality and consumerism on American character. Robert Bellah and colleagues have also joined the criticism of an overly privatized society searching for community; their analysis is reminiscent of studies made by Donald W. Shriver, Jr., in *Is There Hope for the City?* One of the Bellah collaborators, William Sullivan, offers a solid philosophical analysis of the problem in *Reconstructing Public Philosophy,* focusing on the weaknesses of liberalism as currently understood.

56. Gregory Baum, "The State of the Council," *Christianity and Crisis* (Feb. 6, 1989): 11.

environmental factors in the effectiveness of their public witness. Even given the institutional church decline noted in the second section above, the NCC and WCC still seem to have the potential to rally support for their positions — if these bodies pick the right fights for good reasons, and pay attention to their friends. Further, the more diversity the ecumenical movement can handle creatively, the more public space it should be able to influence — wherever this diversity of humanity is located.

The Church and the Political Order: The Role of the Catholic Bishops in the United States

J. Bryan Hehir

The objective of this chapter is to examine the role of the Catholic bishops in the political order during the 1980s. The argument will move in three steps: (1) a review of which issues the bishops addressed and how they addressed them; (2) an examination, in the light of the bishops' experience, of the distinct role of the local, or regional, church in social ministry; and (3) a prognosis of what the sociopolitical agenda of the 1990s will be.

The Bishops in the 1980s: The Issues and Their Method

A *New York Times* Sunday magazine cover story in August 1984 was entitled "America's Activist Bishops." Depending upon the reader's theological and political orientation, the title was either an indictment or a compliment.

More important than how the title was perceived was the pattern of sustained public engagement by the Catholic bishops of the United States that generated the story and title. Before examining that history, I need to make two fundamental disclaimers for this essay. First, it is not an analysis of the Catholic *Church* and the political order; to propose it as such would be a fundamental theological mistake (the bishops are part of the church, not its embodiment) and a basic moral mistake (the views of the bishops on the issues reviewed here do not always and necessarily bind the consciences of the Catholic community — dissent is both legitimate and likely). Second, the focus on the national activity of the bishops through the U.S. Catholic Conference (USCC) in the 1980s is not meant to imply that prior to this decade the bishops were either absent on social issues or less effective in pressing the social agenda. The history of the National Catholic Welfare Conference from 1919 to 1967 and the USCC from 1968 on would belie such a notion. The 1980s are used in this paper as a case study in a wider pattern of social witness.

With these limits, it is now possible to look at the issues of the 1980s, and the questions the bishops had to face when they engaged the issues.

The Issues of the 1980s

From 1980 through 1989 the Catholic bishops of the United States were visibly and vocally engaged in public debate about four major questions: the moral and legal status of abortion; the morality of nuclear strategy; the justice of economic policy and practice in the United States; and the content and consequences of U.S. policy in Central America.

Each issue had a distinct history and public advocacy was pursued by diverse means.[1] The bishops had been involved in the abortion question since the 1973 *Roe v. Wade* decision of the Supreme Court; they had a prior history of addressing both peace and economic questions, but raised the level and method of engagement in the pastoral letters of the 1980s; and they entered the Central America debate in 1979-80 as U.S. engagement in the region increased significantly.

While each of the issues was irreducibly different, a similar pattern of engagement could be found in the bishops' activity. In each case they drew upon a distinct part of Catholic social or moral teaching, and then brought the issue in question under public analysis. The bishops used the mechanism of the USCC to produce a variety of forums of commentary and teaching documents: pastoral letters, statements and resolutions, congressional testimony, and legislative activity were all part of a broad pattern of public advocacy.

The position on abortion was set forth in the 1970s and sustained through the 1980s. It drew upon both Catholic moral teaching and social philosophy based on a natural law jurisprudence.[2] On moral

1. For journalistic accounts of the engagement of the bishops in the 1980s, cf. J. Castelli, *The Bishops and the Mob* (New York: Image, 1983); E. Kennedy, *Reimagining American Catholicism* (New York: Vintage, 1985).

2. For a sampling of statements, cf. National Conference of Catholic Bishops (NCCB), *Documentation on Abortion and the Right to Life II* (Washington, D.C.: U.S. Catholic Conference, 1976).

grounds the bishops have opposed all directly intended abortions, and on legal grounds they have advocated the reversal of the Roe decision of the Supreme Court. The moral-legal position and the public strategy supporting it have been "classically Catholic" not only in their jurisprudential foundations but also in their ecclesiological grounding. Faced with a political and legal challenge to a deeply held religious and moral teaching on abortion, the bishops responded with a "church-type" strategy. In Troeltschian terms, they refused to adopt sectarian tactics. Rather than concentrate their efforts solely on the community of the church, they took their case simultaneously into the ecclesial community and the civil community. They sought both to shape the conscience of the faithful and to reshape the constitutional order of the society as a whole. To the dismay of friendly political critics like Gov. Mario Cuomo and friendly theological critics like Stanley Hauerwas, the bishops refused to focus exclusively on the consciences and decisions of church members. They were determined to address the social system as well as personal conscience. By 1989 they had not fully succeeded at either level, but they were clearly the most significant institutional voice in the public arena opposing the principles and the consequences of the 1973 Supreme Court decision.

The surprising feature to many in the 1980s was the equally visible role of the episcopal conference in the three other issues. Critics of the bishops tried to depict them as "one issue" advocates, but that was increasingly difficult to sustain in the light of the public record.[3] For example, *The Challenge of Peace,* the pastoral letter on the nuclear question, propelled the bishops into a major church-state controversy with the Reagan administration — the most openly antiabortion presidency since the 1973 decision. James Reston described the Second Draft of the nuclear letter as "an astonishing challenge to the power of the state."[4]

The substance of the moral challenge had, like the abortion debate,

3. The public record included the two pastoral letters on social issues and a string of congressional testimonies on Central America; cf. NCCB, *The Challenge of Peace: God's Promise and Our Response* (Washington, D.C.: U.S. Catholic Conference, 1983); NCCB, *Economic Justice For All: Pastoral Letter on Catholic Social Teaching and the U.S. Economy* (Washington, D.C.: U.S. Catholic Conference, 1986); also, K. Briggs, "Catholic Bishops Oppose Administration on Central America," *New York Times,* Feb. 21, 1982.

4. J. Reston, "Church, State and Bomb," *New York Times,* Oct. 27, 1982.

a "classically Catholic" character. While the "just-war ethic" was not exclusively Catholic property, it had been most consistently cultivated in the church's teaching. The policy section of the peace pastoral involved testing the range of nuclear questions — from use through deterrence to arms control — in the light of just-war criteria. The results of the testing were conclusions that placed radically restrictive limits on use and a narrow "conditional acceptance" of deterrence.[5]

Both the "just-war" history of Catholicism and its "church-type" style of public advocacy added to the force of these moral restrictions on policy. Because the tradition legitimated some use of force by the state, the prohibitions on nuclear weapons could not be regarded as rooted in an absolutist position insensitive to the requirements of just defense. Because the church-type advocacy challenged both the substance of policy and the situations faced by personal conscience, the positions of the pastoral letter established two distinct kinds of restraint on the state. Writing two days after Reston's comment, Steven Rosenfeld said of the bishops: "Their logic and passion have taken them to the very foundation of American security policy. And they are doing so on a basis — a moral basis that admits of little compromise once you accept it."[6]

It was undoubtedly the case that the positions held by the Reagan administration on both military and economic policy sharpened the public awareness of the bishops' positions. The dominance of the president — at least until the Iran-contra revelations — left few public institutions capable of raising a substantial challenge. Both the moral content of the bishops' arguments and the traditional conception of Catholicism as a conservative political force enhanced public awareness of the positions the bishops advocated.

In *Economic Justice for All,* the pastoral on the economy, the bishops used traditional Catholic teaching on the moral responsibility of the state, on the imperatives of distributive justice, and on the international obligations of wealthy nations to fashion a broad critique of Reaganomics in its domestic and international dimensions.[7] In the face of a "New Deal/Great Society" policy, the critique would still have been viable but not perceived as such a frontal attack on existing practice.

5. *The Challenge of Peace,* #186.
6. S. Rosenfeld, "The Bishops and the Bomb," *Washington Post,* Oct. 29, 1982.
7. *Economic Justice for All,* cited, ##136-292.

The bishops' address to Central American policy had actually begun as a critique of the Carter policy toward El Salvador in 1980. The letter of Archbishop Romero to Mr. Carter asking for a cut off U.S. military aid, the subsequent assassination of Romero, and the murder of the four women missionaries in December 1980 catalyzed a church response on Central America that extended far beyond the bishops, but built upon their frequent policy statements and congressional testimonies from 1980 through 1986. While the heart of their policy critique was cast in moral terms of social justice, human rights, and nonintervention, the added characteristic provided by the Central America engagement was the ecclesial ties between the U.S. bishops and the church in Central America. This ecclesial solidarity, the sense that the criticism offered of U.S. policy by the U.S. bishops was rooted in advice and insight from the local church in Central America, gave the bishops' position a distinctive role in the wider U.S. policy debate.[8]

Often the episcopal position, on any of the four issues, would overlap with standard secular commentary, invoking ethical analysis used by others and empirical data commonly available in the policy debate. Yet there was never any doubt that the four positions espoused by the bishops were the voice and views of a church convinced of its public role. The scope of the issues addressed and response generated — pro and con — by the episcopal voices compelled the bishops to go beyond their chosen issues and justify how they saw their public role.

The Method

The justification of a public role for the church required a response to three questions: the constitutional question (whether the church should be in the public arena), the theological question (why the church enters the public debate), and the pastoral question (how a public church should engage social and political issues).

1. The *constitutional question* is usually posed in terms of "the separation of church and state." Strictly speaking, the "separation

8. Cf. M. Crehan, "International Aspects of the Role of the Catholic Church in Central America," in *Central America: International Dimensions of the Crisis,* ed. R. E. Feinberg (New York: Holmes and Meier, 1982), pp. 213-35.

clause" is not found in the First Amendment, but the idea of "separation" has served to structure the understanding of the role of the church in the political process.

In the face of "activism" by the largest single religious denomination in the country, the constitutional question inevitably arises. Is such activism appropriate legally and politically? When faced with this question the U.S. bishops have responded with a blend of Catholic theology and American political theory. Their response to the constitutional question involves three steps.

First, a working definition of the political meaning of the First Amendment is needed; essentially it says that religious organizations should expect neither favoritism nor discrimination in the exercise of their civil or religious responsibilities. It is important to stress that the separation clause is meant to protect against both favoritism and discrimination. There is little or no indication in law, history, or policy that silencing the religious voices of the nation was the intent of the First Amendment. Given this definition of the meaning of separation, the Catholic response is to agree with it.

Such agreement was much easier to achieve in the 1980s than it would have been prior to the Second Vatican Council. It was precisely the achievement of Vatican II's *Declaration on Religious Liberty* to replace the normative status of "the Catholic state" with the principle that all the church expects from the political authority in society is the freedom to fulfill its ministry. The argument of the conciliar document that led to this conclusion brought the church to accept religious pluralism as the context of its ministry (i.e., not something simply to resist but a challenge to work with), to accept the constitutional or limited state as the best safeguard of political liberty, and to accept freedom as the principle of political organization that is most conducive to protecting the basic rights of the person. Each of these points had a disputed history in Catholic theology, and the acceptance of them as part of the conciliar declaration constituted a major theoretical development in Catholic theology.[9] In practical terms the conciliar text supports the bishops' acceptance of the separation clause; acceptance is possible because the church should expect freedom, not favoritism, in the public arena.

Second, the acceptance of the separation of church and state is

9. Cf. J. C. Murray, "The Problem of Religious Freedom," *Theological Studies* 25 (1964): 503-75.

to be understood — politically and theologically — in the light of the distinction between society and the state. Accepting the separation of church and state should not be understood to mean accepting the separation of the church from society. The church-state relationship is a crucial but narrowly defined question; it governs the juridical relationship of the institution of the church to the institution of the state. But beyond this relationship are a whole range of issues governing the church's presence in the wider society. The activity of the bishops on the four issues of the 1980s was directed at policies set by the state, but the forum for the episcopal voice was the wider civil society in which established channels exist for democratic expression of views by individuals and groups.

Third, in the wider society the church fulfills the role of a voluntary association. Voluntary associations are central features of a democratic polity; they exist to provide a buffer between the state and the citizen, and they also provide structured organizations that have the capacity to influence the polity and policies of society. Voluntary associations encompass professional, cultural, and labor organizations; they bring different contributions to the public arena usually linked to the specific issues that interest them. The church brings a systematic capability to raise and address the moral dimensions of public issues, and it also brings the capability to engage the members of its constituency in public discussion about these issues. In its engagement with the four issues of the 1980s, the USCC sought to fulfill this dual role of a religious actor in the public arena.

2. The *theological question* asks, What is the basis in Catholic teaching for an activist social role? The bishops' response to this question is crucial; failure to establish the theological legitimacy of their public activity can undercut them in the church and in society. For this reason, the bishops have responded in some detail to the theological question. Their response has essentially been to describe the activity of the episcopal conference as an extension and application of the social teaching of the universal church. This theme is found in both of the pastoral letters and in major addresses of the presidents of the episcopal conference over the last several years.

In Catholic teaching, the foundation of the social ministry is the religious conviction about the dignity of the human person. The reason why the church addresses issues of a political or social significance is to protect and promote the transcendent dignity of the person. The pivotal text on this theme is found in Vatican II's document, the *Pastoral Constitution on the Church in the Modern World:*

> The role and competence of the church being what it is, she must in no way be confused with the political community, nor bound to any political system. For she is at once a sign and safeguard of the transcendence of the person.[10]

The decisive contribution of Vatican II to the social ministry of the church was to locate defense of the person, and — by extension — the protection and promotion of human rights, at the center of the church's life and work.

The quote from the Council, however, highlights the persistent tension in the church's social ministry. It is to maintain the transcendence of the church from any particular political system, and yet to engage the church in issues directly affected by the political process. The *Pastoral Constitution* has been the fundamental reference point for the universal church in keeping the balance of an engaged public ministry without compromising the church's religious origin, nature, and destiny. The key texts are paragraphs 40-42 in the *Pastoral Constitution,* which affirm the following principles:

a. The ministry of the church is religious in origin and purpose; the church has no specifically political charism.

b. The religious ministry has as its primary objective serving the reign of God — the church is, in a unique way, the "instrument" of the kingdom in history.

c. As the church pursues its religious ministry it should contribute to four objectives that have direct social and political consequences: protecting human dignity, promoting human rights, cultivating the unity of the human family, and contributing a sense of meaning to every aspect of human activity.

These three principles define a role for the church in the world that is religious in nature and finality, but politically significant in its consequences. The mode of the church's engagement in the political arena is indirect. Since the church has no specifically political charism, its proper competence is to address the moral and religious significance of political questions. This indirect address to political issues also sets limits on the means the church should use in pursuing its four designated goals. Means that are expected and legiti-

10. Vatican II, *Gaudium et Spes* (1965), #76.

mate for properly political entities are not necessarily legitimate for the church.

The casuistry of keeping the church's engagement in the political order indirect involves an endless series of choices and distinctions. But the effort must be made precisely because the alternatives to an indirect engagement are equally unacceptable: either a politicized church or a church in retreat from human affairs. The first erodes the transcendence of the gospel; the second betrays the incarnational dimension of Christian faith. The bishops are engaged in the public arena on the basis of this activist but indirect understanding of public ministry.

3. The *pastoral question* asks how the bishops should fulfill this indirect role vis-à-vis the community of the church and civil society.

A case can be made that the pastoral style of the U.S. bishops on social issues has been "democratic" in its process and its product. This democratic style has been most evident in the preparation of the pastoral letters, but it has applicability in analogous fashion to all four of the issues addressed in the 1980s.

The process of the pastorals involved not only the hearing of witnesses but also the circulation of drafts for public commentary. Those who have followed this process know the significant impact such commentary had. This process should not be taken as an indication that the bishops were conducting an opinion poll. The core of these pastoral letters was a normative doctrine that is in place; the commentary related much more to the persuasive quality by which the moral doctrine was conveyed, the quality of the empirical analysis in the letters, and the wisdom of the policy recommendations.

The affirmation of this democratic component in a Catholic teaching document must be carefully described. The bishops themselves distinguished different levels of religious authority within the same pastoral. This differentiation allowed them to protect the status of binding general moral principles, but also to make specific moral choices without expecting the entire community of the church to be bound by the concrete policy options proposed in the letters. The fact that the bishops endorsed a given option ("No First Use" of nuclear weapons, job training programs, a constitutional amendment on abortion) gave it visibility and a certain weight in the public debate, but the very specificity of the choice guaranteed and invited debate within the church and the society. The democratic component of the process is a reflection of several characteristics of the *Pastoral Constitution:* the effort to respect empirical analysis and to abide by the laws and procedures of secular disciplines, the desire to elicit the voice of the laity on secular questions, and the willingness of the church to continue the dialogue with the world begun at Vatican II.

While I argued above that the democratic process could be analogously applied to all four issues, it needs to be explicitly admitted that the bishops do not provide much endorsement of a democratic component in their advocacy about abortion. But it should be pointed out that the distinction between moral principles and policy applications can be used in this area also. The moral position ruling out all directly intended abortion is clearly taught as binding Catholics in conscience. The policy proposal for reversing the Supreme Court decision (i.e., a constitutional amendment) flows coherently from the moral principle, but it cannot be invested with the same authority as the principle. Here too the specificity of means chosen guarantees and invites debate within the civil and ecclesial communities.

The product of the bishops' proposals is democratic in the sense that they are designed as a contribution to democratic debate within society. The specific purpose of the bishops is to create space for the moral factor in the wider political argument. The bishops believe, in the style of the *Pastoral Constitution,* that they have something to learn from the world and something to teach the world. Although they enter the specifics of policy debate often, the bishops cannot expect that their policy choices will finish the debate. The specific choices of the bishops call others into the moral argument. In this way the moral dimensions of the policy debate are given more visibility, more time and space by the press and policymakers, and, they hope, more weight in the determination of policy.

This democratic style makes the bishops actors in the democratic process. Their initial arena of influence is their own community, but the projection of both principles and policy choices in the public arena gives their ideas public currency. By using a democratic style they purposefully enter the world of public opinion. The church's role in a democracy provides it an opportunity to join a teaching role within the church to a different mode of witness in the wider public. Public opinion does not dictate public policy. But it does set a framework — establishing limits, giving weight to key values or issues — within which policy choices are made. By shaping public opinion it is possible to influence the direction of policy without necessarily dictating policy choices. On all four issues of the 1980s the bishops — with varying degrees of success — fulfilled this function.

The Local Church and the Public Order: Definition and Debate

The primary instrumentality that the bishops used to address the issues of the 1980s was the episcopal conference. The role of the episcopal conference in the social ministry may be seen as a response to two actions of the wider church. First, the decree of Vatican II, *Christus Dominus,* which gave episcopal conferences canonical status, in effect enhanced the role and position of the already existing National Catholic Welfare Conference, an agency the U.S. bishops had used for four decades. Second, Paul VI's apostolic letter *Octogesima Adveniens* in 1971 explicitly invited the local ecclesial communities to become creative agents of social teaching and social ministry. The pope highlighted the indispensable role of the papacy in social teaching, and then he reflected upon its limits:

> In the face of such widely varying situations it is difficult for us to utter a unified message and to put forward a solution which has universal validity. Such is not our ambition, nor is it our mission. It is up to the Christian communities to analyze with objectivity the situation which is proper to their own country, to shed on it the light of the Gospel's unalterable words and to draw principles of reflection, norms of judgment and directives for action from the social teaching of the church.[11]

The phrase "Christian communities" is surely broader than the bishops, but it does not exclude them. The theme that runs through the conciliar text and the apostolic letter is the idea of the local church. Joseph Komonchak has made the point that the term "local church" is open to an analogous interpretation.[12] While the primary analogue is the diocese, it is not out of order to refer to the local church in a national setting. Nor is it distorting key ideas to see the episcopal conference of a country as one means of expressing a position of "the local church." This is particularly appropriate when applied to the

11. Paul VI, *Octogesima Adveniens* (1971), #4.

12. J. Komonchak, "Ministry and the Local Church," *Proceedings of the Catholic Theological Society of America* 36 (1981): 58.

U.S. episcopal conference, which has a history of public engagements reaching back at least seventy years.

Even with this historical record, however, the recent public advocacy of the U.S. bishops has provoked debates about the proper function, competence, and style of a local episcopal conference. Two events of the 1980s illustrate how the specific experience of the U.S. bishops pushed their episcopal style into the postconciliar debate about episcopal conferences. First, in the meeting held in January 1983 at the Vatican to discuss the draft of the peace pastoral, questions were raised about the *mandatum docendi* of an episcopal conference.[13] The tenor of the discussion, in which Cardinal Ratzinger was a significant voice, was to diminish or deny the idea of a *mandatum* for the episcopal conference. Second, at the time of the Extraordinary Synod in 1985, Bishop James Malone, president of the U.S. episcopal conference, made a vigorous intervention stressing the convictions of the U.S. bishops about the theological identity and pastoral utility of the episcopal conference.[14] At the conclusion of the Extraordinary Synod, Pope John Paul II identified the theme of the episcopal conference as one of two topics requiring particular study.

Both by word and action, therefore, the U.S. bishops have become key participants in the process of shaping an appropriate role for the local church as an agent of social ministry. I will comment on two questions that have arisen in the light of the activism of the U.S. hierarchy.

Status of Episcopal Conferences and Style of Teaching

The theological status of episcopal conferences is a question that has been in need of clarification since *Christus Dominus*. Like other issues in conciliar teaching, the action of the council opened a debate even as it made a decision. The theological status of an episcopal conference is a broader issue than its style of teaching, but the two are related and both surfaced in the Vatican consultation of 1983 on the peace pastoral.

In the United States no one has given more careful attention to these questions than Fr. Avery Dulles. Since I both agree with his fundamental approach and differ on some conclusions, I will use

13. J. Schotte, "Vatican Official's Report on Meeting to Discuss War and Peace Pastoral," *Origins* 12 (April 7, 1983): 692.

14. J. Malone, "The Intersection of Public Opinion and Public Policy," *Origins* 14 (Nov. 29, 1984): 388.

Dulles's contributions to comment on the topic of the status and teaching style of episcopal conferences.

Dulles's basic position is to affirm the theological status of episcopal conferences as an expression of the principle of collegiality:

> It is quite true that bishops' conferences are not directly mandated by divine law, but divine law gives the hierarchy the right and duty to establish structures that are found helpful for the exercise of their divinely given mission as individuals and in groups. Entities such as parishes and dioceses, in their present form, or for that matter the Roman Congregations, are not essential to the church as such, but they have real authority based on the divinely established order of the church. The same may be said for bishops' conferences.[15]

In response to the argument that episcopal conferences do not possess a *mandatum docendi,* Dulles points to the need and justification for a level of teaching situated between the individual bishops and the universal teaching authority of the pope and the full college of bishops.[16] He compares this role to the particular regional councils in an earlier period of the church's history, although he does not see an exact parallel with them. Rather, Dulles outlines a functional role for natural episcopal conferences that is pastoral in character and geographically specific in its focus:

> In view of its particular responsibility the conference, it would seem, will speak by preference on matters pertaining to faith and morals that are neither internal to a particular diocese nor common to the universal church.[17]

Dulles goes on to illustrate how, in his view, the U.S. bishops have fulfilled appropriately their teaching mandate as an episcopal conference. It is in the context of these very supportive remarks that Dulles comes to the one point where I would dissent from his position. In addressing the bishops' teaching on social issues, particularly in the pastoral letters, Dulles commends both the process of the pastoral letters and aspects of their teaching. He then raises two critical comments. First, that the letters became too specific, probably overstep-

15. A. Dulles, *The Reshaping of Catholicism: Current Challenges in the Theology of Church* (New York: Harper and Row, 1988), p. 212.

16. Ibid., pp. 215, 216.

17. Ibid., p. 222.

ping the legitimate role of the bishops and giving a partisan flavor to their teaching. Second, that the energy, emphasis, and visibility given by the bishops to the pastorals may "unwittingly give the impression that what is truly important in their eyes is not faith or holiness that leads to everlasting life but rather the structuring of human society to make the world more habitable."[18] Dulles grounds both of these reservations in his concern to protect the transcendence of the church.

Protecting this transcendence must be a constant element in the church's social teaching. I disagree with Dulles not on the objective but on the means required for it. First, his preference for episcopal teaching that is confined to principles may sacrifice the moral weight of the principles in broader policy debates. Principles offered without specification of where the principles lead in the complexity of public policy arguments can doom the principles to a marginal role: honored by all, but seldom followed. Second, Dulles's goal of drawing experienced laity more directly into the social ministry may never be realized if the bishops do not give high visibility and high priority to the issues of social justice, human rights, and peace, precisely as themes that are part of "faith and holiness."

Scope of Competence

The issues of the status and teaching style of episcopal conferences have a doctrinal character. I now turn to a more operational issue — the scope of activity open to a local episcopal conference. This theme has relevance throughout the church, but it has had specific significance for the U.S. bishops because of *where* they minister.

The impact of the policy and practices of the U.S. government and other institutions based in the United States on the lives and welfare of other nations and peoples creates a distinct challenge for the U.S. bishops in their social ministry. In brief, the church in the United States cannot confine its social ministry to domestic affairs.

This local church must address foreign policy issues for at least two reasons. First, recent papal and conciliar teaching has stressed the need to see the "social question" in its global or systemic dimensions.[19] Second, other local churches, themselves involved in protect-

18. Ibid., pp. 170-83, 223.

19. Paul VI, *Populorum Progressio* (1967), #3; John Paul II, *Sollicitudo Rei Socialis* (1987), #9.

ing human dignity and promoting human rights (e.g., in Poland, Lithuania, El Salvador, Chile, South Africa, and the Philippines), call upon the church in the United States when they become aware of U.S. ties to their government or possible influence the United States has with their government or with key international institutions (e.g., the World Bank or the International Monetary Fund).

Just as the degree of social involvement of these other local churches has increased since Vatican II, so the different ways in which the U.S. episcopal conference has had to address foreign policy issues has correlatively increased. The list of issues is extensive. In the 1970s the U.S. bishops took positions on human rights in Brazil and Chile, on the Panama Canal, on the issues of security and human rights in Korea, on the Zimbabwean civil war, and on the Middle East. In the 1980s, while the focus of attention was on Central America (El Salvador and Nicaragua), the bishops were also engaged in questions affecting the Philippines and Lebanon, and they issued major statements on human rights in the Soviet Union and Eastern Europe as well as on the Third World debt problem.

In almost all these cases there has been substantial consultation between the U.S. episcopal conference and the other episcopal conferences. This degree of foreign policy engagement by a local church and the method of bilateral episcopal coordination are both quite different from preconciliar styles of episcopal activity. Issues of international affairs were usually regarded as the sole concern of the Holy See, and bilateral coordination on issues of a political character was not encouraged. It should be noted that the Holy See's role, of course, remains unique in the diplomatic field, and that transnational episcopal cooperation is still regulated very carefully.

At the same time, there have been changes, most visibly illustrated by the human rights activity of the U.S. conference. When the emphasis on human rights in U.S. foreign policy was first initiated by the U.S. Congress, the USCC played an active role. Cardinal John Dearden testified at the hearings of the House Foreign Affairs subcommittee that drafted the human rights legislation and called for the creation of a Human Rights Office in the Department of State. When the Congress passed legislation that established human rights criteria for U.S. foreign aid — both military and economic aid — the USCC testified frequently on specific cases of human rights violations in Latin America, East Asia, and Eastern Europe.

The USCC has had to formulate criteria for determining when it should address a human rights issue. The general policy guidelines used are that three tests have to be met: (1) evidence from reliable sources that human rights abuses are occurring in a systematic pattern; (2) U.S. policy is related to the situation in a substantial fashion; and (3) the local church in the country has a position on the human rights issues, and some consultation will precede a U.S. bishops' statement.

These are stringent tests, but even they do not solve all problems. If division exists in the other local church (either within the hierarchy or within the wider ecclesial community), it may prevent the U.S. bishops from speaking lest they exacerbate the divisions. Even when all the conditions are met, at times it is not clear that an open public statement by the church here will positively affect the human rights situation in another country. It has been a process of experimentation, a continuous testing of both principles and prudential judgments for the U.S. episcopal conference, as it tries to fulfill a role of solidarity and support for other local churches.

The Agenda of the 1990s: More Change than Continuity

The four fundamental issues that the bishops addressed in the 1980s will continue into the 1990s, but on all four, significant shifts are occurring that will require a development in the bishops' position. Because of the activist record of the 1980s, the bishops are well positioned to contribute to the wider political debate, but each of their major positions will require modification and development to meet the fundamental political challenges of the 1990s. In this concluding section of the chapter, I will sketch those developments that mark the difference between the 1980s and 1990s.

Foreign Policy: The Superpowers Shift

Of all the areas of change between the last decade and this one, the foreign policy agenda has experienced the most profound alteration. The 1980s began with analysts describing a "new cold war" between the superpowers; the decade ended with a consensus that the cold war era was over.[20] The consensus was based upon changes within

20. Cf. S. Hoffmann, *Dead Ends: American Foreign Policy in the New Cold War* (Cambridge, Md.: Ballinger, 1983); M. Mandelbaum, "Ending the Cold War," *Foreign Affairs* 66 (1988): 16-36.

the Soviet Union, the collapse of communist rule in Eastern Europe, the movement toward a reunified Germany, and the effect of all these realities on U.S. foreign policy.

The change within the former Soviet Union is an ongoing process and its outcome is far from clear. But even at this stage the shift in Russian foreign policy toward "New Thinking" has had an effect, and its significance was noted in the United States by one of our foremost Soviet analysts, Prof. Seweryn Bialer of Columbia University:

> Far from being a breathing spell designed to facilitate improvements in Soviet economic performance, "New Thinking" represents an innovation as radical as *perestroika* and *glasnost* (openness). Moreover, "New Thinking" as a process of profound reassessment of the Soviet approach to international relations has only started. It holds the promise of further evolution and long-term change in Soviet international behaviour.[21]

The transformation of Eastern Europe in the last six months of 1989 was symbolically and substantively the sign that the cold war concepts could not sustain policy in the 1990s. While a plethora of political, economic, and security questions remain about the future of Eastern and Central Europe, the movement of these countries out of "the Soviet bloc" at the end of the cold war is irreversible. These changes will affect the two issues the U.S. bishops addressed in the 1980s, and they will open a third question for consideration.

The arms control agenda, a major focus in the *Challenge of Peace,* will be placed in a new setting and will take on new content. In the cold war, arms control was the principal barometer of U.S.-Soviet relations because the possibilities of political change seemed so remote. Because ongoing political hostility was the presumption of the superpower relationship, arms control became the hope for "stability," expressed in the classic concepts of crisis stability, arms race stability, and political stability. Stability was a major achievement under the conditions of the cold war, but it was also a minimalist goal. Its purpose was to avoid nuclear war. The post–cold war era opens the chance to go beyond stability, to recast the political fabric of superpower relations toward a "normal" interstate relationship. In this larger picture arms control will still remain central, particularly in

21. S. Bialer, "New Thinking and Soviet Foreign Policy," *Survival* (July/August 1988): 294.

reducing substantially the strategic arsenals of the superpowers, but arms control will fit within the wider political context.

Arms control must also include the new possibilities and the new problems of the 1990s. The opportunity and necessity to proceed with conventional arms control in Europe means that nuclear and conventional arms control must be carried forward together. The political changes in Central Europe have opened possibilities for conventional arms control (and misuse!) that have not existed for thirty years. We now face the larger, more complex, but very hopeful possibility of a European security system.

This optimistic possibility for the European theater must be placed alongside the more troubling arms control challenge of the 1990s: proliferation of nuclear and chemical weapons and ballistic missiles. The proliferation question moves arms control to the systemic level, encompassing a much greater diversity of political and strategic issues than the superpower relationship encompassed. Because the Nonproliferation Treaty must be renewed in 1995, and because the prospects for proliferation are growing, the 1990s will be a crucial decade for this dimension of arms control.

Neither the *Challenge of Peace* (1983) nor its companion document, the 1988 *Report,* provides an adequate policy framework to address the changed context and content of arms control. Both documents provide a foundation, but both stand in need of development, especially on the political and ethical issues of conventional arms control and proliferation.

The conflict in Central America is not rooted primarily in superpower politics; it has its own sources and its own dynamic. But changes in the superpower relationship will undoubtedly influence regional conflicts in the 1990s. Superpower involvement fueled the destructive capacities of regional actors, intensifying the stakes of local conflicts and adding to the arsenals of each side. Both the shift in superpower relations and the initiative of the Central American presidents have created — in spite of the continuing violence in El Salvador — the possibility of a regional diplomatic settlement. The USCC's objectives of the 1980s — preventing military intervention and protecting human rights — remain important, but are best achieved through pressing the United States to support fully and creatively a regional peace, to be followed by a commitment from the United States (and Europe?) to rebuild the devastated economies of Central America.

The third major area that changing superpower relations could influence is less a concrete problem than it is a possibility. The definition of the possibility is found in John Paul II's encyclical *Sollicitudo Rei Socialis* (1987), where he calls for a redefinition of East-West competition to provide the context for addressing the needs of the South.[22] This conception of joining the East-West security agenda to the North-South development agenda hardly has a place intellectually or politically in the U.S. foreign policy debate. The pope's call is just that — an invitation without a road map. In the 1990s, "the East" means something different than it did in the 1980s, and "the South" is a broad term encompassing very different realities, from South America to Sub-Saharan Africa.

The papal conception is fundamentally important, however, since it seeks to place the fate and future of the developing countries at the center of international politics. To get that kind of attention in the U.S. policy debate, the papal invitation must be pressed beyond its present content. Connecting the security agenda of the 1990s with the development agenda requires a different policy framework than the cold war has produced. The interest in the security debate in creating a "new order" opens the possibility for broadening the concept of order to include the papal linkage of security and development. The USCC has the elements of such a position but not an articulated policy vision as yet. It will take some formidable intellectual effort to make the security-development connection in the U.S. public discussion.

Domestic Policy: The Old and New Social Issues

The domestic policy efforts of the bishops in the 1980s were focused upon (although not exhausted by) the economic pastoral and the policies that flowed from it in the areas of employment, housing, health care, and civil rights. One way to illustrate the shifting context of the 1990s is to discuss the "old and new" social issues.

The "old issues" have roots in the New Deal era (economic opportunity and security for workers, the aged, and the disabled), in the civil rights movement of the 1960s (overcoming the fact and the consequences of racial discrimination — extended later to sexual discrimination), and in the Great Society programs (a systematic effort to overcome poverty in America). While each of these broad move-

22. *Sollicitudo Rei Socialis,* cited, ##20-24, 37-39.

ments has registered some success, it is clear that each area has a legacy of unfulfilled promises.

On the threshold of the 1990s many people express fears of a resurgence of racial discrimination and a continuing pattern of socioeconomic inequality between blacks and the rest of American society. In terms of economic security the crisis in health care cuts across racial and class lines with no systematic approach even close to claiming political majority support. Women and children remain the most vulnerable groups in society. These are the classical "social issues" that have been on the political agenda and in Catholic teaching for the last half-century. The United States moves into the final decade of this century with all of them visible and little political urgency for addressing them because of the stringent budget restraints faced by federal and state governments.

Yet the agenda for the 1990s, either for church or state, cannot be defined simply in terms of finding more creative approaches to these questions or new money for them. For the 1980s have brought into view two "new" social questions whose dimensions pose enormous competitive threats to the intellectual energy and political priority needed to address the "old" issues.

These new issues are drugs and AIDS. The first poses a systemic social threat — cutting across class and economic lines, found in suburban and urban schools, destroying families, careers, and lives, generating criminal violence that engulfs inner-city neighborhoods where the "old" issues are most persistently present. The second "new" issue touches a smaller percentage of the population, but it does so with deadly effect. It also constitutes a looming threat to the health care capacity and budgetary priorities of the city, state, and federal government. Caring for AIDS patients is both an extensive and a costly project.

My concern here is not to discuss the specifics of either the "old" or the "new" social issues, nor to exclude others such as the environmental crisis, but to focus upon the *intersection* of the two kinds of problems as the context for domestic social policy in the 1990s. The demand for resources from these two different social agendas is staggering. And the relative paucity of ideas on how to deal with either the old or new kinds of problems is as threatening as the lack of money.

The Life Issues: After Webster

Since 1973 the bishops have been persistent and consistent in their pastoral programs *(Respect Life)* and in their policy advocacy seeking to reverse the constitutional order supporting *Roe v. Wade*. In July 1989, the *Webster* decision of the Court, which permits states to place new restrictions on abortions, opened two significant possibilities.

First, it set the stage for political contests throughout the fifty states, taking advantage of the *Webster* ruling and proposing restrictions that go beyond *Webster* and could be tested in future decisions by the Court. Second, the *Webster* decision reflected a very divided Supreme Court, with at least four justices who seem prepared to impose other restrictions on abortion, up to and including the reversal of *Roe v. Wade*.

The bishops will face both new opportunities and new challenges in a post-*Webster* world. Voting in 1989 and 1990 in some states and in Congress indicated that the *Webster* decision will not provide any automatic legislative victories. On the eve of the Supreme Court's decision in July 1989, a *New York Times* poll found the country deeply divided over the abortion issue: 49 percent supporting *Roe v. Wade;* 39 percent favoring legal restrictions on abortion in all cases save rape, incest, and a threat to the life of the mother; and 9 percent supporting legal prohibition of all abortions.[23]

A democracy that is effectively divided 49-48 percent after sixteen years of public debate is in a delicate — perhaps dangerous — position. Democratic polity lives by debate and by the effort of groups to persuade the public of the wisdom and rectitude of a policy. But democracy also requires consensus on key questions, particularly questions where people are divided on moral issues rather than the empirical dimensions of a problem. A 49-48 percent split does not provide sufficient consensus to support law and public policy over the long term.

The delicacy of the political situation is no reason, of course, for those opposing abortion to withdraw from the contest. But the failure of either side to build a stable majority points to the need for a review of the arguments made and the overarching vision proposed to the public in the name of opposing abortion. The essential moral argument against abortion will not change. But the post-*Webster* political

23. E. J. Dionne, Jr., "Poll on Abortion Finds the Nation Is Sharply Divided," *New York Times*, April 26, 1989, p. A-1.

struggle may provide the setting for examining how the specific moral conclusion is framed and presented as part of a larger and wider concern for protecting and promoting life.

This, of course, has been the effort of the "Consistent Ethic" proposal, first advocated by Cardinal Bernardin and then incorporated into the bishops' pro-life advocacy.[24] The need of the 1990s, I believe, is to continue advocacy of the "Consistent Ethic," but to recognize that more rigorous work is required to fill out the content of this proposal in convincing terms. The rationale for pressing the "Consistent Ethic" involves two dimensions. First, it is an attempt to overcome the stalemate in public opinion by moving the argument to a higher level — not moving away from the opposition to abortion but seeking to relate the fact of abortion to other decisions about protecting human life. Second, the 1990s will likely see an expansion of the debate about how life should be cared for at its beginning and its end. The recent court cases abut treatment of terminally ill patients and the advocacy of "death with dignity" promise a new chapter in pro-life and pro-choice debate. There will undoubtedly be more attempts to provide legal support for action that the Catholic tradition would judge to be euthanasia. This wider pro-life challenge will require the kind of broad framework provided by the "Consistent Ethic" position.

The activist role of the U.S. bishops in the 1980s provides a foundation for the fundamental issues of the 1990s, but the new decade will require more than continuity with the past. At the level of both principle and prudential judgment new tests are ahead.

24. J. Bernardin, *Consistent Ethic of Life* (Kansas City, Mo.: Sheed and Ward, 1988).

Religious Bodies, Workers, and the U.S. Economy

Ron Stief

The U.S. economy is undergoing a profound transition, as important possibly as that now underway in the former Soviet Union. Close to two million jobs in manufacturing (the traditional base for the U.S. economy) were lost forever in the 1980s, on the heels of estimated job changeovers in manufacturing that go as high as thirty million in the 1970s. The low-wage service industry that replaced most of these jobs now employs over 70 percent of the U.S. workforce, according to the U.S. Department of Labor. Some analysts are predicting that companies in the service sector are poised to go through a cycle of "trimming down," internationalizing, and layoffs similar to that which devastated U.S. manufacturing.

Workers who endured one round of layoffs, job searches, and wage cuts as the service economy replaced manufacturing in the 1970s and 1980s are facing a new round in the 1990s. It is doubtful that the U.S. economy can withstand the pressures of further wage reductions; what will be left for U.S. workers, besides record levels of unemployment and underemployment, is not entirely clear to anyone right now. One thing we do know is that unions, the organizations that have historically provided wage and health protections, are at a post–World War II low. In a flurry of anti-union legislation, questionable business practices, and record levels of debt, the policies of the U.S. government and corporations have driven membership in unions to below 16 percent of the work force. In 1945, 35.5 percent of all workers belonged to unions.

The religious community in the United States was quite vocal in raising a voice of protest over plant closures and the dislocation of workers in the 1970s. By the 1980s, at least seventeen major statements from the religious bodies of U.S. denominations placed the religious community on the side of justice for workers. While church commitment to economic justice organizing in the light of these statements was always less than it could have been, an "option for the poor" and a desire to stand in solidarity with workers reemerged as key working principles for the churches in this period. *Economic Justice for All,* the 1986 pastoral letter of the U.S. Catholic Conference of Bishops, was the most widely read of these statements, and it gives good sense of the theological commitments of the church in the light of these documents:

> As a community of believers, we know that our faith is tested by the quality of justice among us, that we can best measure our life together by how the poor and the vulnerable are treated. This is not a new concern. It is as old as the Hebrew prophets, as compelling as the Sermon on the Mount. . . . As bishops, we see too much hunger and injustice, too much suffering and despair, both in our country and around the world.[1]

To evaluate the recent attempts of denominational leaders to educate and motivate their church members to work for economic justice, it is important to understand some of the history of how the religious community in the United States, and primarily the church, has articulated its concern for workers. For, despite all the fanfare of these recent religious statements and the occasional high-visibility, religious-based organizing drive on behalf of workers, the church has little evidence that society is better off now than it was in 1980. On the contrary, the policies of free market capitalism, enhanced by supply-side economics, went virtually unchecked in effecting the most massive redistribution of wealth in this century. This was all at the expense of working Americans (many now unemployed) and future workers, who on the day they are born each now owe tens of thousands of dollars on the federal deficit.

Where in this century has the religious community tried to develop a rationale to stand in solidarity with workers? What were some of the questions and the rationale employed? At which junctures did the religious community attempt to be more effective in advocating for workers? Where were inroads made in articulating a position that the economy is a human creation and a reformable system of values, and as such, subject to legitimate ethical considerations?

1. National Catholic Conference of Bishops, *Economic Justice for All,* Pastoral Letter on Catholic Social Teaching and the U.S. Economy, 1986, p. viii.

Industry and the Social Gospel: 1890–1930s

Much of the framework that is still used today to describe how working people and the religious community can stand together to promote economic justice was established between 1890 and 1930. In this period, organized labor and working people fought specific struggles for many of the benefits that we now take for granted, including a national minimum wage, legal and corporate recognition of collective bargaining rights, programs for social security and unemployment compensation, laws restricting child labor, work rules on hours and safety, and health and welfare protection.

At the beginning of this period, workers were literally in a struggle for their lives as U.S. companies broke strike after strike with violence. In the steel industry, the backbone of the industrial expansion at the turn of the century, workers fought long and hard for gains, only to have them constantly taken away. For example, between 1860 and 1890, U.S. steel production increased from 12,000 net tons to 4,800,000 net tons per year. The Mellons, Carnegies, and other industrialists were realizing unheard-of profits, and the union that represented the skilled steelworkers was the strongest in its day. But with a wave of immigration making cheaper labor available, and the constant desire for more, the Andrew Carnegie Homestead Pennsylvania plant was shut down in 1893, and then — with the help of Pinkerton guards, state militia, and the federal government — was reopened with nonunion labor and new technologies.[2]

This pattern was repeated several times in the industry and continued through the 1920s, as the industrial capitalists attempted forcibly to destroy any inroads made by union organizing and the majority working-class movement that battled to benefit from the wealth created in the industrial expansion.[3] In general, this was the story across steel, automobile, textile, and other core industries that drew millions of workers only to exploit their labor for higher profits.

Thus, while many found opportunity throughout the Industrial Revolution of the nineteenth century, it was equally a time of tremendous dislocation and misery. If, in all the celebration over the

2. Robert Cherry, *Discrimination: Its Economic Impact on Blacks, Women, and Jews* (Lexington, Mass.: Lexington Books, 1989), pp. 52-53.

3. Harvey Wasserman, *History of the United States* (New York: Four Walls Eight Windows Press, 1972, 1988), pp. 135-50.

decline of socialism, one can still quote Marx (a seminal thinker who influenced both the church and workers at this time), it helps to illumine the situation. For it is not easy, as many have done, to write off the Rockefellers and the Jay Goulds, the rail barons and the steel magnates, as evil humans who out of greed and disregard for human life exploited workers. No, the root of the problem was economic, in urging the capitalist system itself toward undreamed-of opportunities for massive profits with the new combination of labor and technologies and the consequent increase in production. In describing the lure of profit in explaining his theory of surplus labor in the context of the African American worker in the South, Marx put his finger on the problem posed by export-led production in the United States and in the economies driven by the developing world:

> Hence the negro [*sic*] labour in the Southern States [of the U.S.] preserved something of a patriarchal character, so long as production was chiefly directed to immediate local consumption. But in proportion, as the export of cotton became of vital interest to these states, the over-working of the negro and sometimes the using up of his life in 7 years of labour became a factor in a calculated and calculating system. It was no longer a question of obtaining from him a certain quantity of useful products. It was now a question of production of surplus-labour itself.[4]

As we can surmise from the situation of the black Southern worker in slavery or later in the nineteenth century, once the labor of the worker was reduced to a formula in the profit-making scheme that stood at the core of the industrial expansion, and new technologies added periodically to the mix, an ethical crisis developed that demanded both restraints and the kinds of checks and balances that could be offered only by unions, the government, and religious and other third-sector institutions. Like many others, Sheila Collins characterizes this as a period of rapid transition that permanently reshaped the economic landscape and the social relationships of this country:

> By the time it [the Industrial Revolution] was over, it had transformed every human relationship, as well as the relation between human beings and the natural order. The dichotomy between public

4. Karl Marx, "The Greed for Surplus Labour," in *The Marx Engels Reader,* ed. Robert C. Tucker, 2nd ed. (New York: W. W. Norton, 1978), p. 365.

> and private, workers and owners, grew. The racial and gender segmentation of labor, the secularization of society, the commodification of everyday life, the emergence of trade unions, the professionalization of functions formerly performed by the family, the separation of knowledge from execution, and the instrumentalization of nature . . . changed the economic patterns that had sustained people for centuries.[5]

In short, the rules for human subsistence and economic relations were being rewritten. At stake were the structure and mission of the entire polis, as power vacuums were created and then filled, as political spaces were opened and then closed. The role of workers in forming the Congress of Industrial Unions and the American Federation of Labor, and historic organizing drives in the mines and the fields as well as in industry are well known. Many excellent histories tell stories of personal heroism and worker commitment to the common good through principles like: "An injury to one is an injury to all."

The religious community was affected by this ferment. Protestant and Catholic industrial missions cropped up to respond to the economic changes — in particular the dislocation of workers. Groups like the Workingmen's Department of the Presbyterian Church, established by Charles Stelzle in 1903, were very active organizers within the churches. Due to the work of Stelzle, the Federal Council of Churches issued a Social Creed in 1908 that would be the basis for organizing church members around labor and work issues.[6] The Federal Council of Churches and denominational efforts to help organize workers added the necessary moral dimension, and arguments were made that human security should be a higher priority than the corporate profits that drove the assembly lines of the industrial manufacturing sector.

Against all odds, church organizers and theologians sought to make their voices heard through the Protestant-led social gospel movement as Protestant pastors, Catholic priests, and active laypersons charted a new course for a theology of justice in the workplace.

5. Sheila Collins, "The Post-Industrial Revolution: Its Implications for Our Jobs, Income and Security," *CALC Reports, Special Issue on Religious Values and Economic Justice*, CALC, PO Box 1987, Decatur, GA 30031.

6. Presbyterian Church (U.S.A.), *Challenges in the Workplace*, Task Force on Issues of Vocation and Problems of Work in the United States, 1990, p. 66.

Christian Socialists and utopian communal movements were articulating and living out a new politics and society based on more egalitarian distribution of power and resources. The reformers were not afraid of politics. In 1886 Father Edward McGlynn of New York endorsed "single taxer" Henry George for mayor of New York and was excommunicated when he refused to travel to Rome to explain his actions. George D. Herron, a preacher and theologian who achieved public visibility in the Christian Socialist movement, was chosen to nominate Eugene Debs for president in 1904. In 1919, Catholic visionary John Ryan applied Christian ethics to the economic order and sought to expand the church's role in arguing for the regulation of public utilities, antimonopoly laws, a national employment agency to guarantee full employment to returning war veterans, and participation of labor in management decisions.[7]

These voices were desperately needed as a counterbalance to the tremendous power that was exercised at the time by the U.S. companies. Even though the buzzwords like "the American century" and "the Roaring Twenties" are how most of us are taught to remember this time, for working people the misery of insufficient wages and the humiliation of the growing gap between the rich and the poor were more accurate descriptions of this forty-year period. At the core of the struggle to get the churches to join more actively with the worker-led campaigns for justice was a theological debate that raged in church halls and in public over how to stand in solidarity with the working class and its growing union movement.

The social gospel movement was a major effort of theologians and laypersons to look out for the interests of the workers and the poor. But since its roots were largely Protestant, it is important to realize that it had a problematic that was both sociological and theological, largely as a by-product of the Protestant work ethic inherited from the Calvinists.

It is no secret that the Protestant work ethic was also one of the primary reasons workers cooperated with the injustices of industrial expansionism in both Europe and the United States in the nineteenth century. Believing that individuals get only what they are worth in God's eyes led average working laypersons to blame themselves, rather

7. John A. Coleman, *An American Strategic Theology* (New York: Paulist, 1982), pp. 71, 89. These demands were made in a paper published by the American Catholic bishops in 1919 entitled "Social Reconstruction."

than the structures of society, for their lack of riches or lack of dignity on the job. In contrast, wealthy churchgoers felt, under this same Protestant work ethic, that they were somehow more vocationally adapted to God's plan and reaping just rewards here on earth. The theologically disastrous notion that one's status as a worker is somehow preordained was popular in the affluent churches.

Commenting on why Christians in general are not more motivated to apply their religious values to changing the economy and instead are willing to gamble that someday they will be rewarded if they work hard enough, Norman Gottwald observes:

> If these [issues of why we do not structure our economy less along competition and more on cooperative terms] seem like undiscussed, even undiscussable, questions in contemporary America, it is in large measure because capitalist ideology has worked well enough to ban them from consciousness and from the public forum. Unfettered capitalism wants to be seen as consonant with — even as the fulfillment of — Jewish and Christian assumptions about human nature and the moral foundations of society.[8]

The Protestant work ethic made it harder for laypersons and church leaders in this period to discover the liberating implications of a radical interpretation of the Christian faith in the light of working-class movements. Those who tried to motivate Christians to take the collective destiny of their economy in their own hands ran up against popular theologies that focused primarily on individual sin and redemption and did little to encourage churches to analyze the structure of capital accumulation and investment and its oppressive role in the hands of greedy industrialists.[9] R. H. Tawney describes this basic ineptitude of the social ministries of the churches and their lackluster response to the moral bankruptcy of capitalism:

> In an age of impersonal finance, world markets, and a capitalist organization of industry, its [the church's] traditional social doctrines had nothing specific to offer, and were merely repeated, when, in order to be effective, they should have been thought out again

8. Norman Gottwald, "From Biblical Economies to Modern Economies," in *Churches in Struggle: Liberation Theologies and Social Change in North America*, ed. Bill Tabb (New York: Monthly Review Press, 1986), p. 146.

9. Donald C. Smith, *Passive Obedience and Prophetic Protest*, American University Studies, ser. 9, vol. 15 (New York: Peter Lang, 1987).

> in new and living terms. . . . The social teaching of the Church had ceased to count, because the Church itself had ceased to think.[10]

Still, some voices in the Protestant community lifted up a new social teaching against the excessive greed and the bankrupt value systems of the capitalist society. Walter Rauschenbusch, a leading social gospel theologian, wrote in 1908 that the competitive spirit of capitalism harms society much in the same way that the disease of alcoholism consumes the individual. Rauschenbusch parodied the ideology of unfettered free market capitalism that was supposed to be the embodiment of all that was good and achievable in the human endeavor:

> Every human institution creates a philosophy which hallows it to those who profit by it and allays the objections of those who are victimized by it. . . . The competitive industry has its own philosophy to justify the ways of business unto men. "Competition is the life of trade." "If every man will do the best for himself, he will thereby do the best for society." In short, the surest way to be unselfish is to look out for Number One.[11]

The selfishness and ruthless competitiveness of the age, in direct contradiction to the Christian values of justice and cooperation, troubled Rauschenbusch deeply. He called on the churches and religious people to engage in the struggle for social justice by opposing this ideology on moral and pastoral grounds. But the social gospel reformers struggled with how to interpret religious solidarity with a working-class people for whom, said Rauschenbusch, "the rest of us may be sympathetic onlookers and helpers, but to them, it is a question of life and death."[12]

Many of the ministers who did have contact with the worker organizers were not welcome, especially when the message was less concrete than the bread-and-butter issues that motivated the worker organizers:

> Long haired preachers come out every night
> Try to tell you what's wrong and what's right;

10. R. H. Tawney, *Religion and the Rise of Capitalism* (New York: Harcourt Brace & Co., 1952).

11. Walter Rauschenbusch, *Christianity and the Social Crisis* (New York: Macmillan, 1908), p. 312.

12. Ibid., p. 319.

But when asked how bout something to eat,
They will answer with voices so sweet;
You will work, bye and bye,
In that glorious land above the sky;
Work and pray, live on hay,
You'll get pie in the sky when you die.

(from the Industrial Workers
of the World songbook)[13]

Another aspect of the times that made it difficult for many churches to work in solidarity with workers was the growing attraction to socialism among rank-and-file industrial workers — never a popular credo among more than the fringe of the U.S. religious community. The suspicion was mutual, as working people perceived the religious institutions to represent accommodationist or reactionary perspectives. The institutional commitment of the churches as social organizations to the status quo further undercut the church's ability to overcome its alienation and to join the increasingly militant working class. Thus, while many of the leaders in the movement were ministers, few could continue to use the church as their platform. As Rauschenbusch noted, "Some of the favorite speakers and organizers of the socialists in our country are former Christian ministers, who use their power of ethical and religious appeal."[14]

It is not surprising, then, that there were only a few examples of church leaders and the institution of the church itself backing the efforts of prominent industrial organizers — Big Bill Haywood, Eugene Debs, Mother Jones, and Sam Gompers.

During a very difficult period for workers in the 1930s, the call of religious bodies to their members was to support the efforts of organized labor to unionize workers. Labor needed tremendous community support as unions tried to rebuild after Great Depression–induced losses in wages and union membership. Unions were in worse shape than they are even now, and they were at a disadvantage against their employers, who kept wages low by utilizing nonunion shops and immigrant labor. Denominational and ecumenical groups at grassroots and national levels supported workers by arguing the rights of workers to engage in collective bargaining. Even the Southern Baptist

13. Wasserman, *History,* p. 159.
14. Rauschenbusch, *Christianity,* p. 312.

Convention made its presence known at a national level in 1938 on the issue of collective bargaining:

> We recognize the right of labor to organize and to engage in collective bargaining to the end that labor may have a fair and living wage, such as will provide not only for the necessities of life, but for recreation, pleasure and culture.[15]

The contributions of the Jewish community to the union organizing prior to the 1930s was profound. In an essay on Jewish statements on social justice, David Biale argues that the great wave of Jewish immigration to America in the period between 1881 and 1924 brought with it a community that was less steeped in traditional (and religious) sources:

> It might be said that the new movements for social change, including liberalism and socialism, were all secular substitutes for earlier religious systems of belief. Many of those Jews who threw themselves into social activism in the Twentieth Century did so in conscious repudiation of the Orthodox Jewish tradition.[16]

Although secular Jews stood heads above the Jewish religious community in siding with workers, the Rabbinical Assembly of America, breaking from the more conservative position of Orthodox Judaism, moved toward the position of the radical secular Jewish organizers in a 1934 statement supporting workers:

> We believe that the denial of the right of workers to organize and form group associations so that they may be treated as economic equals with their employers is tantamount to a curtailment of human freedom. For that reason we favor the unionization of all who labor.[17]

15. David Biale, "Jewish Statements on Social Justice," in *A Cry for Justice: The Churches and Synagogues Speak,* ed. Robert McAfee Brown and Sydney Thompson Brown (New York and Mahwah, N.J.: Paulist, 1989), p. 73.

16. "Church Voices Support Labor Organizing," Commission on Religions in Appalachia and Southerners for Economic Justice, CORA, Appalachia, PO Box 10867, Knoxville, TN 37919.

17. Ibid.

The Catholic Contribution

With advocates for justice like John Ryan and the Peter Maurin–inspired Catholic Worker movement, the Catholic Church spoke strongly to its then predominantly working-class members of how the development of unchecked laissez-faire industrial capitalism would lead to competition, greed, and brutality.[18] In *Option for the Poor*, Donald Dorr traces the history of Catholicism's "preferential option for the poor" back to the church's early stance in solidarity with workers:

> Leo XIII's *On Human Labor* [*Rerum Novarum*, 1891] was the first major step by the Vatican towards putting the church on the side of the poor and the working class. It can be seen as the beginning of a process which has eventually led church leaders, including Pope John Paul II, to approve of the notion of an option for the poor.[19]

Suspicion of capitalist economic institutions is quite strong in Catholic social teaching. Catholic social teaching is generally supportive of efforts of workers to unionize and gain the right to collective bargaining. These teachings undoubtedly had a tremendous influence on the large number of Catholics who participated in the fledgling union movement. Two papal social encyclicals particularly defended the rights of workers, and they serve as a handy bracket for this period between 1890 and 1930, when the Catholic Church influenced the debate.[20] They are *The Condition of Labor* (*Rerum Novarum*, 1891), a statement that serves as the starting point for the tradition of papal social teaching;[21] and *The Reconstruction of the Social Order* (*Quadragesimo Anno*, 1931). John Cort summarizes several major themes

18. Joe Holland and Peter Henriot, S.J., *Social Analysis: Linking Faith and Justice* (Dove Communications; Maryknoll, N.Y.: Orbis, 1980, 1988), p. 67.

19. Donald Dorr, *Option for the Poor: A Hundred Years of Vatican Social Teaching* (Maryknoll, N.Y.: Orbis, 1983), p. 253.

20. John C. Cort, "Social Encyclicals, A Progress Report," *Commonweal Magazine*, May 25, 1956.

21. Gregory Baum, *The Priority of Labor: A Commentary on LABOREM EXERCENS, Encyclical Letter of Pope John Paul II*, p. 5. While much of *Rerum Novarum* is dedicated to a critique of capitalism, it is also focused on the incompatibility of the Christian faith with Marxism's materialism and atheism. Baum notes that it was not until Pope Paul VI's *Octogesima Adveniens* (1971) that socialism was acknowledged as a rational option for Catholics, due in no small part to the changes underway in social conditions and theologies in the Third World at the end of the colonial period.

of these two papal encyclicals that defend the priority of labor over capital:

1. Support for unions and workers organizations.
2. Support for a wage for the worker sufficient to support himself and herself and his or her family (especially strong in *Quadragesimo Anno*).
3. An obligation of the state to pass laws that protect health, life, strength of family and home, the workplace, and wages, and an equal obligation of the state to protect workers, especially women and children, against hazards in the workplace.
4. Advocacy for economic planning that would maintain full employment, and support for planning that would be carried out by the state and business with full representation of labor in the process.
5. Support of the right to hold private property, but also for the importance of the wage contract and of a moderate degree of competition to spur efficiency.
6. Support for profit sharing, stock sharing, and co-management of business.
7. Support for trade associations composed of laity and workers.[22]

From the mid-1930s to the 1960s, a relative détente existed between labor and business. The influence of such strong statements of solidarity with the U.S. worker is hard to determine, but it could have only helped balance out the power between industry and labor. Cort argues that Pope Pius XI's support of labor unions and workers in 1931 was one of the major factors that helped labor to increase its membership from three million in 1931 to more than sixteen million in 1956.[23] But the influence of the church was probably a secondary factor. The advent of the New Deal and the incredible economic expansion that was fueled by the World War II militarization of the economy probably did more to help strike a better balance between organized labor and the industrial capitalists. Profits were up, patriotism was a unifying theme, and even wages stayed on the upside. It

22. Cort, "Social Encyclicals," p. 69.

23. Ibid. Many reasons for the growth of the labor movement during this period were determined by the U.S. economy, although the statements of the pope, especially given the numbers of Catholic working-class people, certainly had an impact.

seemed to everyone as though the American century had finally arrived, and it was thought that the question of who would benefit from the growing economic pie would never again be the subject of pitched battle in the streets.[24]

> On one level, the post-war years were highly conservative, though far from static. As World War II ended, President Harry Truman declared, "I don't want any experiments, the American people have been through a lot of experiments, and they want a rest." The New Deal and the international crisis that had precipitated the war were to be put behind. Americans were again to be free to seek their happiness through economic competition in the free market, without the pressures of ideological or military mobilization, while they retained the considerable benefits of the New Deal's interventions to soften the harshness of the business cycle.[25]

But for African American workers in the steel mills of Gary, Indiana, who were at the bottom of the pay scale and last on the list to get promotions,[26] and for people of color everywhere, the seeds of the civil rights movement were being planted by the obvious racial demographics of who was benefiting from the wealth and who was not. Although class divisions between the rich and the poor began to weaken with the growing middle class in the 1940s, 1950s, and 1960s, racial injustice in U.S. industry and society was as strong as ever. Consequently, even though church solidarity with African American workers can be traced back to antislavery work within most denominations — especially the Quakers; not until the 1950s did church solidarity with workers often include the element of racial justice. Morality tended to follow, not to lead, the law. Martin Luther King, Jr., wrote from jail a decade later:

> I have heard numerous religious leaders of the South call upon their worshippers to comply with a desegregation decision because it is the law, but I have longed to hear white ministers say, "follow this decree because integration is morally right and the Negro is your brother."[27]

24. Robert Bellah, et al., *The Good Society* (New York: Knopf, 1991), "The American Century."

25. Ibid.

26. Edward Geer, "Racism and U.S. Steel," *Radical America* 10, no. 5 (1976).

27. Taylor Branch, *Parting the Waters: America in the King Years, 1954–1963*, p. 742. The quote is from Martin Luther King's "Letter from Birmingham City Jail."

Production Goes International; Theology Goes Global

In the 1960s, the era of the global corporation ushered in what Joe Holland and Peter Henriot call the Third Stage of Industrial Capitalism. The internationalization of capital, financial markets, and production, they argue, has once again created a situation where the corporation is able to reassert nearly total hegemony over national economies (especially in the Third World) and disrupt the balance of power between labor and capital.[28]

Henriot and Holland argue that in this period the churches, both Protestant and Catholic, began moving toward a global theology and a more inclusive commitment to economic and social justice, breaking out of an old paradigm. While it was undergoing a process of liberalization, a new form of church was being born. Catholic social teaching in the 1960s is a good initial gauge of this transition in churches to liberation themes and a more global consciousness of the need for solidarity for workers. Pope John XXIII's teachings reached into all corners of the globe. With his *Christianity and Social Progress* the church turned away from its traditional trust of civil authority, and in so doing "gained new allies and new enemies, in its departure from its traditional defense of the status quo, as it was now seen as an effective opponent of oppressor governments."[29]

In 1968, the Second General Conference of Latin American Bishops at Medellin, Colombia, expanded on this theme that the church should act as the voice of those who have been disempowered in their society. The Medellin Conference sharply focused the issues facing the church in Latin America, and called on the world community to focus its attention on changing the injustice suffered by Third World workers and citizens. Among other things, the conference stressed that structural injustice in Latin America was stripping away the dignity of people. A "church of the poor" *(Iglesia Popular)* created pressure on the institutional church in Latin America, Africa, and Asia, as well as in the First World, to engage in acts of solidarity with the poor and workers to change their oppressive situations and to gain a better chance of succeeding in their struggle for liberation.[30]

28. Holland and Henriot, *Social Analysis.*
29. Dorr, *Option,* p. 263.
30. Ibid., p. 158.

The Fight for Community Survival

I believe that it was this post–Vatican II and Medellin consciousness of liberation themes that propelled the church, both Protestant and Catholic, onto the forefront of the struggle against plant closures. This church-based movement fought against corporate initiatives to replace skilled labor with lower-cost workers in the 1970s, as companies moved everything from steel plants to peach fields into foreign countries to take advantage of cheap foreign labor and tax breaks for international investment. Over the decade of the 1970s, it is estimated that a minimum of thirty-two million jobs were eliminated as a result of private disinvestment in plant and equipment in the United States.[31] According to Dick Gillette, these shutdowns revived church consciousness and stimulated church-related action programs addressing the economic crisis in nearly all parts of the country and "brought the churches back to the concerns of labor and working people they had espoused in the 1930s."[32] But these church organizers who fought arm in arm with labor were not without their detractors:

> The ecclesiastical pronouncements resulting from Youngstown, and from subsequent areas of the churches' engagement with labor in the 1980s, were cast directly into the teeth of a veritable gale of proclamations and policies paying tribute to the glories of the unfettered marketplace as supreme arbiter of justice, jobs, and prosperity.[33]

Beginning with the community coalition that formed around the efforts to fight back against the closure of the steel mills in Youngstown, Ohio, from 1977 to 1979, the struggle of workers and labor unions to hang onto gains made since the 1930s was joined in the streets by churches and ecumenical coalitions in America's industrial heartland. The strategy of plant shutdowns and runaways of the 1970s was accompanied by corporate strategies of conglomeration and capital flight. Millions of jobs were on the line, and local tax bases were devastated. While companies internationalized and set up industrial

31. Barry Bluestone and Bennett Harrison, *The Deindustrialization of America* (New York: Basic, 1982), p. 34.

32. Richard Gillette, "The Church Acts for Economic Justice," in *Churches in Struggle*, p. 269.

33. Bluestone and Harrison, *Deindustrialization*, p. 268

production facilities in low-wage states and countries, workers in traditionally industrialized communities were left with a future having little or no hope.

While conservatives argued that this transitionary period was simply a case of companies exercising their right to migrate toward lower costs and more efficient means of production, few in the grass-roots church organizations that stood up for labor bought that argument. In 1979, concerned steelworkers, union officials, rank-and-file union members, religious leaders, and economic development groups came together in the Ecumenical Coalition of the Mahoning Valley to wage a campaign to preserve the steel industry in the Northeast. The announced shutdown by U.S. Steel of its mill in Youngstown came at the end of a string of shutdowns that closed thirteen plants, laying off thirteen thousand production and white-collar people — a full 8 percent of the company's work force. Two years earlier, the Campbell Works at Youngstown Sheet and Tube had closed, and forty-one hundred workers were without a job. These shutdowns meant a loss of seventy-six hundred jobs to Youngstown at two plants alone, all at a time when the demand for steel was on the rise.[34]

The coalition of steelworkers and religious leaders resorted to direct-action tactics to protest the closure with marches, rallies, and public presentations. They also occupied the corporate headquarters of U.S. Steel and the mill itself. Studies came out (by Policy Management Associates) that the Youngstown Sheet and Tube closing would ultimately result in the layoffs of twelve to thirteen thousand people, and would cause retail sales to drop by $12-23 million each year.[35] The community campaign also helped point out that the company had intentionally disinvested. As a result of the conglomeration process, the Lykes Corporation had acquired Youngstown Sheet and Tube with the intent to shut it down. This action officially put communities everywhere on notice that corporate conglomerates were out shopping for basic industries that could be stripped down and closed in an inhuman profit-taking strategy that rivaled the abuses of industrial capitalism in the 1890s.

Youngstown and the Ecumenical Coalition to Save Mahoning Valley became a symbol of the plant shutdowns crisis for workers, and from the Youngstown experience came a national movement of

34. Ibid., p. 37.
35. Ibid., p. 69.

community-religious-labor coalitions that are still fighting plant shutdowns and Wall Street–induced economic dislocation of millions of workers.

United Farmworkers Organizing: A Rural Dimension

The rural dimension to religious support for organizing efforts of labor in industry came into focus in the 1960s and 1970s with the United Farmworkers organizing campaigns. This movement drew from an historical concern of groups like the Council of Women for Home Missions and the regional and state Migrant Ministries that were begun in the 1950s through the National Council of Churches. With these groups, Cesar Chavez and the United Farmworkers Organizing Campaign moved churches from providing direct aid and services to becoming active partners in an organizing effort that eventually gained worldwide publicity. In California, one of the first acts of the United Church of Christ (UCC), the new denomination formed in 1957 by combining Evangelical and Reformed and Congregational traditions, was to launch a rural ministry to bolster the work of California Migrant Ministries.[36]

The tactics of the churches and the farm workers helped to shape future campaigns, as organizers relied primarily on nonviolent direct action — boycotts, strikes, marches, sit-ins, and nonviolent civil disobedience. Sometimes the first target of their actions were the more established Teamsters locals themselves, which held many of the existing contracts in California agriculture and did not see the need for a new, competing union. The Agricultural Workers Organizing Committee of the AFL-CIO joined forces with the National Farmworkers Association to form the United Farmworkers Organizing Committee, which gave the farm-worker group more clout both among union circles and with the growers.

36. Pat Hoffman, *Ministry of the Dispossessed* (Los Angeles: Wallace, 1987), p. 126. The UCC ordained Jim Drake in 1962 to serve as one of the main organizers, and he helped establish a strong connection to the UCC that benefited the farm workers through several campaigns. (Drake was refused ordination by his home presbytery [Presbyterian Church] in Riverside because his work with the California Migrant Ministries was not considered an appropriate "call" to ministry.) Drake built on and added to the prior work of Fred Ross, Doug and Hannah Still, and others to coordinate membership drives and housemeetings with Cesar Chavez's new National Farmworkers Association.

These large campaigns, begun in earnest in September 1965 when the grape strike in Delano, California, began to produce results. In the spring of 1967, a three-hundred-mile Lenten march for justice for farm workers culminated with ten thousand people descending on the state capital in Sacramento on Easter. Utilizing fasts and a number of other tactics, the struggle moved from the grape fields to the vegetable fields, and the Union signed its first contract later that year with a grower on behalf of workers in the Chancery Office of the Archdiocese of Los Angeles.[37]

The National Conference of Catholic Bishops (NCCB) made a brief but effective statement in support of farm workers in 1968. Its primary purpose was to lend general support to a growing national movement for justice for farm workers and specifically to support the efforts of farm workers to gain the right to form unions, to engage in collective bargaining, and to earn a fair wage. The bishops' statement was linked to a growing national call by the United Farm Workers Union in California to place the farm workers under the National Labor Relations Act.[38] In this statement, the NCCB gave poignant testimony to the human element of the farm workers' struggle to form a union:

> For thirty years, the disadvantaged field workers of this nation have stood by helplessly and listened to other Americans debating the farm labor problem. Burdened by low wage scales, mounting health problems, inadequate educational opportunities, substandard housing and a lack of year-round employment, they have often been forced to live devoid of security, dignity and reasonable comfort. For the past three years, however, many of them have been attempting to take their destiny into their own hands. This is a very healthy development. Farm workers are now very painfully aware that not only do they have to struggle against economic, educational and social inequities, but they have also been excluded from every piece of social legislation as well.[39]

The summer of 1973 was a crucial test of the strong church–labor–farm-worker coalition that had emerged in the organizing ef-

37. Ibid.

38. NCBB, *Quest for Justice: A Compendium of Statements of the United States Catholic Bishops on the Political and Social Order 1966–1980* (Washington D.C.: Office of Publishing Services, USCC, catalog no. 649, 1981), p. 322.

39. NCCB, "Statement on Farm Labor, Nov. 15, 1968," in ibid., pp. 322-23.

forts, since many of the contracts that were won in 1970 were up for renegotiation.[40] In this major labor dispute, once again the churches uncharacteristically took a direct role as local churches and national bodies intervened to support strikes that followed the harvest as it moved from the Coachella Valley in the south to the San Joaquin Valley in the north. The UCC Board of Homeland Ministries, in the process of preparing a statement of support for the strikes at the 1973 UCC's Synod meeting in St. Louis, gathered a planeload of supporters from the meeting to fly to California in direct response to Cesar Chavez's call for church people to protect against violence perpetrated by armed thugs acting for the Teamsters Union and California agribusiness.

In 1974, the Catholic bishops again issued a call for support of legislation favorable to the farm workers, this time seeking passage of legislation that would ensure the right of farm workers to vote for the union of their choice to represent them in collective bargaining.[41] When the California Agricultural Labor Relations Act was enacted in 1975, guaranteeing the right of California farm workers to negotiate a union contract, the bishops immediately congratulated Governor Brown, the legislature, and the United Farm Workers of America, and called on "all concerned — state officials, growers, and union representatives — to cooperate with one another in implementing the spirit as well as the letter of the law."[42]

40. Hoffman, *Ministry*, p. 45.

41. Upon the passage of legislation creating the California Agricultural Labor Relations Board, the bishops commended legislators, calling it a "turning point in the history of farm labor relations in California," and committed themselves to "cooperate with the parties to the fullest extent in their common effort to bring about a new era of peace and justice in the agricultural industry, not only in California, but through the nation" (*Quest for Justice*, p. 329).

42. Ibid., pp. 322-23. Some in the churches went further, drawing from this experience of radical commitment to supporting the farm workers to call for more far-reaching measures than contracts with farm labor. In 1976, the National Catholic Rural Life Conference issued a Call to Action Resolution entitled "The Church and the Rural Community." The Call included taking measures to ensure justice for both the family farmer and the farm worker. Specific issues raised were the abuses of land speculation; the exploitation of agricultural workers, including the undocumented alien; the problems caused by large agribusiness and concentrated land holdings; and the need to give continued support to the family farm. Recommendations were made for Catholic diocesan action as well, which encouraged concrete and progressive measures. Churches were called on to help the farm workers obtain farms of their own ("Call to Action, National Catholic Rural Life Conference, 1976," in *Quest for*

The church's response out of a sense of radical discipleship to the farm-worker crisis is a model of how to fight for the rights of workers that has yet to be replicated. Not only does it show the successes that can be gained when the church and labor organizations pepper their campaigns with theologically trained and politically active staff and members, but it also shows that solidarity with workers at the bottom of the income scale in U.S. industry can be achieved. Now, against the backdrop of models for church-labor organizing that point the way toward solidarity of the churches with workers, we must look at what the future holds for similar efforts. In many ways, the problems are larger, and the task of those seeking to work for economic justice through coalitions more difficult.

What Happened to Industry?

From the 1940s into the 1970s, despite glitches in the social welfare capitalism that brought labor and capital into better balance, by and large some trust had grown.[43] Catholics, Protestants, and Jews alike had a greater acceptance on moral grounds of the need to rely on both the productive mechanisms of capitalism and the government's social safety net to address the needs of working persons and the poor.[44] And, under New Deal liberalism, businesses by and large left the government and other mediating institutions to deliver on the kinds of social safety nets that have historically eased the burden of the working class.

This all came to an end with the Reagan presidency in 1980, as tax cuts for corporations and incentives for nonproductive investments capped a decade of disinvestment in industry with an era of greed that would create a fiscal and economic crisis. While the core of the deindustrialization debate might seem to conjure up images of smokestacks, factories, and heavy equipment in the fields, the ethical (and economic) issues focus more on wage and income inequality that accompanied the deindustrialization of the 1970s and 1980s. In their

---

Justice, p. 408). "Through support of their efforts at unionization, the church has ministered to farmworkers within the prevailing system. Now is the time for a new initiative to aid them in escaping that system. Those who till the land should have the opportunity to own it" (ibid., p. 394).

43. Ibid., p. 75.

44. Presbyterian Church (U.S.A.), *Challenges in the Workplace*, p. 65.

book *The Great U-Turn,* economists Barry Bluestone and Bennett Harrison argue that there is a direct correspondence between manufacturing production and better wages for workers:

> The high rate of productivity growth during the period ending in 1973 corresponds to the rapid growth in real weekly earnings up to that time. Similarly, the slowdown in productivity advance after 1973 corresponds to the decline in real wages, while the small resurgence in productivity in the 1980s corresponds to a slight slowing down in the rate of wage decline.[45]

The result of this maldistribution of income has been to increase income and wealth inequality in the United States. A 1984 report by the congressional Joint Economic Committee shows that the share of the national income for the wealthiest 40 percent of the families in the United States rose to 67.3 percent. The share of income for the poorest 40 percent of all American families dropped to 15.7 percent, the lowest since 1947.[46] The outward, visible signs of this maldistribution are clear as the news media report epidemic proportions of homeless people, a nation of youth who are trapped in the drug economy, and senior citizens going bankrupt because of a lack of basic health care.

All of these social problems can be traced to deindustrialization in manufacturing and the pursuit of greater corporate profits in the face of growing international competition. In the process, the economy we now have, based on the low-wage service industry, was emerging. As Barry Bluestone put it in a 1984 study on the crisis in the labor market:

> There may be a shortage of skilled computer engineers in Silicon Valley and along Route 128 in Massachusetts, but throughout the industrial heartland of America and in large parts of the South, persistently high unemployment among factory workers continues to exhaust family savings and to generate mortgage foreclosures in near record numbers.[47]

45. Bennett Harrison and Barry Bluestone, *The Great U-Turn: Corporate Restructuring and the Polarization of America* (New York: Basic, 1988), p. xix.

46. Kip Tiernan and Fran Froehlich, "Slouching Toward Bethlehem: The Burgeoning American Underclass," *Jubilee Magazine* (Spring 1989).

47. Barry Bluestone, Bennett Harrison, and Lucy Gorham, "Storm Clouds on the Horizon: Labor Market Crisis and Industrial Policy," *Economic Education Project Booklet,* 152 Aspinwall Ave., Suite 2, Brookline, MA 02146, May 1984.

Although the skilled engineers in the work force were keeping their jobs, a 1984 study of jobs in high-technology industries, which is composed primarily of low-wage blue-collar workers, listed forty-three thousand jobs lost and 147 plant closures and incidences of layoffs between 1980 and 1984 in California's Silicon Valley.[48] Most of these jobs were shifted overseas. By 1989, the whole high-tech solution went sour. The "Massachusetts miracle" on Route 128 was on the verge of shutting down, and the unparalleled growth experienced by California's Silicon Valley was skidding to a halt. Analysts now see more layoffs in the future for these areas that were once described as the future of U.S. manufacturing.[49] A low-wage service economy and growing poverty are the most likely fate of the U.S. work force, unless some coalitions can be built to plan for good jobs, reindustrialization, and regional retraining strategies by government and private agencies.[50]

When the Corporate Roof Collapses

The blue-collar work force is not the only group hit hard by policies of the Reagan and Bush era that encouraged corporate disinvestment and the dislocation of workers. There is a growing ethical crisis in American society as business, under the guise of "staying competitive," is paying top dollar to executives who can save the United States' highly debt-ridden companies money — and thereby increase short-term profitability — by laying off middle managers and reducing the payroll. The result has been a stunning increase among the ranks of the unemployed of the very white-collar workers who have typically been the largest supporters of business. These are the same employees who for the most part stood on the sidelines through the 1970s as millions of blue-collar workers lost their jobs. Now these middle-level managers are losing their jobs as companies scale back to fend off hostile takeover attempts or merge with other companies to score short-term profits through job consolidation. One of the seldom-reported results of these massive corporate giants fighting on Wall Street to take over and then strip out the hidden wealth in companies

48. Gilda Haas, *Plant Closures: Myths, Realities, and Responses* (Boston: South End Press, 1985), p. 30.

49. "The end of an era?" *San Jose (CA) Mercury News,* Aug. 30, 1990.

50. Bluestone, Harrison, and Gorham, "Storm Clouds."

across the United States has been that an estimated one million middle managers lost their jobs between 1984 and 1989.[51] While 80 percent found reemployment within six months (usually in a company of less than twenty employees), some ended up with the same menial service jobs created in the Reagan "jobs boom" that pay a fraction of what the old jobs paid.

The ethic created inside the surviving companies is frightening. According to Shann Nix, a staff writer for the *San Francisco Chronicle* who researched this trend:

> Both the ranks of the newly unemployed and the often feeling-guilty survivors who stay behind are struggling to adapt to the new "me-first" loyalties, an ethics system that requires a seemingly treasonous level of self-interest, and the disquieting knowledge that they're all on their own when the corporate roof caves in.[52]

Nix cites Roger Hall, a Harvard MBA who was knocked out of his company and spent eleven months looking for another job: "Once you would never look for one job while you're working another. Now you don't have a choice."

Looking to the Future

With a better understanding of its vocation in this time of major economic transition, the religious community can play a role with workers, community planners, and the growing core of disaffected business people in charting an alternative future that seeks to protect those victimized by industrial decline and the unemployment and poverty of the new low-wage service economy. With planning and a heavy dose of ethics, could we have an economy based on human needs? Social theorist Gar Alperovitz and economist Jeff Faux emphasize one of the central principles of such an economy in *Rebuilding America:*

> [Collaborative] planning is the only way we can hope to survive with our democracy and freedoms intact over the coming decades. Solving this paradox requires economic policies that deal with the

51. Shann Nix, *San Francisco Chronicle,* Business section.
52. Ibid.

> immediate problems of inflation and unemployment yet at the same time reinforce those individual values of cooperation and collective decision-making that increase our ability to plan competently.[53]

Faux and Alperovitz follow this statement by arguing that the solutions to economic problems must be anchored in shared human values if they are to have any lasting significance. Here is where the church can have some influence.

But before anything can happen, people must be aware that the current economic downturn has placed the entire country in a moral crisis that challenges the very core of our self-perception as a nation of equals, a people of justice, and a land of opportunity. A paradigm shift ushered in by the Reagan revolution is moving us away from the American dream. The economy based on goods is being replaced by a more stingy economy of services. Wage income has stagnated and income from wealth has skyrocketed. Workers should not be surprised to learn that they are on the short end of this transition. The progress for the wealthiest one-fifth of the U.S. population (whose income rose by 13 percent from 1978 to 1987) came at the expense of the poorest one-fifth (whose income fell by 8 percent in this same period).

The uneven and undemocratic terms on which this transition beg for a response from religious community advocates who can interject their historical commitment to bettering the condition of the working poor. When concern for workers is combined with the religious community's traditional concerns for stewardship and equitable distribution of the goods of God's earth, one can make a powerful case for involving members of churches and synagogues in what will certainly be a controversial and heated debate over how to better distribute income through reframing industrial, social, and economic development.

To participate in demanding a role in shaping the economy that will succeed post-industrial capitalism in the United States, the church needs to hearken back to its social gospel roots and take the initiative in several important areas of social and economic reform.

(1) Religious organizations and unions need to pay special attention to the just claims of minority workers, especially now that businesses, federal officials, and the Supreme Court seem intent on reversing the gains of civil rights for workers by labeling affirmative action as reverse discrimination.

53. Bluestone, Harrison, and Gorham, "Storm Clouds," p. 277.

Contemporary Catholic social teaching provides a framework by stressing the themes of development, participation, and power in a little-known 1979 pastoral letter on racism. Here the bishops cite evidence that little or no progress has been made to enable greater participation of people of color in the United States since the civil rights movement of the 1960s, and the avenues for participation have actually narrowed. The churches are called to participate in programs to redress the wrongs of past treatment of racial minorities.[54]

Conservatives will continue to argue that the growing poverty that has been experienced by minority youths (African Americans in particular) is due to internal inadequacies of these youths and of their family structures and the harmful effect of government antipoverty programs.[55] But by understanding the economic roots of the poverty that disproportionately affects minority communities, religious advocates armed with the facts can help our society reach a different conclusion. For example, in 1980, when 18 percent of the automotive work force was on layoff, it was estimated that nearly 32 percent of the industry's African American workers were laid off. According to the civil rights department of the United Auto Workers, these layoffs accounted for a one-percent drop in the 1983 average national income for African Americans.[56] Churches must reemphasize their firm support for the gains made for people of color in civil rights legislation and social engineering programs that provide a ladder out of systemic poverty for the poor.

54. "Brothers and Sisters to Us," a pastoral letter on racism of the National Catholic Conference of Bishops, 1979, in *Quest for Justice*, p. 377. A powerful section of the pastoral letter reads: "Racism has been a part of the social fabric of America since the beginning of European colonization. Whether it be the tragic past of the Native Americans, the Mexicans, the Puerto Ricans or the Blacks, the story is one of slavery, peonage, economic exploitation, brutal repression and cultural neglect. All have suffered indignity; most have been uprooted, defrauded or dispossessed of their lands; and none has escaped one or another form of collective degradation by a powerful majority. Our history is littered with the debris of broken promises and treaties, as well as lynchings and massacres that almost destroyed the Indians, humiliated the Hispanics, and crushed the Blacks. But despite this tragic history, the racial minorities of our country have survived and increased. Not only that, but each racial group has sunk its roots deep in the soil of our culture. . . . Each has become a source of internal strength for our nation . . . their struggle has been a pledge of liberty and a challenge to future greatness."

55. Cherry, *Discrimination*, chap. 6, "Black Youth Unemployment Problems."

56. Haas, *Plant Closures*, p. 31. Haas draws her figures from Claude Reed, Jr., "The American Auto Industry and Black Unemployment."

(2) The religious community needs to refocus its priorities and declare an economic and social emergency that calls for special measures. Such a priority will push comfortable churches and synagogues to transcend their social location and, as part of the independent sector, to reassert their roles as public leaders.

Ours is a society divided, where pressures on the life of families and the growing underclass prompt all of us, as Catholic Archbishop Rembert Weakland has said on numerous occasions, to "refocus our ethical concerns and our personal priorities." As mainstream institutions, churches and organized labor share an addiction to their vested interest in the wealth that has been created at the top of society. The cultural effect of this addiction to wealth is to create a system that tolerates, if not requires, injustice and poverty, and that invites the church to withdraw into a therapeutic style.[57]

But beyond this critique, it is time that religious organizations and unions recognize that they share members, constituencies, common concerns. Their commitment to the common good is at stake in quality-of-life arguments for retaining the unionized job sector and the benefits it has traditionally brought. On the other side, the church should be a leader in helping members in business see their vocational task as shaped by the common good and social justice, not simply by the corporate bottom line.

(3) The religious community needs to participate in rebuilding workers organizations.

Unions in this rapidly changing economy have failed to reach out to unemployed former workers or workers in the new nonunion industries. One way to do this is through associate membership programs that reintroduce people to the benefits of collective security without always having to depend on major organizing campaigns, for which there is never enough time and resources. The Communications Workers of America and the Amalgamated Clothing and Textile Workers Unions are piloting such programs for unemployed workers and workers employed in traditionally nonunion jobs.

(4) The religious community must work to promote, support, and even initiate new political coalitions to restore workplace health and safety, wage levels, and community integrity that were lost in deindustrialization.

57. Dieter Hessel, *Theological Education for Social Ministry* (New York: Pilgrim, 1988), p. 5, critiques the boxed-in model of parish ministry.

The loss of human capital and industrial capacity through plant closures and the debt burdens corporations and governmental agencies now carry as a result of the Reagan-Bush era are ethically and economically unsound. The growing gap between the classes that is being fueled by the low-wage service sector strategy needs to be reversed by advocating public policies to foster appropriate industrial manufacturing, democratic participation in community planning, and environmental protection.

(5) The religious community must be vocal in reasserting the necessary role of government in providing basic services and meeting human needs.

New tax laws and public policies to make up for the tax giveaways and the defunding of infrastructure are increasingly regressive in taking a least-common-denominator approach to governmental fund-raising. For example, the funding formula devised by Gov. Pete Wilson for California in 1991 utilizes an "incentive system" of government that so often accompanies a belief in supply-side economics. Many county revenues are now tied to sales taxes and vehicle registration and licensing fees. A Sonoma County supervisor mused that this makes little sense, since in the recessionary years when county government services are most needed by the poor, the revenues will be at their lowest because of the restrained purchasing of nervous consumers and the low sales of new automobiles. In addition, it provides an incentive for local governments to suppport increases in regressive tax policies, which keep the burden for the top rate of the income bracket proportionately lower.

The religious community needs to be informed, educated, and willing to point out publicly the inherent unfairness of these kinds of legislative initiatives and the negative effect they will have on workers and nonworkers alike who still depend on governmental services.

Regardless of how much can be said about the historical role of religious-labor-organizing campaigns, or even religion and business dialogues on ethical guidelines, the religious community is increasingly reluctant to reassert its advocacy role for social reform along with its role as enabler of service ministry.

Jeremy Brecher and Tim Costello argue that we need a "coalescence" among "once insular movements," given new opportunities for groups as different as a church and a labor union to work together:

> The devastation of the human and the natural worlds that marked the 1980's was only possible because the people hurt by it were divided from each other. Whether the 1990's will be a time of continued devastation or an era of creative renewal will depend largely on whether their divisions are overcome.[58]

(6) Finally, a new alliance between the churches and the labor unions is needed. Although both were hit hard by demographic changes of their own in the 1970s and 1980s, their role in charting an ethical course in the midst of the political debate — by stating the moral criterion for economic justice and by standing emphatically on the side of those who are being discarded — is crucial for the future of the U.S. economy in the 1990s.[59] It is hopeful that both religion and labor, in response to the massive economic dislocation, are launching grass-roots education projects that may reach the desired goal of establishing just and humane criteria for future economic programs.

The basic challenge will be whether the leadership bodies and the grass-roots membership of the major Christian and Jewish denominations can follow a decade (the 1980s) of writing and social analysis describing the ills of the economy with a genuine commitment to advocacy for economic justice. This chapter may assist us in rediscovering the heritage of religious social teaching directed toward a concern for the economic life of all members of society. The greatest challenge will be putting it into practice and allowing our vision for a more just economy to be defined by the human needs of the struggling members of our communities.

58. Jeremy Brecher and Tim Costello, eds., *Building Bridges: The Emerging Grassroots Coalition of Labor and Community* (New York: Monthly Review Press, 1990), p. 10.

59. See my article "Churches Talk Economic Justice," *Christianity and Crisis* 52, 9 (June 8, 1992), pp. 193-94, and related articles on reforming the economy.

From Social Gospel to Social Science at the University of Wisconsin

Eugene Y. Lowe, Jr.

The question of the church's public role, as H. Richard Niebuhr pointedly observed in *Christ and Culture,* has been with us for a long time. The relationship between the church and its surrounding community is particularly difficult to characterize when the boundaries between the sacred and secular spheres of life take more the character of permeable membranes between cells of a single organism than the solid barriers separating alien jurisdictions. "When it seems," Niebuhr wrote, in the period following World War II, "that the issue has been clearly defined as lying between the exponents of a Christian civilization and the non-Christian defenders of a wholly secularized society, new perplexities arise as devoted believers seem to make common cause with secularists."[1]

Connections with Secular Social Reform

This dilemma emerges with particular poignancy during the progressive and social gospel period of American history (ca. 1890–1920), when a cultural order based on the values and sensibilities of nineteenth-century Protestant America yielded its hegemony in the face of the intellectual and social challenges wrought by evolution, urbanization, and immigration. A study of how the churches, with sensibilities awakened to the social problems of industrial America, negotiated this transition can take two different approaches. First, one

1. H. Richard Niebuhr, *Christ and Culture* (New York: Harper and Row, 1951), p. 1.

can focus on the denominations, highlighting the extent to which these groups institutionalized responses to the social gospel, taking into consideration the emergence of the Federal Council of Churches and other pandenominational efforts to consolidate an ecumenical social witness for the churches. This strategy sustains the focus of church history with its careful attention to the characters, policies, and structures of the religious institutions themselves.[2]

A second perspective, emphasizing the trajectory of social gospel thought and practice into twentieth-century reform culture, is based on a recognition that there is more to this movement than what happened in and to the churches. Furthermore, because the social gospel was associated with secularization, it is important to look beyond denominational and church structures to appreciate fully what it continues to represent in, and contribute to, American culture. In this essay I will follow the second strategy, focusing on how the social gospel interpreted and mediated in the work of the economist Richard T. Ely wended its way into Wisconsin Progressivism and, through it, to a secular tradition of politics and public service.

In a stimulating rereading of American religious history, William McLoughlin demarcated American religious history along lines that portrayed a series of awakenings as significant junctures in the evolution of American culture. Stimulated by the work of the anthropologist Anthony F. C. Wallace on revitalization movements, McLoughlin suggested that "awakenings are periods when the cultural system has had to be revitalized in order to overcome jarring disjunctions between norms and experience."[3] In his examination of what he termed the Third Great Awakening in the United States (1890–1920), McLoughlin highlighted the destabilizing impacts of the theory of evolution, the rise of biblical criticism, as well as the pressures and consequences of industrialization and urbanization as forces challenging established cultural paradigms and ecclesiastical values. In ethics and social

2. The church history tradition is described in Henry Warner Bowden, *Church History in the Age of Science* (Chapel Hill: Univ. of North Carolina Press, 1971). In the contemporary period Robert T. Handy has made a major contribution to this genre in *A History of the Churches in the United States and Canada* (New York: Oxford Univ. Press, 1977). A recent study of this kind about the social gospel is Donald K. Gorrell, *The Age of Social Responsibility: The Social Gospel in the Progressive Era 1900–1920* (Macon, Ga.: Mercer, 1989).

3. William L. McLoughlin, *Revivals, Awakenings, and Reforms: An Essay on Religion and Social Change in America, 1607–1977* (Chicago: Univ. of Chicago Press, 1978), p. 10.

philosophy, the individualism that had buttressed both theology and political economy was decisively challenged by social ideas based on organic and interdependent values.

For a number of people, these issues challenged the foundations of faith while stimulating new conceptions of vocation. Many struggled to reconcile the assumptions and the convictions that had oriented their formation and development — frequently in the agrarian precincts of Protestant America — with the results of the intellectual revolution and social transformation setting the stage for twentieth-century, pluralistic, urban, and secular America. Such struggles often resulted in decisions on the part of those who might earlier have been inclined toward the ministry to pursue careers in education, scholarship, and reform.[4]

The notions of a progressive revelation, a social gospel, and a God immanent in human history were three useful theological responses to this crisis. Seeking to apply Christian principles to the social order provided an opportunity to redirect intellect and energy toward problems that evolution and criticism could not affect. While the kingdom of God was still a realizable ideal, it encompassed an aspiration that could also be described and sought after by people who were concerned neither about the sovereignty of God nor about the meaning of human depravity. As a utopian goal, it could also be characterized in secular, political, and professional terms. For example, a decision to devote a professional career to the analysis of the institutions and practices defining human relationships in production, exchange, and patterns of urban life (i.e., becoming an economist of some sort) could be justified because it provided a foundation for defining effective modes of human cooperation with God in inaugurating the reign of Christ and the law of love. Such a decision might also, as later was the case for many academics, be justified in ethically disinterested terms: the pursuit of knowledge for its own sake.

4. Cf. Robert M. Crunden, *Ministers of Reform: The Progressives' Achievement in American Civilization 1889–1920* (Champaign, Ill.: Univ. of Illinois Press, 1982), for an illuminating discussion about how the transformation of religious vocation affected the experience of a number of important political, intellectual, and cultural figures — including Jane Addams, John Dewey, Woodrow Wilson, and Frank Lloyd Wright — during this period.

The Example of Richard Ely

The career of Richard T. Ely, professor of political economy at Johns Hopkins University from 1881 to 1892 and at the University of Wisconsin from 1892 to 1925, where the social gospel first stimulated, and was ultimately transformed by, the progressive movement, illustrates significant aspects of this transition, particularly the movement toward the secularization of the self-understanding of the reform-oriented academic.

Born and raised in Chautauqua County in western New York, Ely grew up in a Presbyterian household where his father continued to wait for the religious conversion of his son who, as a young adult, opted to join the Episcopal Church. Augmenting his university connections at Hopkins and Wisconsin with teaching and publication efforts at Chautauqua as well as through the Church (Christian) Social Union of the Episcopal Church, he developed a wide following, particularly after the effects of the economic depression of the mid-1890s had begun to grip the country.

Writing during the winter of 1916 in tribute to Washington Gladden on the occasion of the eightieth birthday of the distinguished exponent of the social gospel, Ely recalled Gladden's cooperation in the founding of the American Economic Association (AEA) in 1885.[5] Gladden, who had served as pastor of the First Congregational Church in Columbus, Ohio, from 1882 to 1914, and Ely had by this time come to represent complementary approaches to social Christianity and to understanding the public responsibility of the church. The cooperation to which Ely referred had been based in large measure on the aspiration that the AEA would contribute both to the advancement of knowledge and to the improvement of living and working conditions for those made vulnerable by the social and technological changes associated with city and factory life. Ely and Gladden had worked together in 1885 to draft a "statement of principles" for the AEA reflecting this combination of professional and ethical motivation. The third point of the statement emphasized the social concerns of the organization: "we hold that the conflict of labor and capital has brought into prominence a vast number of social problems, whose

5. Ely, *The Congregationalist and Christian World* 101, no. 6 (Feb. 10, 1916). Among others — in addition to Ely — Josiah Strong, Lyman Abbott, and William H. Taft offered tributes to Gladden.

solution requires the united efforts, each in its own sphere, of the church, of the state, and of science."[6]

In subsequent years, Gladden successfully used pulpit and pen to advance both the so-called new theology and the social gospel, while undertaking pastoral responsibility for an active, growing congregation in Ohio's capital city. Ely had pursued a different course, based in another state capital — Madison — at a time when the University of Wisconsin, and particularly its school of economics and political science, which Ely had headed since 1892, developed as the fountainhead of "the Wisconsin idea." This phrase, coined by an Ely student, described the cooperation of state government and the state university in the development of the reform program of Wisconsin Progressivism during the administration of Robert La Follette.[7]

Indeed, Ely had suggested on more than one occasion that the task of responding to social change was not a duty that the churches in the United States, divided as they were along denominational and theological lines, could effectively undertake. In *The Social Law of Service,* his 1896 compendium of social gospel essays, Ely had argued that the work of the church consisted of the "redemption of the world, not plucking a few out of the world. . . . It is important to remember that we have something far larger to do than the upbuilding of denominational institutions. . . . It is for us to put the spirit of Christ into all social institutions."[8] Infusing this "spirit" was for Ely the task of the leadership of the civil commonwealth guided by the work of social scientists based in the university. Theological or dogmatic convictions could be the province of the denominations. Social redemption — the imperative of the Christian ethic — would become the objective of the expertise of the social scientist. In Ely's conception, the denominationally riven structures of organized religion yielded responsibility for matters of public concern to the "ecumenical," ethically motivated, but dogmatically indifferent, entities of university and state government. In sum, the social gospel became the responsibility of the secular order.[9]

6. Robert T. Handy, *The Social Gospel in America: Gladden, Ely, and Rauschenbusch* (New York: Oxford Univ. Press, 1966), p. 179.

7. Charles McCarthy, *The Wisconsin Idea* (New York, 1912).

8. Ely, *The Social Law of Service* (New York, 1896), p. 262.

9. J. David Hoeveler has described how the Wisconsin Idea "pledged the University of Wisconsin to serve the state by applying its research to the solution of public problems, by training experts in the physical and social sciences and joining their

While Gladden's influence is uncontested and well represented within the structures that came into being in the various denominations and in such interdenominational bodies as the Federal Council of Churches to carry forward the social gospel, the background of the progressive movement, particularly in Wisconsin, in the social gospel and the new theology has been less well understood.[10] In the next section of this chapter, I will analyze Ely's intellectual development and administrative agenda to focus attention on the transmutation of his interests, inspired and supported by the social gospel, into a strategy of publicly sanctioned secular reform.

Ely's Intellectual Development

When Ely was called to the University of Wisconsin in 1892 at the age of thirty-eight, he was already an established economist, albeit one with a somewhat controversial reputation because of his insistence that practitioners of economics and, more broadly, the social sciences had ethical as well as intellectual responsibilities. As a proponent of the new economics, which he mastered at the University of Heidelberg from which he had received the Ph.D. in 1878, Ely had argued consistently that economics was a dynamic and developing discipline, taking its cues about what constituted its fundamental emphases and imperatives from historical and social experience rather than derivations from abstract principles. On this basis, he had argued in *The Past and Present of Political Economy* that the principles of laissez-faire and the individualism undergirding classical political economy should be superseded as normative standards by a commitment to cooperation and to the well-being of the entire social or-

academic efforts to the public, administrative functions of the state" ("The University and the Social Gospel: The Intellectual Origins of the Wisconsin Idea," *Wisconsin Magazine of History* 59, no. 4 [Summer 1976]: 282-98). While emphasizing the role and theological perspective of John Bascom, president of the university from 1874 to 1887, Hoeveler also gives attention to Ely and to John Commons, both of whom were influenced by the social gospel.

10. Hoeveler (ibid., pp. 285-86) observes that one of John Bascom's students, Robert M. La Follette of the class of 1879, credits Bascom as the "originator" of the Wisconsin Idea. Bascom, who taught moral philosophy, accepted evolution as a basis for theology, argued for an expanded public authority for dealing with social problems, and sought to accommodate the objectives of "evangelical ideology" with the needs of the public sphere.

ganism, particularly to those less privileged.[11] With other economists of the so-called historical school, Ely argued from experience that such an adjustment was necessary, because the enlightened selfishness upon which classical political economy had been predicated would lead to social chaos in the industrial age. That this induction corresponded with his understanding of the social ethic of Christianity provided continuing corroboration for the gospel. Christianity and social science shared a fundamental commitment to empiricism. Indeed, the pragmatic validation of biblical ethics provided new grounds for defending old truths.

A comment in his first book, *French and German Socialism in Modern Times,*[12] revealed Ely's formative fascination with social movements, while also delineating the connection between political economy and Christianity:

> Professors of political economy, finding themselves forced to abandon every hope of reconciling adverse interests of society without a moral and religious regeneration of the various social classes, turn to Christianity, and appeal to it for cooperation in their endeavors to bring about an era of peace and harmony. Professorial socialism terminates in Christianity. Christian socialism seeks in it a starting point.[13]

The coincidence of research and reform was characteristic of Ely's stance throughout the 1880s. It permeated *The Labor Movement in America,* his 1886 study, which appealed alternately to sentiment and to data in order to describe a problem and set forth the idea of cooperation between capital and labor.

Following protracted negotiations about the statement of principles for the AEA, and a lively dispute about motives and methodology in his labor study, Ely attempted to separate his academic and his religious-reformist work. For example, in 1889 he published *An Introduction to Political Economy* — the predecessor to his well-known *Outlines of Economics* — and *Social Aspects of Christianity* — a text that became a standard in the social gospel canon. This separation of subjects should not be overemphasized, however; Ely was able to bring each of these books to the public in connection with his work

11. Ely, *The Past and Present of Political Economy* (Baltimore, 1884).
12. Ely, *French and German Socialism in Modern Times* (New York, 1883).
13. Ibid., p. 187. Quoted in Handy, *Social Gospel,* p. 175.

at Chautauqua, where he had been a regular lecturer and extension faculty member. Chautauqua had been established in 1874 by John Vincent, a Methodist minister, and Lewis Miller, a Cleveland businessman, to train Sunday school teachers. Quickly Chautauqua extended its mission to encompass a range of opportunities for adult learning and continuing education. Thus while Ely muted much of the tendency toward moral exhortation in his professorial work, the Chautauqua context provided him — as well as a number of other social gospelers — a platform and a publishing opportunity throughout the 1890s for the full range of reformist, professional, and ethical interests.[14]

Chautauqua also provided an umbrella of theological legitimacy for vocational concerns and academic interests that soon were assimilated into the curriculum of the state university of Wisconsin. The result of this transition was the secularization of a reform impulse that had been regularly energized by the aspirations and actions of evangelicals of different theological persuasions who believed that the lives of individuals and the experience of communities could be regenerated by conversion and education. H. Richard Niebuhr's prescient analysis of the diminution of the church as a transforming power in liberal Protestantism might well have described the implicit theological immanentalism — the sense that the kingdom of God was a possibility realizable in history — and cultural optimism of Chautauqua, where, without much dispute, the particular tasks of religious nurture and education devolved into general education and the pursuit of knowledge for its own sake.[15]

14. C. Howard Hopkins, *The Rise of the Social Gospel in American Protestantism 1865–1915* (New Haven: Yale Univ. Press, 1940), p. 163. In 1889, Hopkins points out, Gladden, Lyman Abbott, and Ely were featured at Chautauqua discussing various aspects of social Christianity. The role of the Chautauqua movement in social Christianity is inadequately understood, in my view. It exemplifies the syndrome at the center of this essay, the extension of a practical, empirical, and undogmatic Christianity to encompass the whole of life and the commitment to education as a means of social conversion, uplift, and change. In the *Chautauqua Year-Book, 1895* (Chautauqua, 1895), p. 16, John Vincent defined the mission of the organization in this way: "through all her history" Chautauqua has been committed "to two essential elements: the promotion of spiritual life, and the highest culture of a spiritual-minded people for the most effective service in society."

15. Cf. H. Richard Niebuhr, *The Kingdom of God in America* (New York: Harper, 1937), pp. 184-98.

Ely's Contribution to the Social Gospel

Three ideas inform Ely's contribution to the development of social gospel thought. First, in *Social Aspects of Christianity,* he argued that Christianity, while properly and centrally concerned with the duty to love God and neighbor, had devoted insufficient attention to developing knowledge and expertise about loving one's neighbor and, conversely, too much attention to matters of belief and church practice. "The gospel," he argued, "which in its highest unity is Love is divided into two parts: the first is theology, the second is sociology — the science of society." Ely understood theology "as the science of God and his relations to his creatures." This, however, was not the whole gospel. The rest of it, obscured in significance following the Reformation, was the "elaboration" of the second commandment, how one individually and as a member of a community exercises the duty of loving the neighbor.[16] Invoking a secular idiom, Ely could also describe love of neighbor as the principle of rational benevolence.[17] This latter duty provides the rationale for the pursuit of what Ely calls social sciences, which, taken along with theology as he defined it, constitute the full scope of Christian knowledge and responsibility.

The second idea, to which Ely returned again and again, was social solidarity. In religion as well as in economics, the principle of individualism had come to assume heretical centrality. Over and against those who continued to assert the primacy of individual conversion or individual self-interest, Ely countered that human experience is shaped and given meaning in community. In a pivotal section of *The Social Law of Service,* he insisted that social solidarity is *the* formative, central reality of life.

> Social solidarity means the oneness of human interests; it signifies the dependence of man upon man, both in good things and in evil things. Social solidarity means that our true welfare is not an individual matter purely, but likewise a social affair: our weal is common weal; we thrive only in a commonwealth; our exaltation is the exaltation of our fellows, their elevation is our enlargement.

16. Quoted in Handy, *Social Gospel,* pp. 192-93.

17. James T. Kloppenberg, *Uncertain Victory: Social Democracy and Progressivism in European and American Thought, 1870–1920* (New York: Oxford Univ. Press, 1986), p. 238. In this regard, Ely appropriated an interpretation that Henry Sidgwick had employed in *History of Ethics.*

> Social solidarity implies not only fellowship in interests and responsibilities, but that unity of nature which is brought before us by the expression "human brotherhood."[18]

This assertion is historically and empirically grounded; it does not represent an application to experience of a principle that finds its justification outside human experience. It is a conviction that, Ely would have insisted, was gleaned from the Bible and from history, but that was also of immense moral significance for industrializing America. The ministry of the social scientist, if we may speak in such terms, is to learn and teach about the implications of this truth.[19]

Finally, Ely believed in the religious vocation of the state, the *polis* in Aristotelian usage. In his 1895 introduction to the American edition of William H. Fremantle's *The World as the Subject of Redemption,* Ely set forth the view that public and Christian service were one and the same: "The legislator in city, state, or nation is likewise a minister in Christ's church, and he is guilty of violation of a sacred trust if he does not endeavor to bring to pass the kingdom of God in his sphere."[20] Influenced by his own understanding of Aristotle, by Anglican theologians Richard Hooker and F. D. Maurice, and by the Lutheran Richard Rothe, Ely argued that the state represents a culmination of an organic principle of development that built up community through family and church in ever more inclusive jurisdictions. American Christianity, individualistic in part as a result of the revivalist tradition, and denominationally organized by virtue of the pluralism that was also a function of individualism, was theologically and organizationally handicapped to promote and project the renewal that the times demanded.

The social gospel must, therefore, become the responsibility of the state, and the state must succeed the church as the inclusive instrument of divine redemption in the world: "It is true," he wrote, "that the main purpose of the State is the religious purpose. Religious

18. Quoted in Handy, *Social Gospel,* pp. 235-36.

19. As early as 1892, a year before the worst effects of the depression of the early 1890s were experienced in Wisconsin, Ely had lectured to the Milwaukee Ministerial Council and the state Congregational Convention on "The Study of Social Science and the Christian Minister." His efforts to convert Wisconsin clergy to the social gospel did not find much support, a fact that could only have discouraged him about the capacity of the churches to effect social change. Cf. David P. Thelen, *The New Citizenship: Origins of Progressivism in Wisconsin* (Columbia, Mo.: Univ. of Missouri Press, 1972), p. 101.

20. Quoted in Handy, *Social Gospel,* p. 242.

laws are the only laws which ought to be enacted. But what are religious laws? Certainly not in the United States laws establishing any particular sectarian views or theological tenets . . . but laws designed to promote the good life."[21] Ely provided concrete illustration for this contention, suggesting a range of areas for reform legislation and a division of religious responsibility between church and state:

> Factory acts, educational laws, laws for the establishment of parks and of playgrounds for children, laws for securing the honest administration of justice, laws rendering the courts accessible to the poor as well as the rich — all these are religious in the truest sense of the word. The Church can go in many respects far beyond the State. It can place ideals ahead of the State to which the State must gradually approach; it can rebuke and inspire the State. . . . Theology in the narrow sense belongs to the Church and not to the modern State. On the other hand, let the Church see to it that all her actions and teachings strengthen and purify the State. Let all Christians . . . put . . . not . . . doctrine or creed into the State constitution, but . . . Christian life and practice into the activity of the State, working . . . to change the constitution in so far as this may stand in the way of righteousness. The nation must be recognized as a fully Christian nation.[22]

These three ideas — the religious-ethical vocation of the social sciences, social solidarity, and the state as a cooperative, Christian commonwealth — provided the intellectual and theological rationale for the pursuit of what has been termed "secular evangelism" at the University of Wisconsin during the progressive period, particularly during the first decade of the twentieth century.[23]

La Follette and the Progressive Vocation

The election of Robert M. La Follette as governor of Wisconsin in 1900 signaled a new era in the history of Wisconsin and the advent of a period when that state would achieve recognition as a model of pro-

21. Quoted in ibid., p. 249.

22. Quoted in ibid.

23. Arthur J. Vidich and Stanford M. Lyman, *American Sociology: Worldly Rejections of Religion and Their Directions* (New Haven: Yale Univ. Press, 1985), pp. 151-67.

gressive reform and administration. The previous decade had exposed to a degree not known before the precariousness of the post–Civil War industrial expansion and the vulnerability of the economic progress it had generated. As a member of the House of Representatives, La Follette, by his own admission, began during the winter of 1890–91 to see "really for the first time" how the problems of the industrial system ravaged parts of Wisconsin. Violent labor conflict — the railroad strike of 1877 and the Haymarket Riot of 1886 — would soon be recalled by the Pullman strike of 1894.

The depression of that year had sapped the nation's hopes and precipitated a cultural crisis, during which conventional wisdom about self-sufficient individualism was called radically into question. Historian David Danbom put it graphically: "Because English capitalists panicked, Kansas farmers, Seattle grocers, and Pennsylvania miners lost their livelihoods. They did not often grasp the intricacies of why it happened, but many could see that they were not the authors of their own misery."[24] In Wisconsin, public utilities, such as power and water companies, the railroads, and other services maintained high rates in the face of the economic downturn, while cutting back on provision of service, relying for protection from the public on a network of friendly politicians who had been bribed. By the mid-1890s, the social gospel had taken hold in significant parts of the major religious denominations. No longer did Protestantism present what Henry F. May called a "massive, almost unbroken front in . . . defense of the social status quo."[25] Progressivism responded to these incongruities with a call to restore — with the aid of the state — the social balance that had been jeopardized.

In pursuing this goal during the six years he presided over the Wisconsin statehouse, La Follette forged an unusual alliance with the university. The social and philosophical ideas of John Bascom, especially Bascom's willingness to conceive of a positive use of state authority on behalf of the public interest, predisposed La Follette to policies of activism and protection in social and economic affairs and to an interpretation of leadership that was consonant with Ely's ideas about the religious vocation of politics and the state.[26]

24. Danbom, *"The World of Hope": Progressives and the Struggle for an Ethical Public Life* (Philadelphia: Temple Univ. Press, 1987), p. 42.

25. May, *Protestant Churches and Industrial America* (New York, 1949), p. 91.

26. Robert S. Maxwell, *La Follette and the Rise of the Progressives in Wisconsin* (Madison: Univ. of Wisconsin Press, 1956); and Robert S. Maxwell, ed., *La Follette*

During this period, with the assistance of a number of faculty members associated with Ely's department, La Follette and the Wisconsin legislature instituted direct primary elections, enacted antimonopoly laws, and formed commissions to develop and monitor policies about railroads, civil service, and taxes. In addition, the beginnings of the work of Wisconsin's renowned Legislative Research Library under the leadership of Charles McCarthy were undertaken.[27] Changes in policy in state government were based on advances in scholarship in the state university. The linkage of the research agenda of the university with the reform agenda of the governor led to a legacy of innovation and commitment to reform principles, which Robert La Follette would later bring to Washington as a U.S. senator. La Follette's ideas and passions influenced both Theodore Roosevelt and Woodrow Wilson (who had been one of Ely's graduate students at Hopkins in the 1880s), forming a tradition of state activism that became a foundation of the New Deal of the 1930s and the Great Society of the 1960s.

This projection onto the near-contemporary stage should not obscure how much Wisconsin Progressivism was indebted to the revivalist and reform background of nineteenth-century Protestant America. While it was manifestly a response to conditions arising out of the industrialization, urbanization, and immigration of the last quarter of the nineteenth century — conditions that define important contours of modern America — Progressivism can also be understood as an effort to recapture the moral universe and social harmonies of a passing culture. The linkage of knowledge and reform, the respectability of the empirical investigative techniques, and the quest for a more efficient and well-ordered society were concerns central to nineteenth-century moral philosophers such as John Bascom and to the twentieth-century social scientists and public administrators who were trained at the University of Wisconsin, the University of Chicago, and a host of other emerging private and land-grant institutions.

For many Progressives, the turn of the century presented a challenge not only to inherited Protestant Christianity, but more impor-

---

(Englewood Cliffs, N.J.: Prentice-Hall, 1969), provide very useful background for this period. The latter volume includes La Follette speeches appealing for different parts of his reform agenda.

27. Edward A. Fitzpatrick, *McCarthy of Wisconsin* (New York, 1944), chronicles the development of the legislative reference library and the important relationship that McCarthy formed with La Follette.

tantly, to their sense of vocation. With the help of secularizing theological strategies like Ely's, the task of deciding what to do was rendered less complex. Evolution, Ely insisted, was an historical-social as well as a natural process, which had bestowed on the state status as a redemptive instrument in the divine plan.[28] The extension of democracy, education, and research, as well as moral campaigns for human uplift and improvement, constituted crusades for social conversion. Deeds not creeds would regenerate American society!

Strategy for Civic Awakening

In a speech delivered in 1889 before the Boston conference of the Evangelical Alliance on "The Needs of the City," Ely anticipated the convergence of religious and civic zeal in a direct call for a "revival of religion." He argued that such a revival, which was not to be directed toward the concerns of a narrow group or fomented to buttress theological convictions, should in the "broadest, largest, fullest sense" be a "great religious awakening which shall shake things, going down to the depths of men's lives and modifying their character."[29]

As part of his strategy for promoting civic awakening, Ely took up a question that would occupy him in succeeding years about the limits of individual and voluntary group action for redressing social problems. Without denigrating the importance of such organizations as the Evangelical Alliance or the Salvation Army for educating about and responding to specific issues, Ely observed that the public sphere — particularly at the municipal and state level — and the work of government represented the "truest development of the Church." The Alliance, "like other societies, must put itself behind municipal government and recognize the reform and elevation of municipal government as one of the chief features of its work." Indeed, Ely continued, "it must strive to establish among us true cities of God." Christian nationalism, inspired by a moderate appropriation of Christian socialism, would be represented at the local level by what Ely

28. Richard T. Ely, *Studies in the Evolution of Industrial Society* (New York, 1903), pp. 10-11.

29. A copy of the original text of this address is in the Richard T. Ely Papers in the Archives of the State Historical Society of Wisconsin. Ely added this address with an introductory note in the rev. ed. of *Problems of Today* (New York, 1890), from which (pp. 231-33) this citation has been taken.

termed *municipalism*, for whose service and mission it would be the task of social scientists to prepare citizens.[30]

Ely returned many times during the 1890s to this argument. In a decidedly more secular vein, his conclusion to *The Coming City*, published in 1902, articulated clearly his view that the United States was becoming an urban civilization: the time of the old ideal of the "domination of the rural community" had passed. "Is it without significance," he asked, "that Christianity became known in a city, and that the word 'pagan' means dweller in the country?" Or, he continued, "is it without significance that the apostle John saw a redeemed society existing as a city [new Jerusalem], coming down from God out of heaven, prepared as a bride adorned for her husband [Rev. 21:22]?"[31] The ordering and management of civic life — the "civic church" — was a religious vocation; it stabilized and consolidated the results of the awakening.

For many who found themselves unprepared and uncertain about the theological or historical legacy of Christianity, the opportunity to pursue social science, social service, or public responsibility seemed eminently consistent with the expectations and the hopes of earlier generations of American Protestants who had assumed responsibility for education and community leadership. While this development may well appear as an abandonment of the distinctively religious dimension of the crusade, it may also be viewed as a progression of a characteristic tendency with roots in the revivals of the Second Great Awakening that stressed religious experience more than religious thought. Practical, experience-based Christianity had after all been the hallmark and the goal of revivalists such as Charles Finney and culture-Protestants such as Henry Ward Beecher.

A theology centered on sentiment — the cultivation of religious feeling in an environment infused with Protestant cultural confidence — was being succeeded by a theology based on service and learning in an environment on the way to becoming post-Protestant in its fundamental orientation. The work of Ely and others associated with the social gospel, who maintained an allegiance to a Christianity practiced privately and faithfully, obscured "the shift," as one writer has characterized it, "from a religious to a scientific perspective in reform."[32] The kinds of issues Ely addressed, those that also became

30. Ely, *The Coming City* (New York, 1902), pp. 71-72.

31. Ibid.

32. Clyde Griffen, "The Progressive Ethos," in *The Development of an American Culture*, ed. Stanley Coben and Lorman Ratner, 2nd ed. (New York, 1983), p. 167.

the concerns of Progressive politicians, focusing on economic, social, and administrative structures, were problems that did not in and of themselves require theological foundation.

Theologically grounded pastors like Washington Gladden or Walter Rauschenbusch could and did address social problems as a result of what they understood as a divine commission. Such problems could, however, also be confronted quite seriously by committed and ambitious persons who lacked any such religious conviction. Believers, searchers, and skeptics could and did come together on this common ground. That they might describe differently how they got there became less important than the alliances they formed to address and alleviate the problems of the time.

This development also marks a transition taking place in the culture, which, while still firmly Protestant, was reorienting itself to accommodate the aspirations of this-worldly focused, pluralistic, and more-subject-to-dogmatic-doubt community. Reform and secularization walked hand in hand into the twentieth century. They did not, however, walk alone. They carried with them the hope and the dream that the national community, unified and revitalized, might become a moral beacon, sending forth light and truth, as they prepared the way for a more democratic kingdom. Sam "Golden Rule" Jones, the Progressive mayor of Toledo, gave expression to a sentiment shared by many Christian progressives at the turn of the century:

> We are to see in the near future a wave of revival that shall sweep over this country and, indeed, the civilized world, that shall be, in the best sense of the word, a revival of real religion; the setting up of a social and political order that will enable every man and woman to be the best kind of man or woman that he or she is capable of being. The noble, the patriotic thing for each now is to do his best to spread the truth of Equality, of Brotherhood, that alone can bring the better days.[33]

Historical Assessment

The transition described herein not only helps illumine the relationship of the social gospel to progressivism and to the development of

33. Samuel M. Jones, *Letters of Love and Labor* (Toledo, 1900), pp. 7-8. Quoted in Griffen, "Progressive Ethos," p. 177.

twentieth-century American culture, but also highlights the ambiguous character of the reform movement itself. Since the publication of Richard Hofstadter's *The Age of Reform* in 1955, historians have been concerned about the significance of personal status in the motivation of reformers. Hofstadter emphasized the role of the middle-class reformer's quest for a perspective on social change that would preserve class differentiations during a period of rapid transformation. To be sure, Ely and others like him were in part motivated by a concern about their station in life and desirous of self-advancement.[34]

To a significant extent, however, they were also charting a new course, making use of coordinates from an old map. To fail to appreciate the extent of their cultural dependence on, and rootedness in, the ground of nineteenth-century Protestant America is to fail in the fundamental task assigned to the historian — to see our predecessors as clearly as possible in terms that they would have understood, and then to make the connections that can be made to our experience. The social gospel and progressive movements may be as confusing to interpret as they are because we rush prematurely to make them as modern as we are.

In truth they conserve and transmit important — but different — legacies: they conserve and perpetuate a quest for a commonwealth that has a single standard of value, and a common language to describe it. Something about their quest justifies the stress on revitalization and renewal, as William McLoughlin has argued. They frequently give expression to a yearning for an essentially homogeneous Anglo-Saxon community. For example, when Ely discusses race, he is usually referring to problems of strengthening the Anglo-Saxon legacy of the country.[35] He and others like him seldom considered issues of structural racism as it affected the lives of black Americans. In a peculiar sense, while these progressives recognized so many dimensions of change and evolution, they had a difficult time tolerating, much less embracing, differences of background, experience, and culture. The quest for social solidarity was based, at least implicitly, on the assumption that those bound together in the emerging cooperative com-

34. Cf. Thelen, *New Citizenship*, pp. 1-4; and Kloppenberg, *Uncertain Victory*, pp. 271-77, for a fuller discussion of the problem of status, elitism, and social control in the Progressive movement.

35. For example, the discussion of eugenics in Ely, *Studies in the Evolution of Industrial Society*, pp. 179ff., focuses on the importance of controlling the reproductive habits of the unfit.

monwealth would be people like themselves — the descendants of those who had sought two and a half centuries earlier to build, in John Winthrop's words, "a City upon a Hill."[36]

At the same time, this movement definitively challenged the power of laissez-faire individualism, breaking with one of the cardinal tenets of the conventional wisdom by setting forth a model of a society as an organism composed of interdependent human beings, and laying a foundation for a recalibration of the role of government. The idea that public policy could become the vehicle for social change and the relief of distress is a fundamental axiom of twentieth-century politics. It underlies government responsibility for regulation and protection in the economic sphere, health policy, social security, environmental preservation, and, to some extent, human rights. As influential as this idea was to become, we should not forget that Ely and others argued for the positive state on biblical as well as experiential grounds. It was, however, the argument from experience — the terrain charted by the social sciences — that would finally prevail, becoming the basis of the pragmatic, public activism that has been characteristic of twentieth-century reform.

H. Richard Niebuhr worried about the implications of this anthropocentric shift for the church. He understood Christianity to represent a revolution in the world that enabled modern sensibilities to respond to the presence and activity of God without sacrificing the gift of critical reason or the imperative of scientific objectivity. The Christian church was and is called to transform and not become captive to the culture. Ely read, and was to some extent influenced by, F. D. Maurice, whom Niebuhr cited — along with Augustine — as an exponent of the theological model of Christ, the "transformer of culture." By this designation Niebuhr sought to identify a stance, consistent with the incarnational theology of the Fourth Gospel, that did not succumb to a secularity that lost all sight of the continuing dependence of the human community on the saving work of God. The distinctiveness of this position is its combination of serious this-worldliness and faithful recognition that the relationship between creatures and their Creator would never be based on a principle of sameness.[37]

36. In a recent study, Ronald H. White argues that some social gospelers were more concerned about racial issues than historians have noted (*Liberty and Justice for All: Racial Reform and the Social Gospel [1877–1925]* [New York: Harper & Row, 1990]).

37. Niebuhr, *Christ and Culture*, pp. 218-29.

As a group, progressively inclined social gospelers — critical as they could be of certain patterns of abuse — did not transcend the culture; they did not find a common vantage apart from the reality they sought to change. Focused almost entirely on the problems of the new industrial order, they remained captives of their situation, their competence, and their professional aspirations. In the quest to revitalize their culture, they left scarcely a trace of their religious root system. In part as a consequence of this omission, this stream of the social gospel was assimilated virtually without remainder into the secular academic and reform tradition.

Mainline Protestants and the Social Gospel Impulse

Janet F. Fishburn

The social gospel movement was the church-related form of a larger "Progressive" movement in the United States between the Civil War and World War I. The concept of a "social gospel," or "applied Christianity," originated in the late 1870s as a few clergy began to respond to social issues created by industrialization, urbanization, and immigration. Early social gospel leaders like Washington Gladden and Josiah Strong expressed concern about labor problems, workers, and the cities through sermons, lectures, books, and articles.

Gladden, a Congregational minister, established a national reputation for his ability to "arbitrate" labor disputes because of a speech he gave to laborers and labor leaders after the Haymarket Riot of May 11, 1886. In that speech, "Is it Peace or War?" he was critical of the effects of laissez-faire economics of the time. But he never developed a critique of the politics of a laissez-faire economic system. He believed that labor and capital could resolve their differences, and this resolution would lead America toward the next stage in world history, a socialist state with shared ownership of industry.

After the turn of the century, men like former pastor and seminary professor Walter Rauschenbusch joined labor leaders, "progressives," and "muckrakers" of the time in alerting the public to the excesses of laissez-faire capitalism. Like other social gospel leaders, Rauschenbusch believed that political unrest could lead to class warfare if labor conflicts were not resolved.

Theirs was a world in which church members and clergy were unsettled by social and intellectual change, especially talk of socialism, Darwinism, and higher criticism. It was also a world in which it was taken for granted that clergy and the church should not be involved with political issues.

Although historians generally refer to the social gospel as a movement, it is becoming more common to think of the social gospel as an impulse.[1] When seen as an impulse related to modern liberal theology the American social gospel appears to be more than just part of the progressive movement of the nineteenth century. Most Protestants have always been concerned in some way with public welfare and the public good. It is the American context, not the social impulse, that makes the American social gospel unique. Edward Farley claims:

> It was especially the Social Gospel of the early twentieth century that pressed the issue of the social character of the gospel. And while its framework was an optimism and progressivism, which few people now share, its legacy is at work when the church takes its stand against dehumanizing movements of modern culture, when it confronts racism and sexism within itself and the larger society, when it debates issues of militarism and the pollution of the planet. Rare now is the view that the gospel is simply a message about a trans-earthly destiny of individual souls. Few doubt that the Christian gospel has something to do with systematic evil and our social well-being.[2]

Few Protestants doubted that the gospel had something to do with systematic evil and social well-being earlier in the century either. The Prohibition Amendment was supported by a coalition of social gospel leaders and evangelicals with no interest in labor problems. Both believed that a host of related social "ills" would be solved by Prohibition. The issue was not whether the gospel was simply a message about "heaven" and the salvation of individuals. The issue was *how* the gospel is related to systematic evil and what that means for the church. The broader issue was the role of the church in a democratic society.

The social gospel has always been an impulse more than a movement. A movement refers to an organization with political objectives that has leaders who plan strategies and followers who act on

1. William R. Hutchinson, *The Modernist Impulse in American Protestantism* (Cambridge: Harvard Univ. Press, 1976).

2. Edward Farley, "The Modernist Element in Protestantism," *Theology Today* 47, no. 2 (July 1990): 140.

their strategies. The leaders of the American social gospel movement kept a historic Protestant concern for public welfare alive in a time when preoccupation with the conversion of individuals threatened to blind a prosperous middle-class constituency to the wretched living conditions of a growing lower class. They refused to believe that Christians should be concerned only with spiritual welfare and that separation of church and state meant that the church cannot speak publicly about political or economic issues.

Even though social gospel leaders did emphasize the social application of the gospel, they were also evangelicals who believed that conversion was necessary. In general, they expected social reform to occur through the activity of redeemed individuals. Like other evangelicals at the time, they believed that America was, or would soon be, a Christian nation. Like other evangelicals, they sanctioned the activities of the American government as the acts of a Christian nation, including the invasion of the Philippines in 1898.

Social gospel leaders differed from other evangelicals in believing that it was *also* necessary for Christians to speak out against social evil. On the one hand, they did not support legislation unless they thought it embodied public opinion; on the other hand, they worked tirelessly to influence public opinion where they thought new laws were needed.

Social gospel leaders are distinguished from more conservative evangelicals of the period by their belief that "new" theology was needed to undergird the social gospel. They considered confessional statements and the "old" Calvinist theology a hindrance to social and moral progress. The new theology was dedicated to adjusting old Calvinism to "present-day living." At a time when social gospel leaders were writing new theology and books about higher criticism, Presbyterians were caught up in internal theological conflict over this new theology. The General Assembly that officially sanctioned thirteen social principles also adopted a statement concerning the "five fundamentals" of Christian faith.

Social Gospel Theology

Walter Rauschenbusch was the historian of the social gospel movement as well as its theologian. He influenced the writing of all subsequent social gospel history. His theology is still studied in seminaries. The themes of his three major books provide insight into the history of the early movement as he understood it.

Rauschenbusch was pleasantly surprised by the positive response to *Christianity and Social Crisis,* published in 1907. He wrote that, despite the present social crisis, the kingdom of God would come on earth if the church would be the church. He viewed the American democracy as the social system most favorable to creating a social environment in which "good people could be good." He considered freedom of religion essential to the possibility that there could be more social good than evil in America. But the church was the social institution responsible for the moral and social values of the people.

In 1912, Rauschenbusch wrote *Christianizing the Social Order* as a sequel to his earlier analysis of the forces of good and evil in American society. This time he systematically analyzed major social institutions and found all except the economic system to be "almost" Christianized. He believed that the capitalist system would gradually become more socialistic. Otherwise, he found the family, education, the government, and the churches "Christian" insofar as each institution seemed to contribute positively to a social order that increasingly favored cooperation rather than competition as a social principle.

Early in the pages of this book he cited particular movements as evidence of a hastened flow of goodwill toward the coming kingdom. High on his list was the influence of the Men and Religion Forward Movement. Like the writer of a 1910 article in *The Presbyterian* who claimed that America was a Christian nation because there were more Protestants than Catholics, Rauschenbusch was concerned with statistical majorities.[3] He was alarmed that there were more women in Protestant churches than men. Since he assumed that men were responsible for government, politics, economics, and all public affairs, he drew the conclusion that if the kingdom of God was to come in America, the church had to reach more men.

In 1912, anyone looking for evidence of positive social change would have found it. For a man like Rauschenbusch, who interpreted social cooperation as a sign of the coming kingdom, there was a great deal of good news. The Socialist party of America became official in 1901. Presbyterians organized a Department of Church and Labor in

3. "Is Ours a Christian Nation?" *The Presbyterian* (June 15, 1910). Both use empirical evidence to establish their point; both assume that the will of the majority establishes what is right or true.

1903. The Clayton Anti-Trust Act was passed in 1906, the year the Department of Labor and Commerce was established. Adoption of social principles by denominations signaled ecumenical acceptance of a social gospel. For a church historian like Rauschenbusch, the 1908 founding of the Federal Council of Churches must have seemed like a great victory for church unity compared to theological conflicts like earlier Presbyterian heresy trials over higher criticism.

Rauschenbusch considered it possible that theology that did not keep up with present-day events and ideas would die. *A Theology for the Social Gospel,* published in 1917, was written in the conviction that a social gospel movement that would continue to exist and grow. The social values of the movement would be affirmed with or without a theology. His assumption was that religion is essential to human society; theology is not.

Written during the years of World War I, the theology of Rauschenbusch was a response to conservative evangelicals who rejected "new" theology and claimed that the social gospel movement had no theology. Movement leaders had studiously avoided theological and creedal affirmations that they thought worked against ecumenical cooperation. In the book, Rauschenbusch updated the doctrines he considered essential to theology — symbols for God, interpretations of human nature, sin, salvation, and eschatology.

The premise of his new theology was a progressive interpretation of the history of ideas, theology, and the Bible. Rauschenbusch argued that premillennial apocalyptic ideas were socially destructive. The belief that Jesus would return to earth before the millennium kept Christians from seeing that the coming kingdom required their contribution to the social good.[4] Instead, he offered Jesus as moral inspiration to the church. Here was a person who suffered for his role in criticizing the social status quo of his time, but who was ever faithful to the task.[5]

The theological issue between liberals and conservatives was not whether the gospel has social applications. It was how to balance the individual and social aspects of the gospel. It was also a question of the role of the church in a democratic society.

The major distinction between the new (liberal) and old (con-

4. Walter Rauschenbusch, *A Theology for the Social Gospel* (1917; repr. Nashville: Abingdon, 1945), pp. 208-11.

5. Ibid., pp. 277-79.

servative) theology is that liberals considered new truth more valuable than old truth, new ideas better than old ideas. Many had been influenced by Horace Bushnell, who viewed "truth" as a whole known only to God that was gradually unfolding through progress in human knowledge. In other words, human knowledge of truth is considered progressive. On those grounds, social gospel leaders accepted higher criticism of the Bible and dismissed parts of Scripture they found anachronistic. Their criterion for truth was pragmatic. It was the effect of ideas on human behavior.

Regardless of theological differences, especially over the status of the Bible, the conservatives and social gospel leaders all subscribed to an evangelical view of the world. Both parties assumed the reality of "natural law" that guided the moral sense (conscience) of individuals.[6] Both subscribed to a social theory in which they assumed that more people doing good would result in a basically good society. This same logic led both groups to expect that the world could be Christianized in their lifetime. They differed about how and how soon. Conservatives, then as now, saw the social good being achieved by influencing individuals through evangelism and mission. Liberals, then as now, saw a need for the church to act more corporately in seeking social well-being.

Both assumed that truth is self-evident and available to the senses. Knowledge is considered reliable when a group of people agree on an interpretation of reality. This epistemology is very convenient in a democracy where it is believed that the opinion of the majority must be right. Then, as now, faith in the goodness of democratic freedom as an ultimate value makes it difficult to challenge any social status quo. This difficulty is further compounded by belief that America is a Christian nation.

No one questioned the rightness of middle-class prosperity. Although Rauschenbusch was a lonely critic of capitalism as an economic system, he would have agreed with the Presbyterian social principles that what was needed was a responsible use of wealth. Social gospel leaders were not critical of wealth accumulation. They wanted a more just distribution of wealth. There is no indication that they asked whether unlimited wealth is good for people.

6. See Mark A. Noll, *The Princeton Theology: 1812–1921* (Philadelphia: Presbyterian and Reformed, 1983), for a full discussion of the commonsense philosophy foundations of conservative theology. I am suggesting that liberal and conservative theologians shared very similar assumptions about how truth is known.

Rauschenbusch assumed that everyone has a desire to work, but work must be fairly rewarded so the "natural" desire to work can develop. Therefore, social law and governance should be arranged so that everyone can exercise the desire to work and be fairly compensated. He assumed that property must be available to all as a reward for good.

Evangelicals, including social gospel evangelicals, never supported social reform through legislation unless they believed it expressed the will of the majority. They regarded new legislation as an expression of changed public opinion rather than a way to change public opinion. That is why the primary objective of social gospel leaders was that of influencing public opinion rather than more direct participation in legislative, corporate, or political processes.

When these nineteenth-century premises are recognized it becomes obvious that the civil rights movement under the leadership of Martin Luther King, Jr., broke with earlier social gospel tradition. In the world of Walter Rauschenbusch, the tradition of "higher law" on the possibility of civil disobedience as a strategy was (literally) unthinkable.

Earlier Movements and the Social Gospel Impulse

Social gospel history is usually written as the history of an ecumenical movement with attention to leaders from various denominations. Ecumenical commitment to social principles expressed in the founding of the Federal Council of Churches is often regarded as the "flowering" of the social gospel movement. Rapid decline of the movement after World War I is usually explained in terms of a theology too optimistic to address postwar social reality.

Social gospel advocates tend to imagine that the churches have, at some time in the past, been more effective in taking a stand against dehumanizing forces in modern culture. This is the impression given about the role of the movement regarding labor issues. This impression was partially created by a remark of Rauschenbusch that the Progressive party had "simply adopted the Federal Council platform" in 1912.[7] A new study of the social gospel in the progressive era shows, however, that 1912 was the banner year for the social gospel and the

7. Donald K. Gorrell, *The Age of Social Responsibility: The Social Gospel in the Progressive Era* (Macon, Ga.: Mercer, 1988), p. 182.

Federal Council. The council was soon caught up in debate about how an ecumenical agency with a small staff could be involved in social service. Much of the impetus for the debates came from more theologically conservative members like the Presbyterians.[8]

A more likely explanation for the rapid loss of influence of the social gospel movement after 1912 is that it was a movement without a strong constituency among church members. The formal adoption of social principles did not commit congregations or church members to any particular kind of theology or activity. It was not until 1960 that the Methodist General Conference recommended that every congregation have a Commission on Christian Social Concern.

It is inadequate to equate the history of the new theology, or the story of a small group of social gospel advocates, or official acts of denominations with the history of the social gospel impulse. A fuller picture requires attention to all the people who were the church prior to and during the social gospel movement. What happened to the social gospel impulse during the women's suffrage movement? Who were the advocates of rights for women? Who were the advocates of rights for black people after the failure of reconstruction?

The social gospel impulse of evangelical Christianity in the nineteenth century had roots going back to the abolition movement. Although Rauschenbusch described the movement of his time as new, this was not accurate. Clergy addressing social issues in public was new. Social analysis was new. But concern for the well-being of social groups was not. The same evangelical emphasis on acts of piety as signs of salvation that inspired Rauschenbusch had inspired attention to civil rights issues in the 1830s.

During the height of earlier expressions of a social gospel impulse, evangelicals at Seneca Falls in 1848 had declared their support for abolition and women's suffrage. The broadly ecumenical leadership at that time included men and women, black people and white people.[9] This integrated ecumenical spirit had a short life. In 1869 the Female Suffrage Association separated from the National Suffrage Association. The so-called social gospel movement and the suffrage movement — both predominantly white — emerged when reconstruction efforts in the South lost ground.

8. Ibid., parts 3 and 4.

9. Barbara J. MacHaffie, *Her Story: Women in Christian Tradition* (Minneapolis: Fortress, 1986), pp. 102 and 113.

The decade between 1870 and 1880 is known to suffrage historians as "the Women's Decade." It is also the first decade of social gospel attention to labor problems. These were the years in which Frances G. Willard emerged as a national W.C.T.U. leader seeking to resolve "the alcohol problem" through "woman suffrage." Willard, a Methodist, is rarely treated as a social gospel movement leader. Yet her social concerns differed little from those of men who led the movement before the turn of the century. Both worked for a more Christian America. Both believed that solving the alcohol problem would resolve many of the problems of cities, urban slums, and lower-class life. Like the social gospel men, Willard was a public figure associated with the church in the public mind. Willard was bitterly disappointed to discover that men she had supported in the temperance cause did not support her in the suffrage movement.

Social Gospel Leaders and "the Woman Problem"

Walter Rauschenbusch had said very little about suffrage until asked to write an article in 1913. He titled the article "Some Moral Aspects of the Woman Movement." In 1912 both the woman suffrage movement and the social gospel movement came of age. On the day of Woodrow Wilson's inauguration, five thousand suffragettes marched down Pennsylvania Avenue. In July, suffrage leaders carried two hundred thousand signatures with petitions to their senators. By 1913, when Rauschenbusch addressed the issue, it looked as if women were going to get the vote. The tone of his article is one of resignation, not support. When compared to the political activity of women who had garnered the votes to achieve state by state passage of suffrage bills, the concern of Rauschenbusch that women might be morally compromised by participation in the public sphere was patronizing.[10]

A survey of activities of the Methodist Federation for Social Service led by Harry G. Ward after its formation in 1907 shows no interest in "the woman question." Records of Ward's speaking engagements, and a list of topics available from speakers in seventeen states, reveals only one reference to women's issues between 1912 and 1914. The Federation, Methodism's social gospel agency, concentrated its

10. Walter Rauschenbusch, "Some Moral Aspects of the Woman Movement," *Biblical World,* new ser. 42 (Oct. 1913).

resources on educating church members about men and religion, business practices, politics, poverty, and labor issues.[11]

Official Presbyterian commitment to the social gospel was located in the Department of Church and Labor. A one-man office was opened by Charles Stetzle in 1903. Stetzle, the only publicly recognized Presbyterian social gospel advocate at the time, was devoted almost entirely to "the laboring man." He spoke at labor rallies and founded a church in New York City called the Labor Temple.[12] The Department, hailed by social gospel leaders as a sign of progress, was located in the Board of Home Missions. Its demise in 1912–13 is a complicated chapter in the rise of conservative opposition to a Presbyterian social gospel that was not finally silenced until 1936.[13]

The demise of the Department of Church and Labor did not leave Presbyterians without social concerns advocates. Since 1905, the northern Presbyterian Church had a board, with an official publication, devoted to social issues. *The Amethyst,* published by the Board of Temperance and Moral Welfare, took a "strong and supportive interest in . . . women's suffrage. It was presumed that the women's vote would weigh heavily against drink, adding direct political clout to the leadership and energy they had long contributed to the social movement."[14] During the Prohibition crusade that ended with the ratification of the Eighteenth Amendment in 1918, *The Amethyst* had a circulation of 185,000.

The Social Gospel Impulse among Methodists and Presbyterians

Rauschenbusch, the self-appointed historian of the movement, was convinced that Protestant churches lacked social influence because they were not attractive to men. He viewed the movement as work

11. Janet F. Fishburn, "The Methodist Social Gospel and Woman Suffrage," *Drew Gateway* 54, nos. 2-3 (Winter/Spring 1984): 88-91.

12. C. Howard Hopkins, *The Rise of the Social Gospel in American Protestantism* (New Haven: Yale Univ. Press, 1940), pp. 280-83.

13. Lefferts A. Loetscher, *The Broadening Church* (Philadelphia: Univ. of Pennsylvania Press, 1954), pp. 148-56.

14. "Church and Society at Eighty," *Church and Society* 80, no. 1 (Sept./Oct. 1989): 6.

important enough to challenge manly faith.[15] The fact that histories of the movement usually treat only men leaders and public issues associated with men reinforces the idea that "the social gospel" was and is men's work.

A closer look at the range of church activities between 1870 and 1912 suggests that social service agencies formed during that period represent a men's movement with interests similar to those pursued by women's missionary societies and boards originating in the 1830s. Typically, the social concerns of social gospel men fell under the rubric of home mission work, including abolition, temperance and prohibition, reconstruction, poverty, and city mission work. The Presbyterian Department of Church and Labor is the outstanding example of a church agency devoted to the one issue that most clearly distinguished the causes of social gospel men from those of church women.

The leadership and official status of home missions makes a difference in the way the social gospel impulse among Presbyterians has been perceived. During the years that the Presbyterian General Assembly was embroiled in theological controversy, the Women's Boards were engaged in a prolonged controversy with the General Assembly over autonomy and control of their own finances. A first step in reorganizing women's work was taken in 1916 through an incorporating charter that made women's work "auxiliary" to the Assembly's Foreign Board and Home Board.[16] A series of discussions over proposed reorganization began in 1923 when the General Assembly approved a plan that would have, in effect, dissolved the two women's boards.

Bargaining about multiple mission boards did not officially end until 1946 with the formation of a new organization, Presbyterian Women. At issue had been finances and the power of the General Assembly to reorganize the women's boards without consultation or representation. The discussions eventually led to a General Assembly commissioned study of "unrest among church women" and approval of the ordination of women as elders in 1930.

While Presbyterian disagreements about the social gospel and social ministry came to focus in the modernist-fundamentalist con-

15. Janet F. Fishburn, *The Fatherhood of God and the Victorian Family: A Study of the Social Gospel in America* (Philadelphia: Fortress, 1982), pp. 166-70.

16. Lois A. Boyd and R. Douglas Brackenridge, *Presbyterian Women in America: Two Centuries of a Quest for Status* (Westport, Conn.: Greenwood, 1983), pp. 50-54.

troversy and in the status of the Women's Boards, Methodist denominational identity has been associated with the social gospel since the adoption of the Social Creed in 1908. The Social Creed is periodically updated and is part of the Methodist Book of Discipline.

An important chapter in Methodist history is the denomination's stance on racism. When the Methodist Churches, north and south, reunited in 1939 they agreed to the formation of an all-black jurisdiction. In the restructuring of the new denomination an official but semiautonomous Women's Board of Christian Social Relations was created. The Women's Board served as the conscience of the denomination about segregation in the church and in society. As a consequence, Methodist women have a history of studying and supporting legislation, of educating their denomination about social concerns.[17]

The Presbyterian social gospel impulse during the same period was expressed through the Board of Social Education and Action and its journal, *Social Progress.* Racism has been a continuous theme in the journal and its successor, *Church and Society,* since the publication of an article, "Race Relations and the Church," by Roy Wilkens in 1935. Despite the difference in denominational structures, official actions concerning desegregation differ very little. Neither acted with any strong conviction regarding racism until after the Supreme Court ruling of 1954 *(Brown v. Board of Education)* indicated a need for legislation outlawing desegregation in public institutions.

Although Presbyterian leaders have addressed racism as a social problem since the 1930s, a 1984 national survey shows that a majority of Methodists and Presbyterians oppose the use of legislation in race issues. The survey reveals that mainline church members sanction only the voluntary actions of individuals as a response to discrimination.[18]

One may draw several conclusions from comparing official actions and institutional structure of Methodists and Presbyterians during the first half of the twentieth century. If the social gospel is considered an impulse rather than a movement, the expression of that impulse was not limited to a group of white men concerned with labor

17. Thelma Stevens, *Legacy for the Future: The History of Christian Social Relations in the Women's Division of Christian Service, 1940–1968* (Women's Division, 1978), chaps. 2 and 3.

18. William McKinney and Wade Roof, *American Mainline Religion* (New Brunswick: Rutgers Univ. Press, 1987), p. 103.

problems before World War I. The Methodist self-image as a social gospel denomination is related to the continuing role of the Social Creed as a theological commitment. It is also related to the fact that Harry F. Ward, the most visible Methodist social gospel advocate, was actively involved with the Methodist Federation for Social Service from 1907 until 1944. Since 1939 the Women's Division of Christian Social Relations has exerted continuous influence in Methodist congregations through the activity of Methodist women.

Social gospel historians associate Presbyterian identity with doctrine and theology, with an educated clergy, and with protection of white, middle-class values. It has been suggested that Presbyterians are more protective of status quo values because Reformed polity grants equal votes to laity and clergy.[19] The Presbyterians have no equivalent to the influence Methodist women have exercised in their denomination. In addition to the influence of the Women's Division, Methodist women were first seated as delegates to General Conference in 1892. Presbyterian women could not participate in official policy-making until after 1930.

Still, the social gospel impulse has had a broader base in Presbyterian denominational structure. After the emergence of the Department of Social Education and Action in 1936, social concerns were associated with that board, with education in general, and with the mission boards. In 1947, the Department of Social Education and Action opened an office in Washington for the purpose of keeping church members informed about social legislation.

An officially sanctioned creed has no necessary relationship to the values of the people who are the church. Although few Protestants today would claim that America is "an almost Christianized nation," nineteenth-century thinking about the world, God, and the church still influences theological discourse. The values of church members are often those of civil religion. Even though scholars suspect a decline in civil religion in American culture, Protestant religion is still intimately linked to the moral and social aspirations of "a Christian America."[20]

In their study of *American Mainline Religion*, Roof and McKin-

19. Henry May, *Protestant Churches and Industrial America* (New York: Harper, 1949), pp. 192-93.

20. Robert T. Handy, *A Christian America: Protestant Hopes and Historical Reality* (New York: Oxford Univ. Press, 1981), pp. 173-74. Handy's well-documented argument is that the hope for a Christian America was widely shared in the culture and among Protestant church members and their leaders in the nineteenth century.

ney note the close link between religion and core values and ideals. In trying to explain the precipitous decline in mainline denominations since 1965, they point out that "the American religious mainline is very American."[21] A wellspring of religious and moral values lies at the heart of American self-understanding and sense of national vocation. "To be mainline is to relate to this core aspect of American experience, to evoke its symbols and meanings in the collective experience of the people."[22]

A major function of Protestant religion has been to keep the American dream alive. The dream includes belief in democratic values, especially freedom and justice for all. The paradox of the social gospel is that those who have been part of that impulse since the beginning of the twentieth century have taken national rhetoric more seriously than others. They have worked to make freedom and justice a reality. As a minority trying to convince their denominations that majority opinion is not always right, justice advocates are sometimes perceived as un-American or unpatriotic. The irony of the accusation is that representatives of the social gospel impulse are often only saying that America is not Christian enough!

A survey of government officials, senators, and representatives conducted in 1957 showed that they had no knowledge of denominational pronouncements, even when they were members of a denomination.[23] There is little evidence in the history of various expressions of the social gospel impulse to indicate that official representatives of Protestant denominations have actually shaped public opinion. The social gospel was effective because it was one of many progressive movements in favor of better labor conditions. Leaders were motivated by fear of class warfare as well as sympathy for labor. Put another way, they were protecting social order and middle-class prosperity.

The Social Gospel Impulse in a Changing Culture

It is the American separation of church and state that makes the social gospel impulse unique and necessary. Racism, sexism, and classism

21. McKinney and Roof, *American Mainline Religion*, p. 75.

22. Ibid.

23. Janet Forsythe, "The Interests of Protestant Churches in the Legislative Process," unpublished paper, Washington Semester Project, 1958.

are systemic evils related to economic issues. The self-image of justice advocates as lonely prophets is not a fiction. There is no way to seek justice for minority groups in a democracy without asking the majority to yield some of their taken-for-granted privileges. The fact that affluent Protestants have so often equated middle-class prosperity with God's blessing makes it doubly difficult for them to challenge institutionalized injustice.

The disestablishment of religion in America made pastors economically vulnerable to the financial support of their congregants. There have always been a few pastors who were justice advocates, but they are exceptions. Presbyterian Panel surveys regularly show that ordained church leaders who do not serve a parish are more liberal on social issues than their counterparts in the parish. Most of the early social gospel leaders were professors or administrators, men who did not depend on the goodwill of a congregation for their livelihood. It is likely that social gospel leadership among Presbyterians will continue to come from men and women who are nonparish clergy and professors.

The major difference between the earliest social gospel impulse and the mainline Protestant social mission since mid-century lies in the minority status of Protestant churches. Robert Handy claims that the disestablishment of the ethos of "a Christian America" began in the mid-1930s. He is correct if he means that values considered American-Protestant were losing motivating power in American culture. Yet there appears to be little recognition of this cultural shift among pastors, church members, or denominational leaders. Conservative churches may be growing because they still affirm the values of the nineteenth-century Protestant ethos. But denominational leaders have been so preoccupied with membership loss that they rarely look at the relationship between church and culture as a factor in membership loss.

Since 1960, a changing culture would probably have reduced the formative power of Protestant values even if "mainline" churches had been growing. Robert Wuthnow argues that government intervention has displaced Protestant influence in education and social services.[24] Television has become a powerful source of religious and

24. Robert Wuthnow, *The Restructuring of American Religion* (Princeton: Princeton Univ. Press, 1988), chaps. 6 and 7. Wuthnow argues that the restructuring of American religion is related to the expanding role of the state in entitlement legislation,

cultural values. Very few Protestant leaders are now known to the public. Protestant religious leaders and church activities receive little news coverage. These are all aspects of what Handy refers to as a second disestablishment of religion in America.

The mainline churches are caught up, once again, in theological controversy over moral and social values. Nevertheless, as in the past, a social gospel impulse still exists, and there is evidence that Protestant leaders have developed more realistic strategies for concrete social action in recent years. Two outstanding examples are the Nestlé Boycott and interfaith work on corporate responsibility through investment.

The Interfaith Center on Corporate Responsibility (ICCR) is an ecumenical group formed to distribute information, analyze investment portfolios, and coordinate the filing of resolutions.

> In its 20-year history ICCR has filed thousands of resolutions with thousands of companies on issues like Third World debt; tobacco and infant-formula marketing; nuclear weapons manufacture; environment standards; nondiscriminatory employment practices in the U.S., South Africa and Northern Ireland; animal rights; and affordable housing. By 1991 ICCR's membership included 55 Protestant denominations and more than 200 Roman Catholic archdioceses and orders.[25]

These activities acknowledge the connection between economic policies, politics, and dehumanizing movements of modern culture. Some groups, such as the Presbyterian Committee on Mission Responsibility Through Investment (MRTI), publish newsletters that interpret denominational policies to church people who are affected by them.[26]

Early social gospel leaders like Gladden and Rauschenbusch have been criticized by historians and theologians for their naive reading of social institutions and American culture. They have also

---

issues of poverty, aging, and child care (p. 116), and in government funding choices in education and scientific research. He concludes that between the 1950s and the 1970s "the influence of traditional religion . . . seemed to be declining relative to that of other social institutions" (p. 159). His work is an impressive attempt to describe the changing role of religion in American culture.

25. Robert K. Massie, Jr., "Corporate Democracy and the Legacy of Divestment," *Christian Century* (July 24-31, 1991): 717.

26. MRTI Newsletter 1, no. 1, Committee on Mission Responsibility Through Investment, Presbyterian Church (U.S.A.) (Jan. 1989).

been rightly praised for taking a stand, for challenging the complacency of their church constituencies, and for representing the church to the public. Each new generation of social justice advocates can learn from their naivete and from their faith, hope, and courage.

The mix of civil religion with Protestant moral and social values has historically inhibited the ability of mainline church members to see and to acknowledge the dehumanizing power of injustice. An uncritical appropriation of cultural values considered "Christian" has meant that social gospel leaders rarely saw social evil with more clarity than others.

A worldview grounded in the belief that "truth is self-evident" has functioned to perpetuate ways of thinking about moral and social values that have seriously compromised the capacity of Americans to see and hear biblical "truth."[27] The democratic idea of freedom functions as a value requiring no justification. Americans are convinced that a close relationship exists between their freedoms — including freedom of religion — and a free enterprise system.

From the beginning of the twentieth century to the present, most religious leaders have sanctioned the equation of freedom with capitalism and individual self-fulfillment. The economy is usually regarded as a means to other ends: greater prosperity, less suffering, more freedom.[28] It is rare to find a justice advocate challenging the idea of individual freedom, or capitalism as a free enterprise system. It is also rare to find representatives of religious institutions taking the kind of initiatives found in the civil rights movement and the ICCR.

The immediate task for social justice advocates is the education of the people who are the church and continuing advocacy with public decision makers of more just policies. The educational task in the biblical prophetic tradition is "to nurture and evoke a consciousness and perception alternative to the consciousness and perception of the dominant culture."[29]

Since a civil religion is at the heart of the dominant culture, it

27. This is indirectly demonstrated in Christian T. Iosso, "Reformed Economic Ethics in Presbyterian General Assembly Statements, 1900–1987," in *Reformed Faith and Economics*, ed. Robert L. Stivers (Lanham, Md.: Univ. Press of America, 1988), pp. 225-28.

28. Wuthnow, *Restructuring*, p. 261.

29. Walter Brueggemann, *The Prophetic Imagination* (Philadelphia: Fortress, 1978), p. 13.

is incumbent on biblical scholars, theologians, ethicists, and educators to engage in historically informed reflection about the social values associated with the Protestant ethos — the idea of freedom, the effect of freedom on religion, and the effect of capitalist economics on social welfare. Critical reflection about democratic values long thought to be "Christian" is essential to the task of claiming that Christians do see and respond to systemic evil in some way that is different from the dominant culture.[30]

Bibliography

"Boycotts: Policy Analysis and Criteria," Presbyterian Committee on Social Witness Policy. 1979.

Eleanor Flexnor, *Century of Struggle.* Cambridge: Belknap, 1970.

Harry F. Ward, *Social Creed of the Churches.* Eaton and Mains, 1912.

Ronald C. White, Jr., *Liberty and Justice for All: Racial Reform and the Social Gospel.* San Francisco: Harper and Row, 1990.

30. Ibid., p. 59. "The prophet is engaged in a battle for language, in an effort to create a different epistemology out of which another community might emerge." I am suggesting that this task includes a critique of the language of American nationalism especially with regard to government, freedom, and free enterprise.

The Churches on Church and State

Donald L. Drakeman

> "It was the last struggle of the separation of Church and State."
>
> Lyman Beecher on disestablishment in Connecticut (1820)[1]

In the first decade of this century, the Presbyterian Church confronted the issue of religious pluralism in America by pronouncing that this land "was not settled by bands of atheists and infidels . . . nor by Jews or Mohamedans . . . but by colonies of Christian people acknowledging Jesus Christ as Lord." Calling for increased public support of this Christian heritage, the General Assembly lamented that some Americans — men and women labeled "our opponents" — "say that all such exercises as express any Christian theme, even those that breathe the sweet Christmas cheer, should be excluded from the public schools and all other institutions of the state."[2] Yet, by the 1960s, Christianity had indeed been expelled from

1. Quoted in John F. Wilson and Donald L. Drakeman, eds., *Church and State in American History: The Burden of Religious Pluralism* (Boston: Beacon, 1987), p. 95.
2. *Minutes of the 200th General Assembly 1988, Presbyterian Church (U.S.A.)* (Louisville: Office of the General Assembly, 1988) (hereafter, *1988 Minutes*), pp. 581-82.

I would like to thank the following individuals for their help in preparation of this article: James Hudnut-Beumler, Rosemary Brevard, Lisa Drakeman, Alison Gallup, George Gallup, Jr., Dean Kelley, Anne Larsen, and Lori J. Smith. — DLD

the schools and the Presbyterians were fighting, not defending, legislative efforts to reinstate it, proclaiming that "religious observances [should] never be held in public school [and] Bible reading and prayers as devotional acts tend toward indoctrination or meaningless ritual and should be omitted."[3] During this century, then, this church's "opponents" have shifted from atheists and infidels to born-again presidents and pious politicians who seek to send God back to school, keep Christ in public Christmas displays, and assign the Bible as a textbook in science classes as well as in literature and history.

The Church-State Spectrum

From the earliest days of the Republic (and even further back to the Reformation), Protestant views on church and state have fallen at various points along a spectrum, as the Presbyterians have demonstrated in their school prayer policies. This spectrum begins at one end with the position that one or more churches should be formally established by law and should be funded directly by tax dollars. Moving down the spectrum away from this state-church model, there is a broad middle portion in which churches must fund themselves but the government not only accommodates the churches' activities but also sponsors religious observances — such as prayer in the schools and legislatures, public Christmas displays, and the like — in recognition of the inherent religiosity of the American public. Finally, the other end of the spectrum represents an extremely strict separation of church and state where religion is completely limited to private property and even traditional linkages between religion and government — such as "In God We Trust" on legal tender — are forbidden.

The state-church model flourished during the colonial era when formally established churches were often the norm. Episcopalians prevailed in the South, and Congregationalists in New England. Presbyterians and, on rare occasion, even Baptists enjoyed the benefit of tax support in various locales. In the nineteenth century, after the state-subsidized churches were finally disestablished, the government and the churches continued to share the belief that America is a

3. Hearings before the Subcommittee on Courts, Civil Liberties, and the Administration of Justice of the Committee on the Judiciary, House of Representatives, 96th Congress, 2nd session of S.450 (Washington, D.C.: U.S. Government Printing Office, 1981) (hereafter, *1980 Hearings*), p. 296.

"Christian nation." From Sunday closing laws to national days of prayer and congressional chaplains, the government continued to put a Protestant stamp on the national character. For the most part, these practices were welcomed by the churches, which urged the government to "be mindful of its avowed faith in Almighty God as the fountainhead of our rights and on every public occasion to give due and proper recognition of this faith."[4]

Mainline Protestantism thus settled very comfortably in the broad part of the spectrum that supports a Christian nation, and many churches deprecated Thomas Jefferson's concept of a "wall of separation" between church and state as the view of "atheists and infidels." Although the Baptists had long before developed a strong theological commitment to separatism, and were perhaps the least likely to push for governmental support of religion, other churches were actively involved in programs to provide religious instruction in the schools, offer prayers and religious services on public occasions, and generally to give God his "due and proper recognition" in American public life. It is perhaps an historical cliché to observe that Protestantism was culturally dominant in America for much of the nineteenth century and a large part of the twentieth, and countless public prayers and religious displays have served to emphasize the point.

During the last half century, however, Protestantism has been, in historian Leonard Sweet's words, "set upon by troublesome forces tart enough to sour honey."[5] One of these pungent forces was the movement to eradicate from the public schools religious activities, such as prayers and Bible reading, that had a particularly Protestant flavor. The initial skirmishes over school prayer had begun a full century earlier, and almost every state had enacted laws requiring or at least permitting school prayer and Bible reading. But by the middle of the twentieth century the Supreme Court had decided that the states as well as the federal government would be held accountable under the First Amendment, including the establishment clause that prohibited laws "respecting an establishment of religion." In 1962 the Supreme Court declared that the practice of reciting prayers in the public schools violated the Constitution's mandated separation of

4. James D. Beumler, "Social Teachings of the Presbyterian Church," *Church and Society* (Nov./Dec. 1984): 83.

5. Leonard I. Sweet, "The Modernization of Protestant Religion in America," in *Altered Landscapes: Christianity in America, 1935–1985,* ed. David W. Lotz (Grand Rapids: Eerdmans, 1989), pp. 19-20.

church and state; a year later, the Court followed suit and announced that school-sponsored Bible reading similarly contravened the establishment clause.

The Court's action left many with a sour taste in their mouths: fully 70 percent of the American public condemned the decisions; the governors of forty-nine states called for a constitutional amendment to return religion to the schools; and Episcopal bishop James Pike railed that the Court had "deconsecrated the nation."[6] Whether reviled or acclaimed, the Court's pronouncements brought church-state issues into sharp focus throughout the land, and the Protestant churches were forced to decide whether to cling to traditional concepts of a "Christian nation" or to recognize that the force of pluralism required a new vision of the relationship of God and country.

Mainline Protestantism opted for pluralism; for example, the Presbyterian Church (U.S.A.) announced that "we have no right to claim that ours is and always has been a Christian nation."[7] Despite these kinds of straightforward proclamations by denominational leaders, church-state issues remain contested even today. To get a sense of current Protestant approaches to the proper relationship of church and state, we need to plot the relevant points on the spectrum by looking at the attitudes of the churches through their official actions and statements as well as the beliefs of their clergy and their members. While there are many difficult issues on which to focus, I will look primarily at those involving religion in the public sphere, namely, prayer and other forms of religion in the schools as well as religious displays on government property. Many Protestant churches could be studied, but I will focus on the National Council of Churches and the principal churches that many consider to be "mainline" or "old-line" Protestantism and that make up the categories of "Liberal Protestants" and "Moderate Protestants" in Roof and McKinney's sociological work on *American Mainline Religion:* the Northern Baptists, Presbyterians, Lutherans, Methodists, and United Church of Christ.[8] (Episcopalians are excluded only because they have been largely silent on church-state issues.)

6. Quoted in Philip B. Kurland, "The School Prayer Cases," in *The Wall Between Church and State,* ed. Dallin H. Oaks (Chicago and London: Univ. of Chicago Press, 1963), p. 142.

7. Beumler, "Social Teachings," p. 83.

8. Wade Clark Roof and William McKinney, *American Mainline Religion: Its Changing Shape and Future* (New Brunswick: Rutgers Univ. Press, 1987).

National Council of Churches

The National Council of Churches of Christ in the U.S.A. (NCC) is composed of thirty-two religious bodies, with over forty million members, and it has often been considered the voice of mainline Protestantism. (Although many would dispute that the NCC is in fact representative, it has certainly maintained a public presence as *one* voice of Protestantism, if not the only voice.) The NCC has released several policies on church-state issues and has participated as a friend of the court (or *amicus curiae,* in legal terms) in many Supreme Court cases involving the interaction of religion and government.[9] While always affirming the fundamental importance of religious freedom in America, the NCC has consistently called for the separation of church and state dating back to a 1959 pronouncement that the Constitution should not be amended to declare that the United States is a "Christian Nation."[10]

In 1963, close on the heels of the Supreme Court's decisions declaring school devotionals unconstitutional, the NCC issued a statement recognizing the "wisdom as well as the authority of this ruling" and asserting that "neither the church nor the state should use the public school to compel acceptance of any creed or conformity or any specific religious practice." The only hedge on a completely strict separationist position in the statement was the suggestion that the propriety of public prayer "offered at special occasions in the public schools" should be left to the local school board.

Even more important than these public statements has been the activist role in church-state issues undertaken by the NCC through its staff member, the Reverend Dean Kelley. Since the early 1960s, Kelley, acting either single-handedly or with the aid of allies from the American Civil Liberties Union, the American Jewish Congress, and a number of the Protestant churches, can be credited with defeating numerous attempts to overturn the Supreme Court's school prayer ruling by constitutional amendment. He has also caused the NCC to file briefs in numerous Supreme Court cases to let the justices know

9. For a general discussion of the activities of religious groups in church-state cases, see Leo Pfeffer, "Amici in Church-State Litigation," *Law and Contemporary Problems* 44, no. 2 (1981); and Frank J. Sorauf, *The Wall of Separation: The Constitutional Politics of Church and State* (Princeton: Princeton Univ. Press, 1976).

10. "Opposition to the Christian Amendment Proposal" Policy Statement adopted by the General Board of the National Council of Churches of Christ in the United States of America (June 4, 1959).

that the NCC opposes, for example, laws mandating that the biblical account of creation be taught in schools, and does not favor the display of nativity scenes on public property.

The NCC has also exerted a potent organizing force in church-state issues by convening, through Dean Kelley's office, a group now known as the NCC's Religious Liberty Committee. With a membership far broader than the NCC itself, this committee has included many of the key players in the field of church-state litigation: Leo Pfeffer of the American Jewish Congress, Samuel Rabinove of the American Jewish Committee, and representatives of the General Conference of the Seventh-Day Adventists (which have been heavily involved in religious liberty cases) as well as delegates from the Christian Legal Society and the National Association of Evangelicals. Members from the United States Catholic Conference, firm supporters of parochial schools, and the Baptist Joint Committee on Public Affairs, dedicated opponents of federal aid to religious schools, add to the committee's ecumenism in both theological and church-state matters. The committee serves as a valuable clearinghouse for information on important church-state issues and constitutional litigation, and its organizational role adds to the power of the NCC's voice as a representative of mainline Protestantism in matters relating to the separation of church and state.

Baptists

Many Baptists point proudly to a rich theological heritage calling for a high wall of separation between church and state. This tradition began even before the Baptists became American colonists, and in the New World, Baptists such as Roger Williams, Isaac Backus, and John Leland were outspoken and influential proponents of religious liberty and the separation of church and state. The Baptists' theological commitment to church-state separation remained strong throughout the development of the American nation. In the 1930s, when many Protestant churches were still fully committed to the building of a "Christian nation," Southern and Northern Baptists jointly adopted the "American Baptist Bill of Rights," announcing that religious liberty is "indispensable to human welfare," and that Baptists "condemn every form of compulsion in religion."[11]

11. Quoted in Stan L. Hastey, "The History and Contributions of the Baptist Joint Committee on Public Affairs," *Baptist History and Heritage* 20, no. 3 (July 1985): 36.

In 1946, several Baptist conventions formed the Baptist Joint Committee on Public Affairs (BJC) in response to a number of perceived cracks in the wall of separation between church and state, particularly the appointment by President Roosevelt of an ambassador to the Vatican and the growth of federal aid to parochial schools. With financial support from nine Baptist conventions, as well as the strict separationist mantle inherited from Williams, Backus, and Leland, the BJC opened an office in Washington, and has maintained an active presence in Congress as well as in Supreme Court litigation. The BJC has consistently fought government involvement in religion on topics ranging from school prayer to parochial school aid.

Historian and former BJC staff worker Stan L. Hasty has noted that the BJC's "primary strength has been in the halls of Congress, where most Members do not know about intra-Baptist divisions but are naturally impressed when groups numbering some thirty million Americans band together in a common cause."[12] These intra-Baptist divisions on church-state matters have certainly left their imprint on the BJC. For example, the BJC's second foray into constitutional litigation came in 1947 when it filed a friend of the court brief supporting the claims of an agnostic that the Constitution prohibits the public schools from releasing children for religious instruction during the school day. The brief engendered a storm of criticism within the Baptist ranks, and the precursor to the American Baptist Convention went as far as to send a telegram to the Supreme Court asserting that the BJC's brief did not represent the views of its convention or members.[13] Chastened by this controversy, the BJC did not file an amicus curiae brief for another two decades. Nevertheless, it maintained its strict separationist posture in Congress and in the activities of its first executive secretary, Joseph M. Dawson, in the founding of an advocacy group with the felicitous name of Protestants and Other Americans United for Separation of Church and State, which became extremely active in church-state litigation, especially in cases involving aid to parochial schools.[14] Not until 1969 did the BJC renew its amicus filings, but since that time it has filed over two dozen briefs calling for a recognition of Americans' rights to religious liberty in a context of strict church-state separation.

12. Ibid., p. 41.

13. Walfred Peterson, "The Baptist Joint Committee on Public Affairs and the Amicus Curiae Brief," *Mid-America: An Historical Review* 66, no. 3 (1985): 127.

14. Ibid., pp. 129-31.

Intra-Baptist disputes persist, however, and the future of the BJC's role as church-state activist is unclear. Although some believe with Baptist minister Charles G. Adams that "Baptists pervert their own heritage by clamoring for a . . . 'Christian nation,'" many influential members of the Southern Baptist Convention, a body representing half the Baptists in America and providing 85 percent of the BJC's funding, have attacked the BJC's separationist posture.[15] Among other things, the pastor of the largest Southern Baptist church has said on national television that "the separation of church and state is a figment of infidels' imagination."[16] These views, which certainly represent a significantly less strict separationist posture than the one espoused by the BJC, crystallized in a decision of the 1990 Southern Baptist Convention to reduce its funding of the BJC by 65 percent, thus essentially halving the BJC's budget for the next year.

Where are the Baptists, then, on the church-state spectrum? The continuing dissension and potential schism in Southern Baptist ranks makes it clear that some Baptists can be found at virtually every point on the spectrum, and even if the Northern "mainline" Baptists maintain their separationist heritage, the BJC will certainly become less visible in Congress and in the Supreme Court as an advocate of strict separationist policies.

Presbyterians

In the early 1960s, the United Presbyterian Church adopted a policy statement promoting a stricter separation of church and state, particularly in the public schools, thus marking a sharp reversal from earlier statements extolling the benefits of a Christian nation. Noting that this shift along the church-state spectrum was "not a comfortable experience," historian Elwyn A. Smith hailed it as a renunciation of the "tendency of Protestants to act as though the religious composition of the population has not changed since 1830."[17] In that same era, how-

15. Charles G. Adams, "The Scrutiny of History," *Baptist History and Heritage* 20, no. 3 (July 1985): 67.

16. Quoted in G. Hugh Wamble, "Baptist Contributions to Separation of Church and State," *Baptist History and Heritage* 20, no. 3 (July 1985): 13.

17. Elwyn A. Smith, "The Presbyterians on Church and State," in *Religion and the Public Order 1960*, ed. Donald A. Giannella (Chicago and London: Univ. of Chicago Press, 1964), p. 198.

ever, the Southern Presbyterian denomination, named the Presbyterian Church in the U.S., issued a report lamenting that the "absence of any sort of public acknowledgment of God [in public schools] could, in effect, be an unspoken suggestion that education is exclusively a secular pursuit without moral and spiritual considerations."[18] These differences survived the union of the two major Presbyterian churches, and a 1983 report of the General Assembly noted only that "prayer in the public schools, which seems to some to be appropriately excluded and to others to be a legitimate means of religious expression, becomes a matter for concern in an increasingly pluralistic society."[19] Throughout the 1980s, a move toward the strict separation approach appeared to be gaining momentum, however, and representatives of the General Assembly made several pilgrimages to Congress to oppose constitutional amendments to overturn the Supreme Court's school devotionals cases.

Finally, in 1988, the Presbyterians officially resolved their differences as the General Assembly adopted a set of fairly separationist policy recommendations after a lengthy committee review. Among its many conclusions, the comprehensive report, *God Alone is Lord of the Conscience,* strongly disapproved of a constitutional amendment to return prayer to the public schools, and called a Supreme Court decision permitting a municipal nativity scene "regrettable" because the "Court's emphasis on the secular nature of Christmas is offensive to Christians and transparently false to non-Christians."[20] Even "moments of silence" designed to provide time for prayer or meditation in public schools were disapproved, although the report acknowledged that the practice was not inherently unconstitutional. By 1988, then, the Presbyterians had moved officially into the strict separation side of the spectrum, and since then the Presbyterians have had a considerably higher profile in constitutional litigation involving church-state issues.

Lutherans

Shortly after the Supreme Court's school prayer decision, the president of the Lutheran Church in America issued a comment reflecting

18. *1988 Minutes,* p. 582.
19. Ibid., p. 549.
20. Ibid., p. 568.

mixed emotions. Although the "elimination of the devotional practices did not entail much of a religious loss," it did signal that "the United States of America . . . is past the place where underlying Christian culture and beliefs are assumed in its life."[21] By 1964, however, both the Lutheran Church in America and the American Lutheran Church had issued policy statements condemning efforts to overturn the Supreme Court's school prayer decisions as "unnecessary from a religious point of view and unwise from a public policy perspective."[22] In particular, the statement of the Lutheran Church in America posited, "The more we . . . insist on common denominator religious exercise in public schools, the greater risk we run of diluting our faith and contributing to a vague religiosity which defines religion with patriotism and becomes a national folk religion."[23]

Numerous Lutheran conventions have reaffirmed these policies, and at numerous congressional hearings the Lutheran Council (representing the Lutheran Church of America, the American Lutheran Church, and the Association of Evangelical Lutheran Churches) has provided testimony in opposition to constitutional amendments seeking to return prayer to the public schools. In such testimony, the general secretary of the Lutheran Council noted that the churches' views on church-state issues must change with the times. Acknowledging that "the historical situation . . . has changed since the early days of the Republic when underlying religious beliefs were assumed," the general secretary concluded that religious pluralism is a challenge to the church to "articulate . . . our faith . . . rather than cling to practices which may have been appropriate at an earlier stage of our nation's development but which need reevaluation in the light of historical change."[24] Thus the Lutherans, too, have made a shift toward the strict separationist end of the spectrum.

21. Quoted in Donald Giannella, ed., *Religion and the Public Order: The Year 1963 in Review* (Chicago: Univ. of Chicago Press, 1964), p. 294.

22. Hearings before the Committee on the Judiciary, United States Senate, 97th Congress, 2nd session on S.J. Res. 199 (Washington, D.C.: U.S. Government Printing Office, 1983) (hereafter, *1982 Hearings*), p. 303.

23. Ibid., p. 293.

24. Ibid., p. 204.

United Church of Christ

Since 1971, several national agencies of the United Church of Christ have released statements urging a separation of church and state in America and specifically supporting the Supreme Court's school prayer decision.[25] The United Church of Christ has also periodically lobbied Congress on church-state matters, particularly on the issue of school prayer, consistently favoring a strict separationist approach. Once again, however, opposition to school prayer is essentially seen as a sociological necessity rather than a theological commitment. In a written statement to the Senate Judiciary Committee, a staff member from the United Church of Christ's Office for Church in Society observed that religious pluralism and "the disavowal of societal compulsion in religious activities and observances have undermined traditional relations between the public school and the church in many communities." As a result, both church and state must find new ways to discharge "their respective responsibilities for the development of children."[26] This theme echoes throughout many of the Protestant churches' statements on church-state issues: one of the consequences of a move in the strict separationist direction is that the churches must find new ways to communicate their beliefs to the nation.

Methodists

Although several Methodists joined a group of prominent Protestant churchmen in criticizing the Supreme Court's 1963 decision to ban Bible reading from the schools, by 1968 the General Conference of the United Methodist Church had adopted a policy statement (reaffirmed in 1980) supporting the Supreme Court's decision and declaring the church's opposition to "all establishment of religion by government."[27] In particular, the statement proclaimed that the state should not use its authority to inculcate particular religious beliefs (including atheism) nor should it require prayer or worship in the public

25. "A Summary Look at the United Church of Christ" (Cleveland: Office of Communication, United Church of Christ, March 12, 1990).

26. Hearing before the Subcommittee on the Constitution of the Committee on the Judiciary, United States Senate, 99th Congress, 1st session in S.J. Res. 2 (Washington, D.C.: U.S. Government Printing Office, 1986) (hereafter, *1986 Hearings*), p. 166.

27. *1980 Hearings*, p. 290.

schools.[28] Based on this statement, officials of the United Methodist Church have periodically joined with representatives of the NCC, BJC, Presbyterian Church (U.S.A.), and the Lutheran Council to oppose constitutional amendments on the subject of school prayer.

Protestant Clergy and Laity

The twentieth century has witnessed a sea change within the Protestant churches on church-state matters. For most of the century, the churches were either ardent advocates, or at least willing accomplices, of many traditional links between Protestant Christianity and the government until after the Supreme Court overhauled the Constitution's approach to the church-state spectrum. The churches were certainly not major causes of the newly found secularism in the schools and throughout the government, but they have since embraced it with a devotion once reserved for the Virgin Birth and the doctrine of the Trinity. The separation of church and state has become a part of the mainline Protestant creed.

As with many doctrines and policies of the Protestant churches, there is no guarantee that each church member subscribes to the official position. Some individual Protestants undoubtedly favor school prayer, just as some may question the divinity of Jesus or disapprove of the churches' stands on abortion. In the light of the diverse opinions on church-state issues held by individual church members, the general secretary of the Lutheran Council was careful to point out in his congressional testimony that official statements of national Lutheran conventions do not reflect the personal opinion of all Lutherans. Rather, the statements "represent the end result of an organized and democratic process which is acknowledged as legitimate by members of these church bodies."[29] Throughout the churches' official actions on church-state issues, from congressional appearances to Supreme Court briefs and public policy campaigns, the official organizations almost always note that they cannot speak for each individual member of the denomination. This caveat, however, is inevitably accompanied by a recitation of total membership, leaving the Court or Congress to wonder whether the speaker is merely pre-

28. *1982 Hearings*, p. 304.
29. Ibid., p. 292.

senting an institutional perspective or, as noted in a recent amicus curiae brief on behalf of the Mormon Church and several Protestant groups, "The amici joining in this brief represent more than eighty million Americans."[30] This assertion raises an interesting question: do their official positions accurately reflect the beliefs of American Protestants or are these spokesmen mere "generals without armies," as members of Congress periodically ask the denominational representatives who lobby for strict separation of church and state?[31]

To what extent can we determine what the men and women in America's Protestant pews think about church-state issues? Thanks to an enduring interest in these topics by the Princeton Religion Research Center of George Gallup, Jr., as well as a number of other surveys, we can develop a good picture of Protestant church members' attitudes on a variety of church-state questions. Among other church-state topics, the polls survey attitudes about prayer in public schools, the teaching of the biblical account of creation in the public schools, and the display of crèches on public property. The results of a number of studies are remarkably consistent.

The polls make it clear that the American public shares the churches' dedication to the principle of strict separation. In a 1988 Gallup Poll, 77 percent of the public either "mostly" (29 percent) or "completely" (48 percent) agreed that "church and state should be separated."[32] Only 5 percent completely disagreed. Despite this clear mandate for a separation of church and state, the public in general, and Protestants in particular, are not as clear on how that commitment applies to specific issues. Virtually every time the public is surveyed, approximately 70 percent favor prayer in the public schools, with the percentage reaching 81 in 1983.[33] These people were asked whether they would favor a constitutional amendment to "allow voluntary prayer in the public schools," and 84 percent of Protestants in 1983 said they would vote for the amendment. Greatest support came from

30. Brief of the Baptist Joint Committee on Public Affairs, Christian Legal Society, Church of Jesus Christ of Latter-Day Saints, National Association of Evangelicals, National Council of Churches of Christ in the U.S.A., and James E. Andrews as Stated Clerk of the Presbyterian Church (U.S.A.) as Amici Curiae in Support of Respondents in *Westside Community Schools v. Mergens* in the Supreme Court of the United States, October Term 1989, p. 1.

31. Interview with the Reverend Dean Kelley, July 9, 1990.

32. George Gallup, Jr., and Sarah Jones, *100 Questions and Answers: Religion in America* (Princeton: Princeton Religion Research Center, 1989), p. 134.

33. *PRRC Emerging Trends* (Oct. 1983), p. 5.

the Baptists, and the smallest percent of school prayer advocates were the Methodists, 82 percent of whom favored the amendment.

Two years later, another Gallup Poll showed a drop in support for school prayer to 69 percent of all Americans, but 73 percent of Protestants continued to favor prayer. Lest we assume that these numbers are skewed by evangelicals or fundamentalists who may fall outside the mainline, it is worth noting that such nonmainline groups are not unanimously in favor of school prayer. Among those who consider themselves evangelicals, 85 percent favor school prayer. Similarly, 84 percent of Southern Baptists and 78 percent of those who live in rural areas support school prayer. And if we hypothesize that school prayer proponents are either poorly educated or have not thought critically about church-state matters, we should bear in mind that a 1988 poll showed 59 percent of all Americans and *69 percent* of Protestant ministers in favor of prayer at public school athletic events.[34] Even if the poll results are adjusted to exclude, to the extent possible, those falling outside the churches with whom we are concerned, it remains clear that a majority of mainline Protestants — including the clergy — would like to return prayer to the classroom. It is not surprising, in the light of these results, that politicians continually resurrect a constitutional amendment to overturn the Supreme Court's school prayer decisions despite opposition from the official representatives of the mainline churches.

The results of a 1988 poll on church-state issues sponsored by the Williamsburg Charter Foundation demonstrated that 80 percent of the public would permit the government to display a crèche during the holiday season.[35] The Williamsburg survey did not break the data down to give the exact figures on various religious groups, but it is unlikely that mainline Protestants, who constituted 43 percent of the sample, would differ markedly from the general public. In fact, on a purely arithmetical basis, the total of 80 percent favoring crèches on public property requires the support of more than a majority of mainline Protestants. Once again, Protestant ministers supported this collaboration of church and state by a margin even greater than the public at large (85 percent). It is interesting, then, that in the year the survey was conducted, the NCC filed an amicus curiae brief in the Supreme

34. *The Williamsburg Charter Survey on Religion and Public Life* prepared by the Center for Communication Dynamics (Washington, D.C., Feb. 1988).

35. Ibid.

Court arguing that publicly supported nativity scenes violate the Constitution's mandated separation of church and state. Thus displaying a crèche on government property, a practice condoned by 85 percent of Protestant ministers, was attacked by the NCC as an act that "not only secularizes and degrades a symbol of Christianity, but also represents either a presumptuous identification by government with that religion . . . or an equally presumptuous identification by Christians of their . . . traditions with the . . . government."[36]

Finally, there are surprising survey results on the teaching of creation in an age that has been called "scientific" and "secular." Fully 80 percent of Americans think the Bible should receive at least equal time with Darwin's theory of evolution in public school science classes.[37] Moreover, the same number of Americans (11 percent) would have the schools teach only evolution as would have them teach only the biblical account. It is likely that Protestants closely parallel the responses of the general public, especially since 80 percent of the Protestant ministers surveyed would opt for the "equal time" approach. Yet again, mainline ecumenical Protestantism, in the form of the NCC, appeared as amicus curiae to urge the Supreme Court to strike down a law requiring that the Genesis account of creation be taught in the public schools. According to the brief, the nation's largest Protestant organization concluded that a "review of the doctrines of various . . . denominational groups demonstrate[s] that the particular religious view of creation which creationism incorporates is a 'narrowly sectarian' one." Moreover, the NCC opined that "objective study in public schools of the mechanism of creation [such as Darwin's theory of evolution] does not impugn belief in God as Creator."[38]

These three issues — school prayer, nativity scenes on public property, and the teaching of the biblical version of creation as an alternative to evolution — point to sharp differences of opinion between the churches on the one hand and their members and clergy

36. Brief of the American Jewish Committee, the National Council of Churches of Christ in the U.S.A., et al. as Amici Curiae in Support of Respondents in *County of Allegheny v. ACLU* in the Supreme Court of the United States, October Term 1988.

37. *Williamsburg Charter Survey.*

38. Brief of Americans United for Separation of Church and State, the American Jewish Committee, the National Council of Churches of Christ in the U.S.A., and the General Conventions of Swedenborgian Churches as Amici Curiae in Support of Appellees in *Edwards v. Aguillard* in the Supreme Court of the United States, October Term 1986.

on the other. While the churches have shifted their positions on the church-state spectrum toward the strict separation side, their members — and perhaps most surprisingly, their ordained clergy — remain solidly within the "Christian nation" portion abandoned by the churches in the 1960s. In observing this divergence, we should ask two questions that not only apply to the churches' policies on church-state relations, but cut broadly across a variety of theological, social, and political issues: *To whom* do the churches speak? And *for whom* do they speak?

To whom are the churches' carefully crafted church-state policy statements addressed? The answer seems clear: though they are addressed to the church and to the world, church statements on this subject are utilized primarily as testimony before congressional committees and as briefs before the federal courts. Although policies and pamphlets have certainly been made available to those in the pulpits and the pews, the church-state discussions have most often been carried out at the institutional level, with the church speaking to the state. And the churches have been quite effective, especially in blocking constitutional amendments to overturn the Supreme Court's school prayer decision. Despite this institutional effectiveness, the people who make up the churches are yet to be convinced. Church-state questions are often complex and emotional, so it may not be shocking to find the laity unsupportive of separationist policies. But if they are to acquire the churches' institutional fervor for religious and cultural pluralism, it may be necessary first to convince the clergy. However strong the churches' voices have been in the halls of government, they have not been heeded in either the seminaries or the sanctuaries.

This raises the second, more difficult question. For whom do the churches speak when they urge a greater separation of church and state? In Congress and in the courts the churches are careful to clarify the ecclesiastical procedures by which they are authorized to speak only for the organization itself and not for individual church members, *but they never fail to mention how many members they have.* To be sure, senators are more impressed with witnesses who may represent tens of millions of votes than those who merely claim to speak the voice of truth and reason. If the churches' positions are not held by a majority of their members — and the politicians know this — then the power of their lobbying efforts (on church-state issues and many others) will be drastically reduced. The churches do not want to bring to life Martin Marty's slightly tongue-in-cheek suggestion that "when the mainline churches take a position, [everyone knows] it is only six people in a room on Riverside Drive."[39]

A New Antidisestablishmentarianism?

In talking about church-state issues we often refer to them as questions of the establishment of religion. When Virginia, Massachusetts, and several other states cut the churches adrift from state funds in the late eighteenth and early nineteenth centuries, we say the churches were "disestablished." Historian Robert Handy has used the powerful concept of a "second disestablishment" to describe the plight of Protestantism challenged by the forces of pluralism in the twentieth century.[40] Now, in their influential study of *American Mainline Religion,* Professors Wade Clark Roof and William McKinney have described the current state of affairs as yet a "third disestablishment" characterized by "an expanded pluralism in which there is less of a religiously grounded moral basis for society."[41] As a result, various religions "find themselves contending with one another to become the shaping cultural influences."[42]

Disestablishment is indeed a potent description for what has happened to the churches. At its roots, it relates much less to religious faith or doctrine per se than to two other attributes with which the churches have long been familiar: money and power. An "established" church, in the formal sense, is one that receives money from the state and that has access to some degree of power over or through the government. In colonial America, for example, numerous Protestant churches were funded by taxes, and public office in some colonies was restricted to those who affirmed certain Christian doctrines. After formal disestablishment, the Protestant churches continued to play such a strong role in the shaping of America's many institutions, including the government, that countless historians have described nineteenth-century America as a Protestant republic. Through their

39. A. James Reichley, *Religion in American Public Life* (Washington, D.C.: Brookings Institution, 1985), p. 267.

40. See Robert T. Handy, *A Christian Nation: Protestant Hopes and Historical Realities,* 2nd ed. (New York: Oxford Univ. Press, 1984), pp. 159-84.

41. Roof and McKinney, *American Mainline Religion,* p. 38.

42. Ibid.

denominational leaders, influential laity, and a multitude of voluntary organizations, mainline Protestant churches continued to have enough money and power to constitute a de facto establishment. Sometime early in the twentieth century, however, Protestantism lost some of its grip on the American culture, and was replaced initially by a triumvirate Will Herberg has labeled "Protestant-Catholic-Jew."[43] Whether this "disestablishment" occurred in the 1920s, as some historians suggest, or as late as the election of the first Roman Catholic president in 1960, the fact remains that pluralism supplanted Protestantism as a hallmark of the American people, and the influence of the mainline Protestant churches waned as other religious and secular voices joined in the process of setting society's norms.

Roof and McKinney have identified a third disestablishment emanating from the radical pluralism of the 1960s and the decline of the "liberal, mainline churches." This third disestablishment has given rise not only to secularism but to a "crusading conservative wing" of Protestantism seeking to "impose a new unity upon the nation."[44] Once again, as with the two prior disestablishments, the mainline churches have felt the effects of lower membership and diminished financial strength. The first disestablishment cut the churches off from state financial support; the second, from their power to dictate cultural norms. What have the churches lost in this third disestablishment? Roof and McKinney do not offer a clear answer, but they certainly point to an even further diminution of power in society as a result of the many other voices clamoring for attention in a disjointed, radically pluralistic nation.

Based on a review of the churches' views on church-state issues, we may see an even more significant development in modern American Protestantism. The mainline churches' acknowledgment of pluralism is evident, but so is the fact that the churches' official positions differ dramatically from the beliefs of their clergy and members. If the first disestablishment separated the churches from the state, and the second from society at large, does the third disestablishment mean that the churches are now severed from their one remaining constituency — their own members?

The disjunction between the churches' official positions and their members' convictions is not limited to the realm of church-state

43. Will Herberg, *Protestant–Catholic–Jew* (Garden City, N.Y.: Anchor, 1955).
44. Roof and McKinney, *American Mainline Religion*, p. 39.

issues. As James Reichley contends in *Religion in American Public Life,* since the early 1970s "the Washington offices of most mainline denominations have consistently supported the most liberal option available," whereas many surveys show that the laity "have remained predominantly moderate or conservative in their political inclinations."[45] (For Reichley, "liberal" means "favoring an expanded role for the federal government in dealing with domestic problems and a more conciliatory approach in world affairs.")[46] By and large, according to Reichley, official denominational offices espouse the most liberal positions on issues such as foreign policy, abortion, and race relations; the clergy hold a more moderate position; and those in the pews express the most conservative attitudes. The following table shows the results of a 1980 United Methodist survey of lay leaders, clergy, national staff, and bishops. Each "issue" represents a position *contrary* to the United Methodist Church's official position.[47]

Issue	Laity	Clergy	National Staff	Bishops
Policies designed to protect the environment have gone too far	55.4	39.0	25.0	3.7
Favor return of school prayer	74.8	49.5	28.8	15.4
Oppose Equal Rights Amendment	36.9	30.7	13.7	3.8

The diversity of opinion on social issues among these various Methodists is readily apparent, and surveys conducted among members of other mainline churches have produced comparable results. The sea change experienced by the mainline churches in the 1960s seems to have left the churches and their members sailing in very different directions.

Churches need not merely mirror the changing attitudes and prejudices of their members (unless, of course, their polity or theology requires it). But in an era in which few officials of mainline Protestantism are prepared to claim direct divine inspiration or the insight of inerrant Scriptures, the churches need to lay a foundation for the authority of their voices in the public sphere. Otherwise, those with opposing views will be quick to point to public opinion polls, mem-

45. Reichley, *Religion,* p. 267.
46. Ibid.
47. Ibid., p. 272.

bership rolls, and church finances to portray the churches as institutions in decline with leaders who have lost touch with their own members on matters of religion as well as politics.

The gospel of Christ claims the power to change whole governments as well as individual lives. But in bearing witness to that gospel in the public sphere, whether the churches are speaking on school prayer, the homeless, or nuclear arms, they need to be careful not to sound like voices crying in the wilderness of their own denominations. Whether we like it or not, the truth becomes far clearer in the halls of Congress when it is spoken by millions of voters. To the extent that the churches want to maintain a strong authoritative voice on difficult social policy questions, they need to speak (or perhaps listen) to their "constituents," the clergy and the laity, as well as Congress. If the polls cited above tell us anything it is that the churches' leaders are worried about appropriate church-state relations in an increasingly pluralistic secular society, while the clergy and laity are trying to remember whether God brought forth the creatures of the earth on the fourth or the fifth day.

For the mainline Protestant churches to regain some of their force in American culture, they need to reestablish contact with the millions of women, men, and children who make up thrice-disestablished American Protestantism. "Flawed and impossible though they may be at times," McKinney has pronounced, "congregations are the most powerful antidote we have to the radical individualism that pervades American secular and religious culture," and he has urged church leaders to "reassert the central role of the gathered community in the life of faith and the church."[48] To draw on the power and vitality of the gathered community in the churches' public stands on social issues, the churches must first deal with the pluralism in their own ranks. This can be accomplished in two ways. Mainline church leaders may choose to listen more intently to the voices of the laity and to steer the denominations' policies toward the beliefs of their over thirty million members. Or they may turn their evangelical efforts inward and preach their social policy gospel not only in Congress but also in sermons, Sunday schools, and seminaries. Either way, the churches should find themselves reunited, reestablished, and perhaps renewed as well.

48. William McKinney, "Revising the Future of Oldline Protestantism," *Christian Century* 106, no. 33 (Nov. 8, 1989): 1016.

The first two disestablishments are the inevitable results of the diversity of the American people. But this third disestablishment — the one that threatens the churches' own sense of community — is one worth fighting. The churches need to tear down any "wall of separation" that has been erected between the church leaders on the one hand and the local congregations and clergy on the other. This need not entail majority rule in the churches, but it should involve thoughtful consideration of why Protestant laity do not adopt the doctrines pronounced by their leaders. A church bent on influencing the Supreme Court and Congress should also, and perhaps even first, set out to convince its own members. Whether we consider these efforts practical theology, continuing education, spiritual renewal, or home missions, they are crucial not only for addressing society's ills but for the health of the churches themselves.

Conclusion

Have the mainline Protestant churches truly sought to separate church and state? Not really. Although the churches have generally given up on the idea of state-sponsored devotionals (public prayer, Bible reading), they have, if anything, increased their efforts to use the political process (lawsuits, lobbyists, etc.) to enforce certain Christian conceptions of social justice on issues ranging from Latin American politics to economic justice and abortion rights, often promoting positions that are quite controversial in the minds of the laity. They have even exerted their political influence to keep prayer out of schools, Congress, and other public places. Despite the churches' official statements calling for a separation of church and state, they have not shrunk from involvement with the government. Rather, the churches' desire to make governmental policy and practice consistent with their vision of the kingdom of God on earth remains unabated; the goals have simply shifted from keeping prayer in the schools to keeping it out.

For these reasons, I believe that the divergence of beliefs between church bodies and their members on church-state issues is a far more interesting topic than the simple question of how Protestants should think about publicly funded piety. Should public school children be forced to engage in sectarian rituals? Of course not. May history teachers enrich their curricula by including America's colorful and diverse religious heritage? Certainly. If the questions are asked in the right way, the answers to many of the traditional church-state questions are easy. Some of the answers are less obvious — for example, may the state permit a crèche and a menorah to be displayed on public property? — but it is hard to see dire consequences resulting from either permitting or forbidding the displays. It certainly creates confusion, however, when the NCC condemns the holiday displays in a Supreme Court brief while 85 percent of Protestant ministers disagree with the council's position. What happens when the churches set out to use the political process but the parishioners do not vote the gospel ticket? The result is that the churches simply are not as influential as they could be — and certainly not as influential as they would like to be.

A recent survey asked mainline Protestant leaders what groups should have the most influence in American society. Not surprisingly, they placed themselves first, with intellectuals and blacks falling in second and third places. Yet when queried about who, in fact, has influence in America, the same Protestants rank "religious leaders" a dismal seventh out of ten places.[49] How can the churches and their leaders climb the influence ladder? It appears that simply proclaiming their visions of truth and justice has not brought about adequate results. Perhaps a stronger commitment to mobilizing directly the political, social, and economic power of the tens of millions of mainline Protestant laypeople will give the churches the clout they long for, and at the same time give the clergy and denominational leadership a keener understanding of how all the parts of the body of Christ perceive his call.

49. Robert Lerner, et al., "Christian Religious Elites," *Public Opinion* (March/April 1989): 54-57.

Church and State Revisited

Edward LeRoy Long, Jr.

Changing Patterns in Church-State Relations

Practices involving relationships between church and state have been undergoing considerable transformation. I can remember when Bible reading and the Lord's Prayer provided standard elements in quasi-liturgical opening exercises at a public grade school, and when the birth narrative from the Gospel of Luke was read at the public high school Christmas assembly with at least as much solemnity as it was read at church. Since I lived in a major metropolitan area there were certainly Jewish students in both schools and probably a number of persons having no explicit religious identities — but that did not seem to matter. It was assumed that the United States is a Christian (even Protestant) nation and that religion is good for morals and morale. Nobody challenged such practices. Had they done so in the grade school the vehement wrath of an autocratic principal would have descended with an intensity that would make any mistress of novices seem tenderhearted. The high school principal, who was more humane, would probably have been flustered in trying to ward off the challenge, yet persisted with the practice unless ordered not to do so by someone like the local superintendent of schools.

It is doubtful that such things are done in either school today. That is not merely because both schools are now located in areas where Protestants, perhaps even Christians, are a minority. Even in geographical locations where Protestants are a majority, such practices have generally been abandoned because subsequent Supreme Court rulings have forbidden them. Anyone who chooses to do so can take legal action to summarily challenge mandated religious observances in public schools. Courts, not merely superintendents of schools, will step in to stop them.

This autobiographical vignette provides a vivid and concrete insight into a major change in public outlooks and practices in the last half century. The society is undergoing changes in its composition and ethos as well as in its sense concerning the proper place and function of the religious sector. Even ecclesiastical bodies constantly undergo changes in their own self-understandings as well as in their attitudes toward the role that religion ought to have in society.

It should be no surprise that opinions differ as to the trends that have been taking place. Both the nature and the impact of these changes are, quite understandably, matters about which people have an intensity of feeling often reserved for religious convictions. In the preceding chapter, Donald Drakeman has documented those differences of opinion together with the problems posed for the internal life of those church bodies in which the differences of opinion are acute.

His chapter indicates that many leaders of the mainline churches and of ecumenical Protestantism have come to embrace the separation between church and state in a manner that one might more normally expect from a secular outlook. Many such leaders now hold that those spheres of public life in which state authority is available to impose particular practices on captive audiences should be kept free of specifically religious demands. After detailing the movement toward this position within several specific denominations and groups, Drakeman's account provides information from two research centers showing that a large proportion of the members and ordinary clergy of such bodies actually favor a greater public role for certain religious practices than is currently prevalent. He cites three specific practices as cases in point: prayer in the public schools; the erection of crèches at holiday time on public property; and the mandating of equal teaching time in the public schools for the theories of evolution and creation.

Since this portrayal of the gap between certain religious leaders and their constituencies is based on data concerning three specific issues, we should note briefly that the picture Drakeman suggests is not typical of the entire situation. Jim Castelli provides a quite different reading of what is happening. He notes that on several matters — such as support for welfare-type social programs, for the Equal Rights Amendment, for a dovish foreign policy, even for the legitimacy of pro-choice — church leaders and church members agree to a considerable extent.[1] He suggests that those who posit a sharp, decisive split between church leaders and their members have not yet proved their case. Moreover, even the data Drakeman cites can easily obscure the probability that some laity believe in separation and some religious leaders (even in the mainline denominations) are unhappy with the trends toward strict separation.

Nevertheless, the challenge Drakeman raises is to address the split between thinking among high-level ecclesiastical bureaucrats and that among grass-roots constituencies about the three matters he cites, lest the influence of churches in the public arena be entirely vitiated. The important normative question I am raising is whether this split should be overcome by adopting the views of the general constituencies or by moving toward the views attributed to the leaders.

Assessing the Changes Normatively

Many factors need to be weighed in assessing the shift from an unofficial establishment of religious practice to the more self-conscious efforts to guard the principle of separation. All such transformations involve perplexity as well as progress, distress as well as desserts. We cannot expect that such changes will be unchallenged or even that the discussion of church-state matters will proceed any more smoothly or result in any more easily achieved consensus than the discussions of any other major public issues. We must consider many different factors in the debates about the proper relationship between the ecclesiastical and the public spheres. We need to take into account many competing claims and conflicting values in devising normative criteria for judging current practices and for thinking about the patterns toward which we ought to move in the future.

The least satisfactory way to deal with these questions is to count noses. The presence of a gap between the leadership of mainline churches and the rank-and-file membership is an important internal problem for various denominations, but it has no bearing upon the

1. Jim Castelli, "Church Leaders out of Step," *Christianity and Crisis* 50, no. 13 (Sept. 24, 1990): 295-96. See also Dieter T. Hessel, "Mainline Protestantism Sidelined?" ibid., pp. 293-95.

more important issues of public policy, or upon questions as to which positions on the practices in question are most likely to be productive of theological understanding and spiritual depth within the church bodies themselves. The general public often jumps to the superficial assumption that the well-being of both the society and church bodies is dependent upon the mandating of religious practices in public life; but that assumption may indeed be faulty.

An informed perspective on these matters depends in part upon an historical perspective. We need to understand the changes that have occurred in American life across the decades to create an ever-expanding cultural pluralism and to make all efforts by a single religious tradition (or even a dominant constellation of such traditions) to exercise institutional dominance in public life ill-advised and inappropriate. In the early years America was populated mainly by religious groups from Europe who came here seeking the freedom to worship as they wished. Most of the colonies (with the exception of Rhode Island and perhaps Pennsylvania) were founded by groups that officially supported their own tradition so that their desire to worship God in a particular manner could be carried out — even financed. A continuity of practice between private and public life was spontaneous and natural under such circumstances. The idea of separation of churches as official bodies from government was put into the Constitution as a way of avoiding the problems that would have arisen trying to get a single official religion for the new nation when different ecclesiastical bodies had establishments in most of the individual colonies. The stricture was initially against Congress, prohibiting it from establishing a national church.

Meanwhile, because the prohibition against establishment was coupled with a provision for free exercise, many religious groups began freely to carry on their lives within the new nation, even where some other group gained establishment standing. Moreover, the culture as a whole had a largely Protestant flavor. Thus by the time the immigrations of the nineteenth century took place, a dominant Protestant ethos accompanied by a pluralistic pattern of participation in church life was challenged by the influx of both Roman Catholic and Jewish groups, many of which were ethnically different. The new groups were tacitly expected to adapt to the dominant public ethos. They did so more by acquiescence than by approval. By the mid-twentieth century many of the immigrants coming to our shores were from cultures that do not share the Judeo-Christian heritage. Not only have their differences been even more difficult to assimilate than the differences in groups sharing a basically European orientation, but the awareness of those differences has raised our awareness to the probability that the feelings of the earlier immigrant groups had often been callously affronted by a quasi-official Protestant establishment, such as was present in the public schools I attended.

Both good sense and common courtesy require that we exercise a growing sensitivity about these matters. So does the realization that religious institutions are prone to corrupt themselves whenever they assume that their own perspectives furnish an unquestionable basis for a civic unity. Positively exercised, such courtesy might take the form of developing a pluralistic appreciation of the richness in many religious outlooks. Negatively implemented, it requires that the coercive power of the state be prevented from favoring any one religious tradition (or particular constellation of traditions) over any others. We should rejoice in the fact that the leaders of many religious groups have recognized the importance of this openness and have sought to advance it. This posture represents a religious coming of age as well as a political maturity.

Rather than suggest that ecclesiastical leaders have done something ill-advised by looking at this question differently from their constituencies, we should rejoice in their vision. After all, the biblical story would hardly be inspiring had the prophets been required to obtain a public vote of support from their constituencies before proceeding with their activities (which in several instances condemned widespread engagement in religious rituals that were not supported by a deeper concern for social justice and spiritual integrity).

But we need to push the analysis still deeper. Any official interplay between religious groups and civic institutions had quite different dynamics in the early period of American life than it is likely to have today. Let us look at the contrasts that would likely produce that difference.

In its earliest colonial years America understood itself as a new Israel. The experience of people leaving Europe for a new land in order to escape religious oppression provided plausibility for this imagery. The separate but different colonial establishments were expressions of "free exercise" for particular groups that contrasted with the proscription they had experienced as ecclesiastical groups in Europe. Moreover, in the early years the religious understanding of life and culture was generally coextensive with the sophisticated intellectual achievements of the time; for instance, the ministry was probably the most educated profession. Religion served as a force for civility, for order, for public responsibility. It offered the thrust for a viable public dynamic — represented by the desire for a Christian America. The values of the culture were relatively homogeneous; a moral covenant for social interaction was operative.

In later years, and particularly since the 1960s, the United States has increasingly taken on the characteristics of a new Rome. Its military presence is operative in the whole world, and the stadium has become its new circus. Its national life is no longer cohered by ecclesiastical patterns nor expressive of a significantly Christian behavior. Large portions of religion have become distinctive for the extent to which they are either uninformed about or hostile to the intellectual achievements of our time; the ministry has become primarily therapeutic in function, and much of it is unfortunately regarded as intellectually pathetic. Radical disagreements about values have surfaced; the covenant has been severely fractured.[2]

In the first of these cultural situations cooperation between churches and the political sphere was likely to have one kind of consequence; in the second it may very well have another. In colonial America, when church membership was statistically low,[3] recognition of churches actually had the initial effect of giving support to worship by those groups that had been a persecuted minority in Europe; in contemporary America, proposals for breaching the separation between churches and the state can have the effect of affronting the rights of minorities already here. In the first historical situation, giving a voice to religion generally contributed to the value enrichment and intellectual advancement of the culture; in our time the effect of giving religion a special entrée could well be to give political sanction to attitudes and points of view indefensible in the arena of sophisticated public discourse. In the early situation a biblical literacy enabled the favored religious groups to speak in ways that enriched the public ethos and gave some promise of infusing it with appreciation for justice, mercy, and compassion. In our time, any special privilege afforded to religious groups might well involve the use of biblical

2. For a further account of this see Robert N. Bellah, *The Broken Covenant: American Civil Religion in Time of Trial* (New York: Seabury, 1975).

3. For figures that show that church membership was low despite the established status of churches in the colonies, see Franklin Hamlin Littell, *From State Church to Pluralism* (Garden City, N.Y.: Doubleday, 1962), p. 32.

literalism to bless culturally jingoistic stances and rank intolerances. Anyone who cannot perceive the difference between a Puritan divine and a modern TV evangelist lacks historical sensitivity. The current consequences of placing religious ceremonies into public life today would be at least as likely to represent the Americanization of Christianity as movement toward a Christian America.

Some Mutual Benefits of Separation

One concern in thinking about these matters is to advance the common good of society. This requires us to ask whether the society is impoverished or benefited by providing coercive support for certain generalized forms of religious practice. The foregoing observations have already indicated severe doubts about this. To impose mandatory religious observances in ways that require all citizens to participate (or else refrain from participation at the risk of ridicule and censor) is to erode the freedom and capacity for tolerance that are the distinguishing marks of our society as it has developed in a very special way. It is unfortunate if the constituencies of our churches do not realize this. It is even more unfortunate if they do not realize that a biblically grounded perspective can see dangers in externally imposed participation in religious practices, especially if those practices are performed in the absence of deep commitments of faith and understanding. There are religious warrants for supporting that quality of a pluralistic culture which tolerates various faith commitments and honors the right of those adhering to those faith commitments to pursue them in their full uniqueness and integrity. Civically mandated religiosity, however, tends to pressure individual groups either to dilute or to bracket out their unique identities for the sake of participating in a standardized amalgam.

It is for this reason that the separation of church and state benefits not only a society seeking to be free and open but also religious groups seeking to be unique and faithful. Let us spell this point out in more detail with respect to the three specific practices that are the object of Donald Drakeman's concern.

Under the pressures of pluralism, the most acceptable forms of prayer for public ceremonies tend to be so-called nonsectarian utterances that express convictions of the most general sort and allude to the needs, aspirations, and hopes of a people in ways far more attuned to civic values than to confessional commitments. At the point where such prayers are most likely to be acceptable for public ceremonies they are also likely to be least rich and moving as expressions of a religious heritage. This suggests that being invited to offer prayers in civic ceremonies pressures clergy (or others) to portray their heritage in a watered-down and least meaningful version, not in its most special and strongest one. That is not necesssarily a service to religion. The constitutional guarantee of free expression and practice of religion permits and even encourages the most authentic expression of individual heritages and even a proclamation of such uniqueness in a publicly available (but not publicly coerced) manner. In contrast, support for religious observances under state sanction tends to dilute the uniqueness of religious practices and even to co-opt such practices for the endorsement of civic and nationalistic agendas. The mandating of religious practices by the coercive power of the state all but precludes the possibility of a prophetic element to what is sanctioned. No prophet worth the name would be thrilled with a civic form of prior constraint, however vaguely implied.

Publicly erected crèches may place an electric light bulb in a wooden box in a way that might even prompt some members of the public to think that Christ has now been put into the nation's Christmas. Many such displays are sufficiently cruddy, however, to render them innocuous. People can easily ignore them and still more easily give no thought to what they mean. Crèches create less problems for individual consciences than mandated school prayers or the required teaching of creationism because they do not require a conscious participation implying consent. But they still may not be productive of a spiritually sensitized culture.

Suppose these displays of the Christmas saga were pictorial representations of Herod's slaughter of the innocents. Some of the momentous disruptions associated with the first Christmas might be brought vividly to mind, and a good deal of what is still going on in this world might be brought to attention. After all, public leaders — not all of them in other nations — still deem it necessary to slaughter innocents in order to preserve order. Some unexpected theological discourse might well be fostered by such an unusual innovation — but what merchants would want that kind of display on the park or mall during shopping season? In church instruction and in church celebrations both the momentous promise and the horrendous corollaries of the Christmas drama can be examined. When clergy are skillful enough to juxtapose these, a deepening of understanding can result: a contrition of soul for involvement in the world that has been hostile from its inception to a true messianic function; a realization of the incalculable costs entailed in the assumption of a human status by divine benevolence. The typical cardboard figures in crèches do not convey such meanings and, even if a majority of church members would favor erecting them, would do little or nothing to enrich the spiritual depth of public life.

The movement to request that equal time be given in public schools for the teaching of creationism (or "creation science") alongside the theory of evolution poses even more complex and subtle issues. Its main thrust, however, is usually to imply that the scientific theory of evolution and the ideas of "creation science" are to be treated as of the same level of probable validity, indeed, even as the same genre of knowledge. This is full of potential difficulties, many of which can be assessed only by understandings that are developed through the kind of training in epistemology that comes on a university level (if it is learned at all).

It does little to advance the theological meanings of creation to reduce it mainly to an implied description of the earth's origins and the physical formation of the human species. Theological meanings are embodied primarily in interpretative levels of discourse, not in merely descriptive ones. To teach a religiously mandated idea of origins as a supposed science may give an air of respectability to biblical literalism,[4] but it does not necessarily engender understanding of the meanings, purposes, and implied destiny of creation. A noninterpretative treatment of creation, such as can often be seen in the teaching of creation science, will do no more to advance theological understanding than does a flat, unequivocal portrayal of evolution as though it is a fact (rather than a hypothesis). Moreover, state-mandated teaching of creation science would put the weight of the state's coercive power behind an interpretation of Scripture that is not accepted across the religious spectrum. Those for whom the higher criticism of Scripture is an intellectual commitment of crucial importance in the service of religious fidelity would be seriously disadvantaged by a state-mandated policy that implicitly rules out their way of under-

4. Raymond Eve and Francis Harrold, *The Creationist Movement in Modern America* (Boston: Twayne, 1991), pp. 102-3, assess creationism as a movement to defend or reestablish conservative Protestant status in society.

standing the Genesis creation stories as truthful religious myth or saga. Similarly, those who would teach evolution in a way that indicates its ultimately hypothetical rather than purely empirical standing would be placed at a disadvantage by a state edict implying that the theory of evolution and so-called creation science are epistemologically equivalent. Only the intellectual process itself, carried out in an open dialogue and with free inquiry, can deal with the various levels of meaning and insight that must be considered for either good scientific learning or good religious understanding to result. The seemingly innocuous appeal for "equal time" can only confuse issues and compound problems.

The Importance of Religious Values for the Public Good

Nothing about the separation of church and state as embodied in the policies suggested above necessarily precludes religious people from being concerned about the public good. The separation of church and state does not necessarily lead to a divorce between religious concerns and public responsibility. These two relationships are not identical.[5] It is quite possible to favor strongly the separation of church and state, as the Constitution calls for it, and still seek cross-fertilization between religious values and public life.[6] When religious groups seek to influence public life by the very same activities, such as lobbying and pamphleteering, that are available to all other interest groups, they do not thereby become established. They are merely functioning as voluntary associations among other voluntary associations freely advocating social purposes on the same terms as can other groups. Their right to do so is important and should be both defended and exercised.

Religious people would do well to be more concerned with the conditions of the public schools as a whole than with the absence of prayers in classrooms. It might even be helpful if social historians and social scientists would test the hypothesis that public support for quality education varies from area to area inversely with the presence

5. For a helpful delineation of this distinction see Robert N. Bellah, et al., *The Good Society* (New York: Knopf, 1991), pp. 179ff.

6. See *God Alone Is Lord of the Conscience,* a report on Religious Liberty and Church/State Relations adopted by the 200th General Assembly (1988) of the Presbyterian Church (U.S.A.) (Louisville: Office of the General Assembly, 1989, #OGA-88-107).

of vocal demands for prayer in the public schools. Such an inquiry might well show that concern for the establishment type of religious practices is dysfunctional to the deeper values religions ought to support. Similarly, religious people would do better to be concerned with the mandate to seek peace with justice that is embodied in the Christmas message than with erecting crèches on public property. One wonders, for instance, if publicly erected crèches were not most in evidence in those parts of the country with the greatest tendency toward jingoistic nationalism. Finally, those who want to employ religious influence for the public good should seek to learn what is necessary to understand the earth as a fragile habitat of great value for which human beings have to exercise ecologically sound responsibilities, instead of seeking a privileged status for any particular explanation of its origins. Are demands for the teaching of creationism actually strongest in those places where the unbridled exploitation of the earth is carried on with the least sensitivity? If the answer to these queries is what we might expect it to be, then a modern Amos could say, "I hate, I abhor your coerced prayers, your crumby crèches, and the attempt to dictate truth by legislative actions, but let quality learning roll forward like waters and intelligent understanding like an ever-flowing stream."

It is not the secular consequences of excluding specifically religious practice from public life that most threatens our common life. Rather, it is the consequences of allowing religious institutions to claim special privileges that exempt them from challenge. Letting religious institutions dictate civic practices that are offensive to others in the society definitely poses a threat to freedom, whereas allowing the free exercise of religion as the corollary of nonestablishment permits almost unlimited pursuit of confessional commitments within ecclesiastical groups. It also allows those confessional groups to be concerned for the truly important dimensions of the public good and even to be active in pursuing them.

The Public Church in Retrospect and Prospect

Dieter T. Hessel and James Hudnut-Beumler

To discern the "lessons of history" is to play a dangerous game. History tells more about what did not work than about what might work in the future. Its focus is more on describing what succeeded in days gone by than on predicting the fortunes of similar strategies tried again. Living in a continuum of history means accepting that one lives in a changing world where no experiment is repeatable and the future remains open.

We conducted our own experiment by bringing historians and ethicists together in a symposium that was the basis for this book. We discussed what the past and present experience of the twentieth-century church in public affairs might have to say for the future of mainline Protestant and Catholic public witness. In so doing, we did not expect an easy mix of these disciplines. Historians are not given to normative questions, and ethicists — though quite capable of descriptive analysis in their own right — are not generally prepared to accept that what has been should have much bearing on what should be.

Historians are comfortable in the role of expert witnesses about recorded events and evaluators of conflicting interpretations. Fearful of marshalling yesterday's facts to today's causes and engaging in "Whig history" (secular triumphalism in which past facts are made to lead up to a glorious present), they prefer the safe roles of biographers and historians of movements who make only implicit normative judgments. What seems to be required is that historians become ethicists without discarding their reservations about the limitations of moral casuistry.

Meanwhile, ethicists are accustomed to doing social analysis and evaluation in a normative context. As members of the faith community, Christian ethicists expect to reflect on the moral significance of human action. In the light of the biblical story, they scrutinize moral codes woven into religion and culture, and they identify social vision, values, and virtues that are likely to enhance the common good or to reflect what is (universally) right. Ethicists seek to give voice to conscience, to clarify the values at stake in social policy witness and decisions, and to articulate moral reasons for alternative courses of action.

Our history-ethics dialogue has been fruitful. Looking at public church phenomena from the perspectives of two disciplines at one time has allowed us to see several new things. Retrospectively, we have uncovered the tremendous variety that constitutes the public church. We have also been able to take stock of the successes and limitations of the church's cumulative public witness. Prospectively, we believe that the work of the authors represented in this volume point to certain perennial issues and to new "stuck places" that the church faces. This chapter puts some of these gleanings from the past and aspects of an agenda for the future before the reader.

Retrospect: What We Learned

One of the truths that emerged from these studies is that the public church means different things to different writers. At the outset, the authors, both ethicists and historians, called us and asked, "What do you mean by the public church or the church's public role?" We discussed the concept with them but did not provide a final definition, preferring that they discover or ponder the public church in all its variety. The results of their works of narrative and analysis speak for themselves. For Bryan Hehir, a focused location of the public church is the Bishops' pastoral letters — issued by a "local church." For Peter Paris, it is the African American congregation. All the seminar participants would agree that the church gathered in congregations and larger bodies should exercise its public role. But they point to different emphases.

For Eugene Lowe, the church becomes public in the religiously motivated intellectual move from the worshiping community to the public secular academy. For Ron Stief, the public church is present in the action of particular religious groups in solidarity with workers and organized labor. For Gonzalo Castillo-Cardenas, Ronald Stone, James Hudnut-Beumler, and Dana Wilbanks, the public church makes itself known in the underlying religious and ideological struggle over war and peace, liberation and oppression. For Max Stackhouse and Dieter Hessel, a crucial public role of the church is to clarify and communicate a theologically grounded social ethic. For an important group of our authors, the public church is particularly the social policy witness of mainline denominations and their ecumenical instrumentalities (Janet Fishburn, Christian Iosso, Donald Drakeman, and Edward LeRoy Long, Jr.).

A retrospective view allows us to affirm that the public church partakes of all the aspects in which this volume's authors portray it. A look at earlier decades of social witness also provides a vantage point from which to view the successes associated with the public church phenomenon. Comparing the American context at the end of the last century to our common life in the 1990s is instructive. In the 1890s the Supreme Court decided the case of *Plessy v. Ferguson,* making "separate but equal" the law of the land. The white mainline churches did nothing. The president of the United States talked about our Christian reponsibility to "our little brown brothers" in the land of the Philippines he had invaded by military force. Children worked fourteen-hour days in dangerous factories; women could not vote.

In the 1990s, what do we see? Our nation still uses its miliary power to invade other countries for puposes some believe to be moral. Women remain unequal participants in the economy and society. Children are still abused or neglected by individuals and institutionalized systems. Hard times are upon us again, pushing more people near or below the poverty line, as communities deteriorate. Even twenty years ago, who would have guessed that one in ten Americans would be on food stamps now?

Yet critical consciousness has developed, and the church has played the role of fostering social witness that refuses to let the powerful and privileged remain "at ease in Zion." Uneven or modest social impact suggests that the public church, which has often operated on the assumption that it could give impetus to social transformation, was in fact most successful at speaking truth to power or acting as the goad to conscience that will not let the culture be. We have yet to see whether the church will also become a social healer in the deepening crisis of ecology and justice (see chapter 1).

In a curious way, the church's identity problem leads back to the problem of specifying the church's public role(s). Since the time of the social gospel movement, the church has conducted a great deal of its public witness with an operative definition that concentrates on what a denominational or ecumenical body *declares* about public issues. Yet if we look at the accounts of social engagement by the Christian community represented in the chapters of this book, we see that the public church actually consists of acts, theories, ideas, lived commitments, struggles, and statements — that is, action and reflection in a theological-ethical context. Neoconservative gadfly Richard John Neuhaus has challenged Christians to fill "the naked public square." We would challenge his notion that the public square was or is bare of religious ideas, acts, and witness. Yet we also want to acknowledge that the denominational social "pronouncement" of the past is not the only or the sufficient way to occupy the public arena.

How then do we define the public church? It is the church that is not satisfied with being private[1] — it is more than a rescue mission and salvation train for individuals. The private church is habitually revivalistic and individualistic, focusing on Jesus in our hearts. Its social involvement is likely to stop at the point of condemning personal sins and stamping out social vices. This emphasis can lead to hard-nosed, single-issue crusades on "moral" issues. But when it comes to problems of socioeconomic and environmental justice, there is likely to be some voluntary service but little social policy focus.

Over against this tradition of rescuers or private Christians is another tradition of public Christianity that evolved from the Roman Catholic tradition and from the Reformation movement; it reads in the Bible a message of human solidarity oriented to the kingdom promise of world transformation. This message translates into an expectation of personal-social conversion and a call for active church participation in the formation of public policy. The spirituality (or spirited mission) of a public church is concerned with more than healing individual hurts or gathering in believers' communities. It combines faith commitment with civil dialogue, prophetic passion with public sense. To help prepare the way for the full reign of God, it seeks the transformation of the social order that affects, and should

1. Our distinction between private and public Protestantism is informed by our own ecclesiastical experience and by the original discussion of the distinction in Martin E. Marty, *Righteous Empire* (New York: Dial, 1970), chap. 17. Also see D. Hessel, *Social Ministry,* rev. ed. (Louisville: Westminster/John Knox, 1992), chap. 1.

be affected by, people of faith. A church oriented to public ministry is open to the world, speaking and acting beyond its walls for the common good, so that others notice, interact, and respond. It is people embodying their faith in social concert and coalition. It is the followers of Jesus going where his renewing spirit is already at work and where they can make a public difference.

Prospect: Challenges for the Public Church

Maintaining a lively witness in the world of the future becomes a much larger and more exciting task when our inclusive, from-the-bottom-up definition of public church is accepted. It means that to the participatory thinking process represented by church social statements and study papers are added a wide range of coordinate options for making a public difference. In the years ahead we see an opportunity for the mainline churches to find new ways to witness in addition to the old ones. At the same time, we see challenges that lie before those who would seek to be faithful in public witness. From our vantage point, the future vitality of the church's public witness depends on successfully meeting the following key challenges.

Dealing with the Loss of Apparent Power

As we have seen throughout this volume, the supposed power of the public church in the earlier decades of the twentieth century was often illusory. Yet a myth persists that when the churches were filled at the turn of the century or in the 1950s, the churches were publicly powerful. Furthermore, a substantial body of literature has been written by historians, sociologists, and other church observers on the topic of the decline of mainline Protestantism in the United States. Some of this literature blames liberal social pronouncements of the public churches for the decline in membership. As the authors of such accounts would have it, the mainline churches should be quiet or at least avoid being specific on public issues — emphasizing traditional values instead — if they want to reclaim their lost "market shares."

Suffice it to say that our view of the matter is different. Churches and Christians need to reject this line of reasoning with regard to the church's public witness. The main result of deliberately crippling the church's public role will be to diminish the church.

We also question the preoccupation with the power of numbers. Numbers did matter in media reports of the civil rights movement, and then of Vietnam War protest and nuclear freeze marches. Yet it was during the years of their supposed eclipse that the mainline churches, including the Roman Catholic Church, made three of their biggest contributions to American public life: the frustration of Reagan administration war making in Central America, the development of a widespread consensus on South African sanctions and divestment, and an effective challenge to some of the unscrupulous practices of corporations, such as marketing infant formula in the Third World. By contrast, in the 1950s at the peak of their popularity, the mainline churches could succeed only in blocking the appointment of a U.S. ambassador to the Vatican and, to a lesser degree toward the end of the McCarthy era, challenging the national security obsession of American society. Speaking truth to power, articulating commmon sense, and fostering moral commitment congruent with faith — these turn out to be the most relevant qualitative aspects of the churches' public power.

Rediscovering the Place of the Church in Liberalism

It has been said that a liberal is someone who cannot take his or her own side in an argument. The public church has been guilty of an unfortunate ambivalence about liberalism. In recent years, it has too often allowed fear of being labeled with the "L" word to stop it from contending in the public arena for the human rights and civil liberties its faith would seem to require. The mainline churches must come to terms with the extent to which their own public witness in this country is linked with the enlightenment project of liberal democracy and all that goes with it: a free press, rule by the majority, protected rights for minorities, the petitioning for redress of grievances, freedom of belief and association, the rule of law, and the sovereignty of the people over the state. All of these are principles that mainstream Protestantism has fostered — for theological reasons, Max Stackhouse reminds us (see chapter 4). And they are aspects of the social contract on which churches in the United States depend and which they seek for others throughout the world. While no human government will ever satisfy the demands of God's vision of *shalom,* a basic ministry for the churches in the years ahead is to suggest or clarify the kind of world and society in which Christians, and people generally, should want to live. The church will also need to make clear that some approaches are better than others.

In a context where others may be willing to sacrifice certain freedoms or social gains and human rights or civil liberties for (temporary) political stability, the public churches need to make their position on these basic issues more noticeable. They need to reclaim intelligently the mantle of liberalism, and make a Christian case for their social principles, lest they be left holding a bag labeled "out of the mainstream" by those acting to serve narrow self-interest and limited vision.

Accommodating the Rise of Another Public Church

Now that the private party has gone public and no longer relies only on individual action to achieve political aims, the churches that were used to being the sole public church presence now face sometimes well-organized competition. In this volume, we have sometimes referred to the public church as if it were synonymous with the mainline Protestant churches, adding at times the Roman Catholic Church. But if that characterization was true for most of the twentieth century, it is not true now. Instead of proceeding under the assumption that the churches will speak with one voice, those who lead in the church in making a public witness must adjust to the reality that theirs will often be just one set of religious, or even "Christian," voices in a sea of contention for the political will.

Clashing worldviews and voices underscore the importance of mainline churches making known their positions on crucial social-ethical questions in the ongoing public struggle for justice and peace. The rise of a competitive (neoconservative) public church in an environment of sloganizing single-issue networks directly challenges the mainline churches to articulate their posture with clarity and vigor, while refusing to play only the dichotomizing yes/no game. In short, getting the word out about why a certain position is taken — that is, articulating theological and ethical reasons for it — has become every bit as important as making the position itself known to the public.

Avoiding a Sectarian Conception of the Church

In recent years, even as the private churches were going public and the public churches were withdrawing into private fellowship, reinforced by suburban life-styles, some thinkers advocated that the churches stop dealing with social policy issues as such. The most vocal and influential of these is Christian ethicist Stanley Hauerwas. Simply put, Hauerwas's argument with the public church is that the church is to be a foretaste of the kingdom of God and cannot aspire to help bring in the kingdom itself, since that action is God's alone. The church is to be a social ethic, but not to join in coalitional action to reform social policy. If God desired a perfect world, God would make one. The church's task is to tell the biblical story and to build character. What began in Hauerwas's work as an attempt to deal in a Christian pacifist manner with the issue of church complicity in violence and coercion has evolved among many of his readers into a full-blown quietism. In their essays Dana Wilbanks and Max Stackhouse identify alternatives to such withdrawal from public engagement.[2] In the rapidly changing, socially wrenching years ahead, the public church must resist the temptation to do little about the social policy struggle while nurturing Christian virtues. Both are certainly required.

Developing a Wider Concept of Public Church Activity

To define the public church as the sum of many particular public policy stands of national denominational and ecumenical church bodies is exceedingly narrow. When a local church takes in a Central American refugee family in the name of sanctuary, that action deserves to be seen as public church activity. When a black congregation mobilizes in support of the candidacy of one in its community for political office, then, as Peter Paris suggests in his essay, the public church is at work. In fact, the church seems to have the most public effect through grass-roots presence and action that is given focus and direction by national and regional voices of denominations and ecumenical councils. We would highlight the need for a variety and combination of means as most appropriate, indeed necessary, to the fulfillment of the church's public vocation. Ministers need to learn the value of a well-written newspaper editorial as well as the value of a sermon. Laity and clergy alike need to recover a sense that their

2. Chapter 2 by Dana Wilbanks offers a brief overview of Hauerwas's approach to the church as a social ethic, and critiques this approach in the light of the writings of Martin Luther King, Jr., Thomas Ogletree, and Max Stackhouse. Also see chapter 4.

own churches can be voices for the public good and schools for moral formation that have an effect on citizens. Church bodies need to invest in developing and disseminating ethically focused "white papers" on difficult social problems, even as they continue to empower relatively powerless groups to gain a voice in the public arena and with directors of corporations.

Revitalizing and Broadening Ecumenism

The ecumenical movement, which emerged in the early twentieth century and became an effective instrument of social witness, has fallen on hard times, as Christian Iosso shows in chapter 8. But ecumenism, though it appears dormant, is not dead; today it is most likely to be expressed outside or alongside official conciliar bodies in functional groups concerned with particular tasks of mission and ministry, or through alliances of churches with compatible traditions. The more local the church, the more evident this pattern.

The problem with informal or interest-group ecumenism, however, is that it seldom undergirds a reliable presence of the churches in the public square. It allows but does not challenge self-preoccupied denominations to join in united action, and it leaves them vulnerable to being routed by militant single-issue groups or to being neutralized by divide-and-conquer tactics. (As an example of the latter, the fundamentalist Southern Baptist Convention gleefully took the step in June 1991 of fraternally petitioning the Presbyterian General Assembly to reject its human sexuality report.)

Ways must be found for mainline denominations at every level of organization to develop enough revitalized unity to undergird an effective social witness that responds to deepening social pathologies. The challenge to make a public difference together tests the mettle of church leaders. It also requires imaginative changes in the way ecumenical bodies involve grass-roots church members and enter into coalitional partnerships with compatible organizations also working for social change.

Accepting Increased Pluralism

At precisely the same moment that the public church needs to be able to address a wider audience and new realities of racial-ethnic pluralism and racial injustice in a society experiencing rapid demographic change, it is hobbled by reluctance to accept pluralist society. The American public square has become multicultural, multilingual, and multireligious. Mainline Protestantism, which originated in Western Europe, cannot expect to have the position of cultural dominance that it once held. Nor should it want to. But if it is to have any constructive part in the public life of the future, it must overcome the temptation to substitute emotive responses for reasoned moral discourse and constructive social problem solving.

Under the sway of deconstructionism in the humanities, communitarian moral philosophy, and antifoundationalist epistemologies, the leaders of the public church are pushed — consciously or not — to the view that no one can truly convince anyone else of anything, unless they agree on worldview and beliefs beforehand. Translating Christian moral viewpoints into terms that can be understood and appreciated — if not accepted — by the members of the larger culture is one of the most difficult tasks of the public church in this time of doing "ethics after Babel."[3] Yet it is a public responsibility of the church to interpret the implications of the gospel in terms that hearers can understand.

Perhaps the difficulties of translation — real as they are — have been overrated. There are no functioning societies that lack a concept of murder or of truth. There are no places where people believe, independent of other factors, that children should be made to starve. In the past, such areas of overlap led philosophers, theologians, and anthropologists to posit an Ur-religion, or a single source of morality. Even if that effort must be abandoned, a conversation can and must go on — across distinct ethnic and religious communities — about basic human moral obligations to all neighbors in the earth community. The public church thus faces the obligation to reexamine and own its beliefs, while learning both to listen and to speak in the languages of others, for the common good.

One challenging set of conversation partners are persons in movements also committed to justice and peace who do not share Christianity's complex views of covenanted being, human nature, personal-social sin, and the process of renewal. On any major issue, there is a temptation to reduce issues to slogans and to join those in the camp of the "politically correct," or conversely to side with those who use the epithet defensively to resist pluralism in education, the

3. See Jeffrey Stout, *Ethics After Babel* (Boston: Beacon, 1988).

arts, and the workplace. Yet simply assigning elements of the world to good/bad categories is not in the public church's theological or moral interest.

Religion's cultured despisers, the nonbelieving intellectuals of contemporary culture, represent another translation challenge. For here too the public church may find itself in agreement with secular scholars and social leaders about the complexities of the situation, the policies the public should embrace, and even the democratic means through which to realize those policies; but the church is likely to have different reasons for arriving at those conclusions. The church must continue to reach out in public discourse with secular individuals and coalition partners while refusing to allow its posture to be translated into vague terms that evaporate Christian theology and ethical norms.

Fostering the Eco-Justice Perspective

In the years just ahead, more of the chickens of the "advanced" industrial societies will come home to roost. A poisoned environment that threatens personal and community well-being as well as numerous other species will test the integrity of every religion and culture. Relatively affluent activists in church and society may continue to push a "green" agenda without much regard for justice to low-power people. Meanwhile, a real decline in the standard of living for middle- and lower-income Americans may trigger habitual responses to the economic distress of isolationism and nativism.

The magnitude of global enviromental peril will mock human institutions even as it requires cooperative international responses. Forced options will confront a society previously characterized by overabundance. Framing these earth-community problems and North American society's special responsibility in terms of the eco-justice perspective (see chapter 1) will require lively covenant awareness and continuing perseverance on the part of the church. The public church has a solid record of supporting policies and practices for the good of the environment while seeking justice between human beings and between human beings and the rest of creation. The realities of eco-injustice challenge the church to elaborate and embody that ethic.

Focusing on Priority Needs after the Cold War

The end of the cold war has already turned bittersweet. Even during it there were no fewer wars worldwide than before the Soviets also learned to build atomic weapons. Indeed, low-intensity conflict — a kind of war making particularly deadly for innocent civilians — has increased as the century has progressed. The United States has had a hand in most of these wars, but Americans continue to count only those shooting wars in which U.S. combat troops are directly deployed. The end of the cold war heightens the possibilities of such warfare, using ever-more destructive "conventional" weapons. The public church has a major task before it if it is to keep the United States from being drawn into more adventures like the Persian Gulf War. It will have an even greater role to play as a voice of conscience questioning the nation's involvement and support of death-dealing policies, including low-intensity conflict that uses surrogates. A breakthrough for the church would come when it has convinced the American public of its moral responsibility not only for the wars its citizens fight but also for the ones subsidized by U.S. citizens.

There is an urgent need for the mainline churches to recover a mission to the nation that concentrates more of its resources and the attention of its relatively privileged members on deprivation and suffering in the United States. The denominations have overinvested in local church facilities and overseas mission personnel and underinvested in training and supporting educators, organizers, and social welfare workers to grapple with the problems of deteriorating institutions and community life. The challenge is to seize the opportunity to make more of a public difference by specifying major societal needs illumined by Christian ethics, to project an alternative social vision and policies to embody it in the United States, and to take up urgent tasks of social witness and ministry that contribute to community and national renewal.

Focusing on the Public Vocation of All Christians

Some portion of the agenda of the public church is tending its own garden, or more accurately, tending to its own gardeners. For unless the churches are staffed and led by people committed to a public role for the church, the church will languish in social irrelevance.

The challenge here is to stop living off borrowed theological and educational capital and to reinvest in leadership development for social ministry. While the church was schooled under the politically realistic new reformation theology of Reinhold Niebuhr and European theologians, and then brought to political consciousness under the civil rights and urban mission movements, many of its ministers have settled into a therapeutic model of professional activity, and church officers have gone along. It is no accident that the ministry is classified as a "helping profession," and many ministers, happy to be numbered among doctors and psychotherapists and drawn toward helping individuals live better lives, see themselves in these terms as well. But the ministry is about other things too, as reflected in models of shared leadership and community transformation.

The institutions concerned with ministerial formation need to spend more learning time on the arts of public leadership for social betterment. The motivation of the next generation of leaders also needs to be examined. The numbers of second-career persons enrolled in today's seminary classes is cause for some concern. While it was once thought that such students would bring to the church a less cloistered, more relevant approach to the real world than do first-career clergy, some students have come to seminary from other walks of life precisely to exchange the all-too-familiar real world for the sanctuary.

Meanwhile, the needs of the people of God for individual pastoral attention can overwhelm any practitioner (the problem is particularly acute in the Roman Catholic Church, with its shortage of priests). A hierarchy of demands operates in the life of individual ministers and their churches to make public ministry a very low priority. Yet even the in-church activities of liturgy, preaching, education, and pastoral care present important occasions to (re)form the moral conscience and to clarify the social responsibility of parishioners. Given the declining financial ability of denominational bureaucracies to mount large-scale public church programs centrally, the public role of parish leaders and creative initiatives by their regional associations will be more important in the years ahead than at any time earlier in the century.

Professional church workers and church members together need to clarify and to exercise their public vocation in their articulation of faith and politics. The public church succeeds best when it is both faithful to its principles and broadly representative. The contributions Christianity can make to public life are considerable. The faith offers positive accounts of the good life, of the place of human beings in the created world, of right relations between rich and poor, neighbors and strangers. It also offers an account of the sinful limits of human capabilities and of goodness. The challenge for the church is to enable its members to embody these beliefs outside the confines of a church building. The church has responsibility for a major healing ministry among its adherents to foster a coherent worldview — faithful to the Word and pertinent to the needs of the time — that will bear fruit in daily life and political action.

C 3 3/4